Obsessive-Compulsive Disorder

FOR

DUMMIES®

**by Charles H. Elliott, Ph.D. and
Laura L. Smith, Ph.D.**

WILEY

Wiley Publishing, Inc.

Obsessive-Compulsive Disorder For Dummies®

Published by
Wiley Publishing, Inc.
111 River St.
Hoboken, NJ 07030-5774
www.wiley.com

Copyright © 2009 by Wiley Publishing, Inc., Indianapolis, Indiana

Published by Wiley Publishing, Inc., Indianapolis, Indiana

Published simultaneously in Canada

For general information on our other products and services, please contact our Customer Care Department within the U.S. at 877-762-2974, outside the U.S. at 317-572-3993, or fax 317-572-4002.

For technical support, please visit www.wiley.com/techsupport.

Wiley also publishes its books in a variety of electronic formats. Some content that appears in print may not be available in electronic books.

Library of Congress Control Number: 2008936636

ISBN: 978-0-470-29331-7

Manufactured in the United States of America

10 9 8 7 6 5 4 3

WILEY

About the Authors

Photo by Barbara Warren,
www.barbarawarren.com

Charles H. Elliott, PhD, is a clinical psychologist and a Founding Fellow in the Academy of Cognitive Therapy. He is also a member of the faculty at Fielding Graduate University. He specializes in the treatment of adolescents and adults with obsessive-compulsive disorder (OCD), anxiety, anger, depression, and personality disorders. Dr. Elliott has authored many professional articles and book chapters in the area of Cognitive-Behavioral Therapy (CBT). He presents nationally and internationally on new developments in the assessment and therapy of emotional disorders. Dr. Elliott and Dr. Laura L. Smith are coauthors of *Seasonal Affective Disorder For Dummies, Anxiety & Depression Workbook For Dummies, Depression For Dummies,* and *Overcoming Anxiety For Dummies,* all published by Wiley, as well as *Hollow Kids: Recapturing the Soul of a Generation Lost to the Self-Esteem Myth* (Prima Lifestyles), and *Why Can't I Be the Parent I Want to Be?* (New Harbinger Publications). He also is coauthor of *Why Can't I Get What I Want?* (a Behavioral Science Book Club selection from Davies-Black Publishing).

Laura L. Smith, PhD, is a clinical psychologist who specializes in the assessment and treatment of adults and children with obsessive-compulsive disorder (OCD), as well as personality disorders, depression, anxiety, attention deficit hyperactivity disorder (ADHD), and learning disorders. She is often asked to provide consultations to attorneys, school districts, and governmental agencies. She presents workshops on cognitive therapy and mental-health issues to national and international audiences. Dr. Smith is a widely published author of articles and books for the profession and the public, including those coauthored with Dr. Elliott.

The work of Drs. Elliott and Smith has been featured in various periodicals including *Family Circle, Parents, Child,* and *Better Homes and Gardens,* as well as popular publications like the *New York Post,* the *Washington Times,* the *Daily Telegraph* (London), and the *Christian Science Monitor.* They have been invited speakers at numerous conferences, including the National Alliance for the Mentally Ill (NAMI), the Association for Behavioral and Cognitive Therapies, the International Association for Cognitive Psychotherapy, and the National Association of School Psychologists. They have appeared on television networks such as CNN and Canada AM, and, in radio, they are often featured as experts on various NPR programs as well as You the Owner's *Manual Radio Show* and *The Four Seasons Radio Show.* They have committed their professional lives to making the science of psychology relevant and accessible to the public.

Drs. Smith and Elliott are available for speaking engagements, expert interviews, and workshops. You can visit their Web site at www.PsychAuthors.com.

Dedication

To Joey, who helped build our coyote fence, inspired our efforts, and always gave us a laugh when we desperately needed one.

Authors' Acknowledgments

We'd like to thank our excellent editors at Wiley: Project Editor Stephen Clark, Acquisitions Editor Lindsay Lefevere, and Copy Editor Christy Pingleton, as well as our agents Elizabeth and Ed Knappman.

We also want to thank our publicity and marketing team, which included David Hobson and Adrienne Fountain at Wiley and our personal publicist, Diane Lewis of Common Sense Consulting.

We appreciate the hard work of Erika Hansen for helping us track voluminous amounts of literature about OCD. Thanks to Scott Love of Softek, LLC for his usual care and expertise in keeping our computers running and our Web site humming. Thanks to Trevor Wolfe for giving us feedback and updating our knowledge of current culture.

We want to thank Deborah Wearn and Pamela Hargrove for their support and encouragement as well as helping us to see that the time was right for an encore career as authors.

To Drs. Brad Richards and Jeanne Czajka from the Cognitive Behavioral Institute of Albuquerque, thanks for listening to our compulsive jabbering about obsessive-compulsive disorder. Oh, and thanks for the Chateau Lafite-Rothschild!

Finally, we are especially grateful to our many clients over the years who suffered from OCD. They helped us understand OCD in ways that we could not have without them. They demonstrated resolve, determination, and courage that inspired us.

Publisher's Acknowledgments

We're proud of this book; please send us your comments through our Dummies online registration form located at www.dummies.com/register/.

Some of the people who helped bring this book to market include the following:

Acquisitions, Editorial, and Media Development

Project Editor: Stephen R. Clark

Acquisitions Editor: Lindsay Lefevere

Copy Editor: Christy Pingleton

Assistant Editor: Erin Calligan Mooney

Technical Editor:
Rebecca Moredock Mueller, MD

Editorial Manager: Christine Meloy Beck

Editorial Assistants: Joe Niesen, David Lutton

Cover Photos: Steven Errico

Cartoons: Rich Tennant
(www.the5thwave.com)

Composition Services

Project Coordinator: Kristie Rees

Layout and Graphics: Reuben W. Davis, Nikki Gately, S.D. Jumper, Christin Swinford

Proofreaders: John Greenough, Nancy L. Reinhardt

Indexer: Claudia Bourbeau

Publishing and Editorial for Consumer Dummies

Diane Graves Steele, Vice President and Publisher, Consumer Dummies

Joyce Pepple, Acquisitions Director, Consumer Dummies

Kristin Ferguson-Wagstaffe, Product Development Director, Consumer Dummies

Ensley Eikenburg, Associate Publisher, Travel

Kelly Regan, Editorial Director, Travel

Publishing for Technology Dummies

Andy Cummings, Vice President and Publisher, Dummies Technology/General User

Composition Services

Gerry Fahey, Vice President of Production Services

Debbie Stailey, Director of Composition Services

Contents at a Glance

Table of Contents

Introduction

*O*bsessive-compulsive disorder (OCD) was once thought to be very rare. Now, most estimates suggest that from 2.5 to more than 3.5 percent of adults suffer from OCD. That means that more than 3 million people in the United States and many millions more throughout the rest of the world have OCD. Furthermore, the diagnosis of childhood OCD has been mushrooming in the past several decades.

So, why the apparent increase in OCD? Well, part of the reason is that we do a better job of diagnosing the disorder. Another reason we see more OCD today is that people are more willing to admit to having problems. Other factors may be involved as well, such as stress associated with modern life. Perhaps even advertising makes a contribution, as we explain next.

For example, when your flight is delayed for hours, filling the time can be quite a challenge. Like us, you probably dread coming to the end of a novel, magazine, or movie brought to distract yourself from the endless waiting.

Perhaps, after hours of waiting, you resort to mindlessly pulling out the catalog of gadgets, gizmos, and gifts found in every seatback. Next time you're bored, reach for that catalog and take a look at the advertisements for sanitizing devices. Many of these devices use UV lights and are touted as portable tools for disinfecting all sorts of surfaces, such as countertops, keyboards, cellphones, handrails, public toilets, toothbrushes, desktops, doorknobs, and even armrests on airplane seats. With the wave of a wand, the lights apparently destroy 99.9 percent of all bacteria, viruses, and molds — including E. coli, SARS, and salmonella — in about ten seconds.

Picture the world if everyone carried one of those light wands around. Imagine millions of people scanning everything in their environment that might have some hidden contaminants. Would the world become a safer, cleaner, less contaminated place? What if you added spray disinfectants, hand sanitizers, and face masks to the mix? You might avoid a few colds or bouts of the flu. But hold on, if you avoid all germs, studies show that your body's immune system may not develop antibodies that combat illness. So maybe all that decontaminating isn't so great after all.

Nevertheless, those ads can make you feel a little creepy with all their claims about germs, microbes, and bacteria — especially when you're sitting on an airplane, maybe sweating a bit, smelling the bad breath of the guy next to you, and listening to the hacking coughs, sneezes, and other enjoyable noises of your fellow passengers. We're not saying that travel hassles cause OCD or that advertising makes it worse. However, media's obsessional attention to the dangers of dirt and germs sells lots of products and provides grist for the OCD mind.

About This Book

This book is about OCD. Our goals are to help you understand OCD as well as give you strategies for getting help and getting better. We also tell you what you can do to help a child or someone you care about who has OCD. We discuss the symptoms of other conditions, such as anxiety or depression, that can occur at the same time as OCD. In addition, we explain the differences and similarities of disorders that can be considered cousins of OCD.

Throughout the book we give you tips on when to consider getting more help from a mental-health professional. We provide sources and ways for you to choose the right person to assist your recovery.

This book covers the primary strategies used to treat OCD, including Cognitive-Behavioral Therapy (CBT), mindfulness, exposure and response prevention (ERP), and medication. The information is based on the latest scientific research.

An Important Message to Our Readers

This is the fifth book we've written in the *For Dummies* series. As with our other books, our intention is to share the latest and most accurate information about OCD, as well as to provide tools for effectively dealing with the symptoms.

We also want to keep your interest and provide a little entertainment, so we try to put a bit of humor in our writing. Sometimes we laugh at what we write, and we hope you will, too. But keep in mind that we are very aware that OCD is a serious and painful disorder. We only want to make you smile.

Conventions Used in This Book

Case examples are used throughout this book to illustrate points. These stories are based on symptoms, thoughts, and feelings from real people with OCD. However, the individual illustrations are composites of people rather than recognizable examples. The case examples leave out or change many details so that privacy and confidentiality are protected. Any resemblance to any person, whether alive or deceased, is entirely coincidental. We bold the names of people the first time they appear in order to alert you to the fact that we are presenting a case example.

Other conventions you'll see throughout the book include the following:

- ✔ In addition to introducing examples (as noted previously), **bold** indicates the action parts in numbered steps. It also emphasizes keywords in a bulleted list.

- ✔ *Italicized* terms are immediately followed by definitions.

- ✔ When we use acronyms (like OCD), we tell you what they mean the first time they're used in each chapter. If we miss one or two, please complain to our editors — after all, they're really the ones at fault!

- ✔ Web addresses show up in `monofont`.

- ✔ When this book was printed, some Web addresses may have needed to break across two lines of text. Rest assured that we haven't put in any extra characters (such as hyphens) to indicate the break. Just type in exactly what you see in this book, pretending the line break doesn't exist.

What Not to Read

This book is full of information and every word is well worth reading (and recommending to your family and friends). But you really don't have to read every single word, sentence, or chapter to benefit. You can use the table of contents or index to look up what you want to know. There is no predetermined order to the chapters; you can read them in any order you choose. Sometimes, we suggest going back or checking out certain chapters or sections for more information, but that's up to you.

Sidebars throughout the book provide you with what we think are interesting bits of information. Feel free to skip one or all of them if you're in a hurry. Along the same lines, we have some technical stuff (indicated by the icon of the same name) that explains material in greater detail; don't feel like you have to be obsessional about reading that, either.

Foolish Assumptions

If you're reading this paragraph, we suspect that you may be holding this book in your hands (now that was a brilliant deduction). Maybe you're interested in OCD because you think you have some symptoms. Or maybe you worry that someone you care about has OCD. Perhaps you're simply intrigued by this very interesting disorder (possibly having seen it portrayed in movies or on television).

You may be a mental-health professional who wants to find out more about specific treatment options for OCD or look at books that may be helpful to your clients. Or you may be a student of psychology, counseling, social work, or psychiatry hoping to get a clearer picture of this complex problem.

Whatever reason you have for picking up this book, we promise a comprehensive depiction of everything you need to know about OCD.

How This Book Is Organized

We divide *Obsessive-Compulsive Disorder For Dummies* into 7 parts, 25 chapters, and 2 appendixes. Following is a brief overview of the content of each part.

Part I: The Ins and Outs of OCD

Part I describes what OCD looks like. It tells you about the different types of OCD and some of the common and not-so-common symptoms. The third chapter describes other disorders that some professionals believe are related to OCD. We tell you what they are and why they may be part of what is known as the OCD spectrum. Chapters 4 and 5 tackle the biological and psychological causes of OCD. The specific causes of OCD remain a mystery, but many believe biology and psychology both play a role.

Part II: Starting Down the Treatment Path

Chapter 6 explains why so many people want to get help but can't seem to get going. Mental-health professionals call it resistance — putting the brakes on change. Some people are afraid of change, while others believe themselves incapable of change. We help you find the motivation for moving forward and tackling OCD.

Chapter 7 tells you who's who in the treatment field. It spells out what to expect if you decide to seek professional help. This chapter also shows you how to evaluate your choice of a mental-health professional.

Part III: Overcoming OCD

This part contains the meat and potatoes — the different treatment approaches to OCD. We cover in depth the techniques that are usually referred to as Cognitive-Behavioral Therapy (CBT). *Cognitive* refers to how you think and how that can contribute to OCD. How the way you think effects you and how to change are discussed in Chapter 8. Chapter 9 looks at how *mindfulness,* becoming more aware of the present moment, can help you decrease symptoms of OCD. The gold standard of OCD treatment, exposure and response prevention (ERP) is the behavior part of CBT. We explain how it works and how to implement ERP in Chapter 10.

Chapter 11 takes a close look at the different types of medication that are commonly prescribed for OCD. Finally, Chapter 12 tells you about relapse — what to watch out for and how to deal with relapse if it occurs.

Part IV: Targeting Specific Symptoms of OCD

The seven chapters in this part take a closer look at specific types of OCD and how to treat them. We give you examples of treatment plans for widely diverse problems, such as a need for symmetry or counting, doubting and checking, hoarding, and superstitious thinking. The final chapter gives you advice on treatments for related disorders, such as hair-pulling and skin-picking.

Part V: Assisting Others with OCD

OCD often begins in childhood. The first chapter in this part helps you determine whether your child has symptoms that suggest OCD. It also helps you find a good mental-health professional for evaluating and treating your child. Chapter 21 describes how parents or concerned family members can help a child with OCD. Although we suggest that parents enlist the help of a professional, there are many things parents can do to support therapy and their child. The last chapter in this section gives you tips on becoming a coach for someone else with OCD, including the dos and don'ts.

Part VI: The Part of Tens

Turn to these quick chapters for a little fun. You can read about quick fixes, find out how to move beyond OCD, and get some dirt on dirt.

Part VII: Appendixes

Appendix A contains important additional resources about OCD. We give you lists of books and Web sites you may want to review. Appendix B provides a few forms that you can use for some of the exercises we describe in various chapters. Feel free to make copies for your own use.

Icons Used in This Book

This icon highlights a specific strategy or tool for beating OCD, or an idea that can save you time and effort.

Watch out for this icon. It alerts you to information you need to know in order to avoid trouble.

This icon gives you information that you want to take from the discussion and file away in your brain, even if you remember nothing else. It's also used to remind you of important information that appears elsewhere in the book.

This icon lays out material that we think is rather interesting or cool, but not needed for understanding the essentials.

This icon indicates lists that can be used to develop ERP staircases. This technique is introduced in Chapter 10 and repeated in a number of chapters that address specific forms of OCD.

Where to Go from Here

We expect that reading this book will thoroughly inform you about OCD and related disorders. The book spells out the major treatment strategies for OCD. We hope you find the text interesting and, at times, entertaining.

If you are reading this book to help you overcome OCD, we encourage you to get a notebook, write out the exercises, take notes, and reflect upon your efforts.

Unless you're reading this book for your own interest or education (and not because you have OCD), you're likely to want to consult a professional as well. We expect that most trained mental-health professionals will welcome the opportunity to work with you on the strategies outlined in this book.

Part I
The Ins and Outs of OCD

"Oh, Martin, I do wish you could control these little rituals you need to do before leaving the house."

In this part . . .

In this part, we give you an overview of the symptoms and types of OCD. We cover the major treatment options that are available and most effective for OCD. We also tell you about some other emotional problems that may be related to OCD. Finally, we discuss the varied biological and psychological causes of OCD.

Chapter 1

Reviewing Obsessive-Compulsive Disorder (OCD)

Depending on how you define the terms, everyone has a few obsessive or compulsive traits. In popular vernacular, *obsessive* is a word often used to describe someone's intense interest in something. For example, a man who stalks a movie star is totally obsessed with her. Or a woman who spends hours putting on her make-up and doing her hair obsesses about her looks. An obsession also can refer to an intense interest in a sport, a hobby, or a career. On the other hand, *compulsive* often is used to refer to rigid patterns of behavior, as reflected in descriptions such as "He is compulsive about keeping his house clean," or, "She compulsively balances her checkbook every week without fail."

But mental-health professionals define these terms quite differently. In the mental-health field, obsessions are considered to be unwanted thoughts, images, or impulses that occur frequently and are upsetting to the person who has them. Compulsions are various actions or rituals that a person performs in order to reduce the feelings of distress caused by obsessions.

You can find examples of obsessions and compulsions in lots of places. For example, many major-league pitchers have elaborate good-luck rituals that can look pretty strange. Some feel compelled to hear the same song prior to the game; others eat exactly the same food. You probably have watched pitchers straighten their hats, smooth out the dirt on the mound, and spit in the sand before each pitch. Many baseball hitters have elaborate rituals they carry out with their bats. Other athletes have strange beliefs, good-luck charms, or compulsive acts that they must perform, allegedly to help their performance. If you are a major-league sports player making zillions of dollars to play a game, you can indulge in a few weird behaviors. No one will bother you.

Anyone can have a few obsessions or compulsions, and, in fact, most people do. But it isn't obsessive-compulsive disorder (OCD) unless the obsessions and compulsions consume considerable amounts of time and interfere significantly with the quality of your life.

In this chapter, we introduce you to OCD. We reveal how it debilitates individuals who have it and what it costs society. We also provide an overview of the major treatment options — much can be done for OCD nowadays. Finally, because OCD treatment can be greatly enhanced by the help of friends and family, we provide tips on what you can do to help someone you care about who has OCD.

What Is OCD?

OCD has many faces. Millions of people are held prisoner by the strange thoughts and feelings caused by this disorder. Most people with OCD are bright and intelligent. But doubt, uneasiness, and fear hijack their normally good, logical minds.

Whether or not you have OCD, you can probably recall a time when you felt great dread. Imagine standing at the edge of an airplane about to take your first parachute jump. The wind is blowing; your stomach is churning; you're breathing hard. Suddenly the pilot screams, "Stop! Don't jump! The chute is not attached!"

You waver at the edge, terrified, and fall back into the plane, shaking. That's how many people with OCD feel every day. OCD makes their brains believe that something horrible is going to happen. Some people fear that they left an appliance on and the house will burn down. Others are terrified that they may get infected with some unknown germ. OCD causes good, kind people to believe that they might do something horrible to a child, knock over an elderly person, or run over someone with their car.

Those with OCD almost always struggle with two major issues: shame and the intense desire to avoid all risks. We discuss these issues in the next two sections.

Suffering shame

Because the thoughts and behaviors of those with OCD are so unusual or socially unacceptable, people with OCD feel deeply embarrassed and ashamed. Imagine having the thought that you might be sexually attracted to a statue of a saint in your church. The thought bursts into your mind as you walk by the statue. Or consider how you would feel if you stood at a crosswalk and had an image come into your mind of pushing someone into oncoming traffic.

However, the frightening, disturbing thoughts of OCD are not based on reality. People with OCD have these thoughts because their OCD minds produce them, not because they are evil or malicious. It is extremely rare for someone with OCD to actually carry out a shameful act.

 Throughout this book we often refer to the "OCD mind" rather than you or someone you care about with OCD. The reason we do that is to emphasize that *you are not your OCD.* You have these thoughts, urges, impulses, and rituals because of a problem with the way your brain works. OCD is not your fault.

Wrestling with risk

The OCD mind attempts to avoid risks of all kinds almost all the time. That's why those with Contamination OCD spend many hours every single day cleaning, scrubbing, and sanitizing everything around them. People with Superstitious OCD perform rituals to keep them safe over and over again. Interestingly, most OCD sufferers focus on reducing risks around specific themes such as contamination, household safety, the safety of loved ones, or offending God. But those with contamination fears don't necessarily worry about damnation. And those who worry about turning the stove off usually don't obsess about germs.

Risks of all kinds abound in life. We don't know of any human who has avoided the ultimate worry — death. And no one can ever know when death is about to knock on the door. The following famous people were living their lives with normal precautions and died of random, unexpected events:

- ✔ **Felix Faure:** The president of France died in 1899 from a stroke while having sex.

- ✔ **Isadora Duncan:** A dancer, Isadora was strangled to death when her silk scarf was entangled in the wheel of a car in which she was a passenger.

- ✔ **Sherwood Anderson:** This famous author died after he accidentally swallowed a toothpick at a party.

- ✔ **Tennessee Williams:** A playwright, Williams accidentally choked to death on the bottle cap of his nose spray.

- ✔ **Vic Morrow:** An actor, Morrow was decapitated while making a movie when a helicopter went out of control and crashed.

Given scenarios like those in the preceding list, it's hard to imagine how OCD rituals and behaviors could actually anticipate and save anyone from similar circumstances. But the OCD mind tries to create the illusion that almost all risks can be anticipated and avoided.

In truth, OCD doesn't provide significant protection in spite of extraordinary efforts to reduce risks. In chapters to come, we give you ideas about how to accept a certain amount of risk in order to live a full life, no matter how long or short that life is.

Counting the Costs of OCD

People with OCD suffer. They are more likely than others to have other emotional disorders such as depression or anxiety. Due to embarrassment, they often keep their symptoms secret for years, which prevents them from seeking treatment. Worldwide, it is estimated that almost 60 percent of people with OCD *never* get help.

The pain of OCD is accompanied by loneliness. OCD disrupts relationships. People with OCD are less likely to marry, and, if they do, they are more likely to divorce than others. Those who do hang on to their families often have more conflict.

OCD also costs money. A study done in the '90s reported that the estimated price tag of OCD was over 8 billion dollars in the United States alone. This amount represents the cost of treatment, lost productivity on the job, and lost days at work. Even with improved treatments, these costs have no doubt risen along with increased population and healthcare costs.

Encouraging OCD through the Media

OCD is not a new disorder. However, you can't help but think that the appetite for sensation in the media accelerates OCD concerns. Recently, we saw a television special about people buying used mattresses. Reporters used special lights and took cultures to find all sorts of horrible matter (bed bugs, fecal matter, and body fluids) still clinging to supposedly refurbished bedding.

In another show, zealous reporters burst into hotel rooms armed with petri dishes and black lights to help them find filth and grime on the glasses left in the room, as well as on the carpet and bedding. Media also warns about such dangers as inadvertently inhaling gasoline fumes while pumping gas (of course, who can afford that anymore?) and kindergarten children inadvertently becoming intoxicated from magic markers.

Furthermore, the sales of cleaning products, sanitizers, personal hygiene products, and mouthwash have soared over the years. You can find antibacterial ingredients in products designed to clean your refrigerator, mop your floors, scrub your body, and disinfect your toilets. Antiviral ingredients are also becoming quite the rage.

Yet, try and find solid evidence about deaths from refurbished mattresses, less-than-pristine hotel rooms, incidental exposure to fumes, and homes not cleaned with every antibacterial and antiviral ingredient known to humans, and you'll come up wanting. In fact, a clever study conducted by researchers at Columbia University in Manhattan provided households with free cleaning supplies, laundry detergent, and hand-washing products. All the brand names were removed. Half of the households were given products with antibacterial properties and the other half was provided supplies without antibacterial properties. The researchers carefully tracked the incidence of infectious diseases (runny noses, colds, boils, coughs, fever, sore throats, vomiting, diarrhea, and conjunctivitis) for almost a year. They found no differences between those who used antibacterial cleaning agents and those who did not.

If you spend loads of time cleaning and using antibacterial disinfectants, you may be doing yourself more harm than good! Scientists now believe that excessively clean environments may actually be causing an increase in allergies and asthma. Furthermore, excessive use of antibiotics appears to run some risk of encouraging the development of new, resistant bacteria.

No, we are not suggesting that people stop washing their hands — especially in hospitals! And we're well aware of the long-term dangers posed by prolonged exposure to air pollution, insecticides, and toxic chemicals. Furthermore, we're grossed out by a dirty hotel room as much as anyone else. At the same time, the media and advertisers have shown a disturbing obsession with issues involving excessive cleanliness and minimal exposure to low-level risks.

Germs: Resistance is futile

Some people with OCD spend hours vacuuming in hopes of defeating dust and dirt in their homes. However, research led by Dr. Charles Gerba at the University of Arizona found that household vacuum cleaners not only may spread germs throughout the house, but also may be a safe haven for accumulating bacteria. Vacuum brushes apparently harbor fecal material, mold, and even E. coli. What to do about this situation? One recommendation has been to spray antibacterial disinfectant on your vacuum brushes after every use. Another solution is to buy a new breed of vacuum that purportedly kills bacteria and germs through the use of an ultraviolet, germicidal light.

Other researchers have found bacteria and fecal matter in ice machines at restaurants and on restaurant menus. Therefore, some suggest not using ice machines, not allowing a menu to touch your plate, and washing your hands after selecting your food from the infected menu.

The problem with these studies and recommendations is that no one has proven that any of these sources cause significant amounts of illness or disease. Though reasonable precautions are always a good idea, you can easily start down the disinfectant road and never return. Bacteria and germs exist everywhere. You cannot eliminate all of them, and you can spend huge amounts of time and money trying.

Exploring Treatment Options for OCD

If you had OCD during the Middle Ages, you very well may have been referred to a priest for an exorcism. The strange, violent, sexual, or blasphemous thoughts and behaviors characteristic of OCD were thought to derive from the devil. If you had OCD during the dawn of the 20th century, you may have been sent for treatment based on Freudian psychoanalysis, which purportedly resolved unconscious conflicts from early development. For example, if your OCD involved sexual obsessions or compulsions, you were assumed to have unconscious desires for your mother or father. In fact, the common use of the word "anal" to describe people who are overly rigid, controlled, and uptight came from the Freudian idea that strict, early toilet training caused children to grow up with excessive concerns about neatness and rules.

However, neither exorcism nor psychoanalysis ultimately proved to have much impact on OCD. Only in the last 40 years or so have effective treatments evolved for OCD. And some of these treatments have only become widely available quite recently.

In the next few sections we provide an overview of the major treatment options for OCD that have shown significant promise based on scientific studies. For clarity, we have divided these therapies into the categories of CBT, mindfulness, ERP, and medications. In reality, rarely are any of these therapies used as a single, exclusive treatment for OCD.

TECHNICAL STUFF

What's in a name?

Cognitive-Behavioral Therapy (CBT) is a general term referring to a collection of techniques that aim to improve well-being by bringing about specific changes in the way you think and behave. Throughout this book, we use this more encompassing term. (We discuss CBT in detail in Chapter 8.) But sometimes we in the mental-health field get a little persnickety. So, just to keep things straight, we provide a bit more information here than most readers really need.

Cognitive Therapy (CT) refers to methods primarily aimed at changes in thinking. *Behavior*

Therapy (BT) focuses on making various behavioral changes. Exposure and response prevention (ERP), the subject of Chapter 10, is one specific form of BT. Just to confuse you a little more, mindfulness, which we cover in Chapter 9, is often considered a variant or offshoot of CBT. You will almost always see at least some small degree of ERP or other CBT techniques included in any given treatment of OCD, even if the approach goes by a single term such as ERP or Cognitive Therapy.

Changing the way you think with CBT

Cognitive therapy was developed by Dr. Aaron Beck in the early 1960s and is a major component of the broader term, Cognitive-Behavioral Therapy.

Originally, this approach was used to treat depression. Cognitive therapy is based on the idea that the way you feel is largely determined by the way you think or the way you interpret events. Therefore, treatment involves learning to identify when your thoughts contain distortions or errors that contribute to your misery. After you've identified those distortions, you can learn to think in more adaptive ways. Soon after it was adopted for treating depression, cognitive therapy was applied quite successfully to anxiety disorders and, ultimately, to a dizzying array of emotional problems, including eating disorders, oppositional defiant disorder, and even schizophrenia.

In the early years, cognitive therapy was not applied to OCD, perhaps because of the success of ERP (described in the section "Modifying behavior through ERP"). However, in recent years, the cognitive therapy component of CBT has been found to be quite effective in treating OCD. Usually, CBT includes at least some elements of ERP. Some practitioners believe that applying cognitive strategies first may make the application of ERP somewhat more comfortable and acceptable to the person contemplating that approach. See Chapters 8, 9, and 10 for more information about the various subtypes of CBT.

Approaching OCD mindfully

The OCD mind focuses on possible future calamities. The predictions almost never come true. Yet, the obsessive thoughts keep coming and demanding attention.

- *I worry about shouting obscenities, so maybe someday I'll lose control and do it in church.*
- *Maybe my thoughts of death will cause harm to someone I love.*
- *Perhaps touching that doorknob will make me sick.*

When it isn't thinking about the future, the OCD mind dwells on possibilities from the past. The mind fills with thoughts about what might have occurred.

- *Maybe I left the stove on.*
- *Maybe I ran that person over with my car.*
- *Perhaps I was poisoned by that tuna fish sandwich.*

Furthermore, the OCD mind judges people, the world, and even OCD itself harshly.

> ✔ *A bad thought is just the same as doing something bad.*
>
> ✔ *Having OCD thoughts means that I'm crazy.*
>
> ✔ *I am a weak person for having these thoughts.*

Mindfulness is the practice of existing in the present moment without judgment or harsh evaluations. Thus, as you acquire a mindful approach to OCD, you understand that thoughts are truly just that — thoughts. Thoughts do not make someone good or bad. See Chapter 9 for more information about how to apply mindfulness to your life and your OCD. As you do, you will become more self-accepting and better able to quiet your OCD mind.

Modifying behavior through ERP

A true breakthrough in the treatment of OCD occurred in the mid 1960s when Victor Meyer tested a treatment called exposure and response prevention (ERP) with two patients suffering from severe cases of OCD. These patients had not improved with shock therapy, supportive therapy, or medication. The drastic measure of brain surgery was even being considered. One of the patients was obsessed with cleaning. Dr. Meyer and a nurse exposed this patient to dirt and did not allow her to clean (ergo, the term "exposure and response prevention"). This radical treatment was the first to help decrease the patient's symptoms. The other patient was obsessed with blasphemous thoughts. She was told to purposefully rehearse those thoughts without doing the rituals that she had used to decrease her obsessions. Like the first patient, this woman was helped by ERP after years of other unsuccessful therapies.

ERP resulted in a substantial reduction in both patients' OCD. The mental-health profession took notice because OCD treatments previously had shown little ability to ameliorate this disorder. Suddenly, the prognosis for OCD turned from utterly grim to quite hopeful.

However, ERP requires patients (and sometimes therapists) to get down-and-dirty — literally. Thus, patients may be asked to:

✔ Not check the door locks

✔ Refrain from cleaning up

✔ Repeat blasphemous thoughts over and over

✔ Say the number "13" over and over again

✔ Shake hands

✔ Stop arranging their closets in certain ways

✔ Touch grimy surfaces

You may wonder whether carrying out ERP causes some distress. Indeed it does. Perhaps that's why the strategy took quite a while to be embraced by large numbers of mental-health professionals. However, the discomfort is worth it because ERP is very effective. You can read all about this strategy in Chapter 10.

Controlling OCD with medications

Medications given for OCD had shown almost no effectiveness until Anafranil (Clomipramine) was found to work in 1966, a date roughly corresponding to when ERP was first tested. Thus, prior to 1966, about the only known strategy for treating OCD was psychosurgery — a rather radical approach involving the cutting of certain connections in the brain. Such surgery sometimes left the patient with devastating side effects, such as an inability to function normally. Obviously, psychosurgery was reserved for the most severe cases. Others were left to fend for themselves.

Today, some of the same medications used for depression (specifically, selective serotonin reuptake inhibitors or SSRIs) frequently work for OCD. However, they are thought to work in a different manner for OCD than they do for depression. The good news is that if medication is going to work, it will work fairly quickly for OCD.

Electrifying news in OCD treatment

Electroconvulsive Shock Therapy (ECT) has been used to treat severe cases of depression. In case you're wondering, ECT does not seem to help OCD. However, a treatment that involves placing electrodes deep into brain structures shows some promise in the treatment of OCD, as well as depression, Parkinson's disease, and other neurological disorders. A small continuing study at Brown University, the Cleveland Clinic, and the University of Leuven (in Belgium) found that deep brain stimulation brought at least some relief for all participants with severe OCD. However, the improvement varied a great deal, with study patients averaging about a one-third reduction in their symptoms. Nevertheless, these patients had proven to be highly resistant to other treatments, including ERP and medications. Unlike psychosurgery, deep brain stimulation can be adjusted or reversed.

However, the number of studied patients remains small and the research is quite preliminary. So we don't recommend that you sign yourself up for this strategy quite yet. Give the researchers a few more years to study this approach — many studies are underway at this time.

The bad news is that a substantial number of people do not seem to benefit from medications for their OCD. And those who do benefit find that they relapse quickly if they discontinue the medication. Furthermore, side effects can be significant. For more information about the pros and cons of taking medication for OCD, see Chapter 11.

Helping People with OCD

If you're reading this book because your child, a family member, or a close friend has OCD, there is much you can do to help. Here are a few points to keep in mind if you want to do more good than harm:

- **Don't try to be a therapist.** Generally speaking, we recommend that those with OCD consult a mental-health professional. Those with a very mild case may want to try some of the techniques described in this book on their own. However, treatment plans should either be designed by a professional and/or the person with OCD. At the most, you can make a few suggestions. Even if you are a professional therapist, you don't want to take on that role for a friend or family member.

- **Understand OCD.** Even if you're not taking on the role of a therapist, knowing a lot about this disorder helps a great deal. Understanding OCD can help you feel compassion and acceptance for the one you care about. You will also know that your family member, child, or friend didn't ask for OCD. No one wants to have this problem.

- **Encourage; don't reassure.** You want to encourage the one you care about to participate in treatment. At the same time, you don't want to do what seems natural — reassure the person that everything will be okay. Please read Chapter 22 to find out how to devise alternatives to giving reassurance.

- **Don't get sucked into rituals and compulsions.** Those with OCD often try to elicit help with their rituals and compulsions. For example, they may ask someone to recheck that the doors are locked or that the oven is turned off. Though complying with the request may seem caring, doing so only makes matters worse.

Another mushrooming approach to OCD treatment?

The *Journal of Clinical Psychiatry* recently reported on a study involving psilocybin, the psychoactive substance found in psychedelic mushrooms. Psilocybin was provided to nine people with severe OCD. All nine participants reported that they were symptom-free for periods ranging from 4 to 24 hours. A few patients reported sustaining symptom reductions for several days. However, the primary investigator, Dr. Moreno, indicated that daily ingestion of this drug would likely be problematic. You see, psychedelic mushrooms can also trigger trips to past lives and other planets. Therefore, this is not a treatment that we would recommend at this time. Perhaps some chemical cousin or derivative of psilocybin will ultimately prove to be an effective treatment approach to OCD, but don't hold your breath.

Chapter 2

Scrutinizing OCD

Although it goes by a single name, obsessive-compulsive disorder (OCD) is actually a diverse disorder with multiple presentations. OCD can manifest itself as quirky behavior, exaggerated fears, or seriously disturbed thinking. Thus, in one instance, the diagnosis of OCD may be assigned to someone with the odd habit of hanging clothes exactly 1.2 inches apart in the closet, whereas in someone else, OCD may show up as excessive worries about germs and constant hand-washing. Alternatively, OCD could cause someone to adopt an endless number of cats and live in the midst of feces and filth.

You may be surprised to know that *everyone* occasionally has a few signs of OCD. And some symptoms of OCD are perfectly normal. For example, you may worry about whether you turned off the coffeepot, put the boarding pass in your briefcase, or left a light on as you rush off to the airport for an important business trip. Your mind tells you to stop your car and turn around to check. But usually you don't because you realize that the odds are pretty much in your favor that your worries are exaggerated.

Occasionally feeling compelled to count steps, knock on wood, or arrange items on your nightstand in a particular pattern is also normal. These actions, although possibly unwanted or a little strange, are common. Just because you have one or more symptoms of OCD doesn't mean that you have the disorder.

In this chapter, we explain OCD in plain words and provide clear examples of its symptoms, sorting out what's normal and what's OCD. OCD has two components — *obsessions* and *compulsions*. We describe obsessions, and then we explain compulsions. Finally, we introduce and briefly describe the wildly divergent mutations of OCD.

OCD can steal the minds and dismantle the lives of those affected. Therefore, we take a serious and respectful approach to reviewing the diagnosis and treatment of OCD. At the same time, let's face it, the OCD brain can come up with some wild thoughts and strange actions. These thoughts and behaviors may look downright bizarre, and occasionally funny, but we assure you that they are real and serious. Finally, we do poke fun at ourselves and occasionally take a lighthearted look at OCD. However, we never, ever poke fun at those who suffer from this serious malady.

Coming to Terms with What OCD Is

People with OCD have obsessions and/or compulsions. Well, duh! How's that for stating the obvious? These obsessions and compulsions can vary in both intensity and content over time. Thus, someone may have a terrible problem with compulsive hand-washing for two hours every day. After a year or so passes, the hand-washing may fall off, but compulsive rituals involving excessive cleaning of the house and arranging the furniture precisely emerge in its place.

OCD has been considered to be one of the anxiety disorders (which include generalized anxiety disorder, phobias, post-traumatic stress disorder, and panic disorder, among others) because people with OCD usually complain of *feeling* anxious, uneasy, or distressed. This feeling is often brought on by obsessive fears, thoughts, or images. See our earlier book, *Overcoming Anxiety For Dummies,* for more information about anxiety disorders. However, OCD involves more than anxiety. It also includes distorted thinking, and repetitious urges and impulses. Therefore, some professionals now believe that OCD should be categorized separately from the anxiety disorders.

The OCD anxiety cycle

In OCD, an obsessive thought, urge, or image occurs, sometimes out of the blue and other times triggered by an event, such as being near someone who sneezes. Once the obsessional worry about germs pops up in response to the sneeze, the person magnifies the risk or threat that the obsession poses. For example, the sneeze may be viewed as a spew of serious pathogens sprayed in the air. The OCD mind believes this threat is very serious and anxiety surges. The rising anxiety causes the person to feel desperate to reduce the distress. The OCD solution is to carry out a compulsion, such as spraying lots of antiviral gel in the nose to quell the anxiety. Completing the compulsion results in a short period of relief, which, in turn, actually increases the likelihood that the compulsion will be used again. To illustrate this OCD anxiety cycle, we use the following example of Cyan.

Cyan is a bookkeeper who worries excessively about getting AIDS from touching anything that other people may have touched. Thus, she avoids touching doorknobs, shaking hands, and using public restrooms. She works at home to avoid unnecessary contact with germs. She carries hand sanitizer and disinfectant in her purse. Even at home she disinfects her countertops and telephone dozens of times each day. She worries that germs float in the air and invade her home.

Whenever an obsessional worry about contamination pops into her mind, Cyan believes that she is at high risk for acquiring AIDS or some other serious illness. Her overestimation of risk leads Cyan to feel intense anxiety and overwhelming dread. That distress causes her to immediately wash her hands with sanitizer and disinfect her computer keyboard, kitchen countertops, and phones. Once she has done "enough" cleaning, she feels greatly relieved, but only for a short while. The power of that relief keeps the cycle going. Her obsessive thoughts soon return.

Cyan's cycle is common in OCD and is depicted in Figure 2-1.

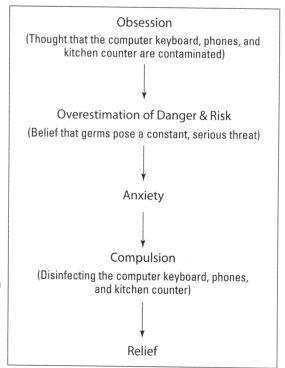

Obsession
(Thought that the computer keyboard, phones, and kitchen counter are contaminated)

Overestimation of Danger & Risk
(Belief that germs pose a constant, serious threat)

Anxiety

Compulsion
(Disinfecting the computer keyboard, phones, and kitchen counter)

Relief

Figure 2-1: Cyan's OCD anxiety cycle.

Cyan's obsession about getting contaminated leads to anxiety. Her cleaning rituals reduce her anxiety. However, the thoughts about germs keep coming back.

This cycle explains why OCD is typically considered to be a type of anxiety disorder. Obsessions are interpreted as serious dangers which lead to anxiety and a compulsion to do something to reduce the risk in order to alleviate the anxiety. But OCD is actually more complicated and the symptoms often appear to involve *more than feelings of anxiety*. A couple other culprits need to be considered in the quest to understand OCD. People with OCD have problems with the way they think and with their ability to control impulses.

Thinking and believing

OCD is really a disorder of belief or thinking. People with OCD lack complete insight into the truth of their obsessions or compulsions. They may be able to admit that their obsessions or compulsions are unreasonable. But they don't fully believe the obsessions or compulsions are completely irrational because their minds are full of doubt.

For example, a woman with OCD may believe that putting soup cans in a certain order on her shelves protects her children from getting sick — not an especially logical thought. If you ask the woman what evidence she has that her ritual protects her children, she doesn't have much to tell you. But she has enough doubts that she feels compelled to continue with her compulsive ritual. After all, she wants to keep her kids safe.

Or a man with OCD may worry about the possibility of leaving the stove on. He may admit in a calm discussion that his beliefs are not completely consistent with reality. He's never actually left the stove on, even though he's checked hundreds of times. But he continues to act as if his beliefs about needing to check are true. He has just enough doubt to continue checking again and again.

Delusional thinking

OCD thinking sometimes goes to such extremes that it appears delusional or completely out of touch with reality. For example, some cases of OCD involve worries like becoming contaminated and infected by molecules emanating from things made out of stainless steel. Other sufferers may feel compelled to perform an elaborate ritual involving counting and precisely arranging items — firmly believing that if the ritual is not performed correctly, a loved one will die. When OCD thinking becomes this distorted, treatment and diagnosis can become more complex.

Extreme doubting

People without OCD also experience doubt. Consider the common superstition that knocking on wood after stating something positive will ward off bad things happening in the future. Is it really true that knocking on wood keeps someone safe? Where is the evidence? Have there been studies about not knocking on wood? Most people would agree that the superstition is sort of silly. Yet, many people continue to knock on wood. Why not, just in case, right?

Those who continue to engage in wood knocking technically have a disorder of thinking and believing, but it's hardly a serious one. At least we hope it isn't serious, because we've been known to do it ourselves on occasion.

What makes wood knocking okay and *not* a compulsion are two characteristics that make OCD a disorder:

✔ The first characteristic of OCD is that when a compulsion is blocked, there is a great deal of distress. However, "wood knockers" don't usually get too upset when they can't find wood to knock on (besides, wood laminates will do in a pinch!).

✔ The second aspect of OCD that makes it different from wood knocking is that it interferes with life and takes huge amounts of time — most people don't spend hours each day knocking on wood.

Inspecting impulses

Some people have described their OCD like a "brain itch" or a "brain hiccup." In other words, OCD can feel impossible to suppress. An obsessive thought intrudes into the mind like a bolt of lightning. A compulsive action, such as arranging food alphabetically in the refrigerator, can feel as necessary as breathing. The impulse often involves an intense feeling or need for things to be just right.

For some people, this driven impulsivity seems to underlie their OCD more than anxiety or worry. That's why some experts suggest that problems such as trichotillomania (uncontrollable hair-pulling) and tics (uncontrollable jerking, body movements, or sounds) are related to OCD. See Chapter 3 for more information about OCD's relatives.

Seeing the Two Sides of OCD

Technically, OCD involves either obsessions or compulsions, or a combination of both. We say "technically" because in reality, almost everyone with OCD has both obsessions and compulsions. Distinguishing between obsessions and compulsions can seem a little tricky, but here goes.

The difference between an obsession and a compulsion is that obsessions are *intrusive mental events* that make a person feel terribly upset. Compulsions, on the other hand, are behaviors or actions someone engages in either mentally (like counting or repeating words) or physically (like washing hands) *in order to feel better*. In other words, obsessions start in the mind and then create a negative emotional response, while compulsions are actions (either mental or physical) targeted to soothe negative emotions.

The next two sections examine the nature of obsessions and compulsions in more detail.

Obsessing about obsessions

Obsessions are like uninvited houseguests who refuse to leave. They barge into your mind like mental terrorists. Obsessions make you feel uncomfortable, uneasy, angry, and sometimes frightened. Obsessions come in three forms:

- **Thoughts:** Thoughts are the words that clang around in your head. For example, if you touch something dirty, you may have the thought "I'm sure to get sick if I don't do something immediately." Other obsessional thoughts come in the form of doubting whether you've locked the doors or concerns about things not being arranged correctly.

- **Urges:** These are feelings, impulses, or worries that you're going to do something inappropriate or undesirable. For example, you may have an urge to harm someone you care about or a need to have everything in a very specific, "just so" order. Other examples of obsessive urges include worries that you may shout out obscenities during a religious ceremony or that you may turn your car into oncoming traffic.

- **Images:** These are uninvited pictures that form in your mind, often depicting violent, horrifying, morally reprehensible, weird, and unwanted scenes. Disturbing images may include scenes involving sex with animals, child abuse, or gruesome murder.

Obsessive thoughts, urges, or images seem to pop into the mind without warning. When they do appear, they cause a lot of distress if you have OCD. Lonnie's story illustrates how an obsession is experienced by someone who suffers from OCD.

> **Lonnie** forces himself to attend his niece's wedding. He's not particularly close to his family and finds himself seated at a table with seven of his elderly aunts. The reception has barely started and he's already anxious to get home.
>
> The best man toasts the bride and groom and Lonnie's mind wanders. Suddenly, he looks around at his tablemates and a picture of what they would look like *naked* pops into his mind. His mind envisions seven women, over 75, with sagging breasts, wrinkled faces, and much worse. Horrified, Lonnie gulps the sweetly spiced punch in front of him. "My God," he thinks, "Why do I have thoughts like these all the time? I must be a sick pervert!"
>
> Just as suddenly, his mind suggests a slow, sensual dance with his 85-year-old aunt seated next to him. Then, a second later, comes an image of a steamy hotel room scene with his elderly aunt. We won't give you the details of the rest of Lonnie's imagery. Lonnie has a sudden urge to shout out, "Baby, you are so hot!"

"Ick, what's wrong with me? Am I losing my mind?" Lonnie blushes with embarrassment and almost jumps out of his skin when his aunt touches his arm and asks kindly, "Lonnie, are you okay? You look flushed — is there anything I can do for you?"

Lonnie experienced intrusive, unwanted thoughts, impulses, and images. These are obsessions. Lonnie's rather strange incident is not an uncommon example of an obsession. His thoughts represent the _essential characteristics_ of obsessions (as opposed to normal, mildly worrisome thoughts and doubts). The thoughts Lonnie associates with his obsession are

- **Disconnected:** The obsessive thoughts, urges, or images jump into conscious awareness. They seem disconnected to what the person had been doing or thinking. These are not pleasant daydreams; people don't willfully ask for obsessions.

- **Unacceptable:** The thoughts are unwanted and unacceptable to the person who has them. Obsessions involve actions or thoughts that are totally silly, uncharacteristic, morally upsetting, violent, or uncomfortable.

- **Uncontrollable:** The thoughts capture attention. Wow, do they! When an obsession comes along, it's difficult to think about anything else. Thus, they interfere with whatever a person was trying to think about or get done. Obsessions overpower the mind and feel uncontrollable.

- **Highly upsetting:** Feelings after the obsessive thoughts, images, or urges are highly upsetting. Worry, guilt, fear, anger, disgust, or sadness often follow obsessions.

- **Frequently reoccurring:** An obsession tends to reoccur often. People who have obsessions work hard to suppress them. They may avoid situations that they associate with their thoughts or perform rituals to keep their thoughts at bay. Untreated, obsessional thoughts spread like unchecked weeds, choking out healthy, adaptive thinking and increasing the distress of their victims.

This final characteristic truly separates the "obsessions" (that is, mild worries) almost everyone occasionally experiences from obsessions experienced by people with OCD. For those who suffer from OCD, this piece of the obsession is what makes life miserable.

The informal use of the word "obsession" often conveys a positive, enthusiastic focus on something pleasant or desirable such as a passion for fishing, coin collecting, a new relationship, or art. The word "obsession" as used in OCD has nothing to do with such positive interests.

When your ear has worms: Read this sidebar at your own risk!

If you have attended a wedding in the last ten years, you can probably conjure up the melody to "Y.M.C.A." or, worse, "Macarena." Can you recall the jingle that starts with "I love my baby back, baby back . . ." or how about the song on the ride at Disneyland with the lyrics, "It's a small world. . . ." Have we ruined your day?

Scientists study and label everything. So, they've come up with a term for getting a song stuck in your mind. That term is "earworm." Now, think about an earworm, a slimy parasite, digging into your brain. What does it look like? Imagine one crawling through your ear. Yuck!

When you consider these musical annoyances, the earworm has many of the same characteristics of an obsession. Segments of songs, like obsessional images and thoughts, flood your mind over and over and feel both unwanted and obnoxious. The more you try to get rid of the melody, the more entrenched it becomes. Like obsessions, earworms occur more often in people who worry a lot.

So, how do you get rid of the nuisance? That's the bad news. To date, no sure and successful earworm exterminators have been found. Some people try to substitute one song for another. Others get unstuck by passing the worm onto someone else. Here we go, we'll try passing this one along that's been bugging us since we started writing this sidebar . . . Y.M.C.A. . . .

Considering compulsions

Compulsions are actions people feel driven to complete in order to deal with obsessions. These actions frequently take the form of behaviors, such as hand-washing or repeatedly checking locks, or rituals, such as lining up everything in a cupboard in an unusually precise manner. Unlike obsessions that merely heighten anxiety and distress, compulsions are intended to neutralize obsessions or reduce distress. Compulsions can also come in the form of mental acts (such as counting or repeating phrases).

Compulsions are attempts to:

- ✔ **Reduce anxiety:** For example, after suffering from an obsessional worry that the doors are unlocked (thus inviting unwanted intruders) a person may feel compelled to return and recheck his door locks. Once he's done so, he feels briefly relieved. But then he leaves his house again, and the obsession returns, thus compelling him to go back to check. This cycle may continue numerous times before he's able to let go and continue with his day.

- ✔ **Respond to an urge:** After using the public restroom a person may obsess about possible germs, contamination, and sickness. She may feel an irresistible urge to scrub her hands. She carries a powerful disinfectant and spends 30 minutes washing her hands, even though they're red, raw, and oozing from all the washing she does.

✔ **Decrease discomfort:** Some compulsions appear out of a need to feel more comfortable or "just so." For example, a person may have a ritual she feels compelled to perform in order to go to bed. She arranges items on her nightstand over and over until they feel "just right." In addition, she touches her shoulders five times each and repeats these touches until she feels comfortable. Only then can she allow herself to go to bed.

✔ **Seek certainty:** A person may have an obsession that he might run someone over in his car. Almost every time his car goes over a bump in the road he starts to worry. He often feels compelled to turn his car around to check. Even then sometimes he drives off and feels he must return to check again to be absolutely certain he did not injure someone. This compulsion consumes hours of his time each day.

✔ **Obtain reassurance:** A 10-year-old may worry obsessively that her parents might not still love her. So every night, after she's been put to bed, she gets up and goes to her parents' bedroom and asks if they still love her. She feels compelled to repeat this ritual many times seeking this reassurance. Before she stops, her parents become upset and irritated. But they always give her the reassurance she asks for.

✔ **Increase a sense of safety or well-being:** Someone may have frequent obsessional worries that his thoughts might cause harm to his family. So, if he has the slightest negative image or thought about anyone in his family, he feels compelled to repeat the words "Hail Mary; I love my family so much," 50 times in his mind. Sometimes he loses count and has to start over.

Categorizing the Types of OCD

Unlike depression and some other disorders, OCD is variegated. People who suffer from depression look a lot alike. Although their symptoms differ somewhat, most depressed folks feel sad and gloomy, have low energy, and lack enthusiasm. By contrast, OCD looks more like breeds of dogs that differ in appearance the way that dachshunds, Great Danes, cocker spaniels, Saint Bernards, and Yorkshire terriers do. In other words, OCD shows up in very different forms from person to person.

Experts have struggled to come to an agreement on the various breeds of OCD and have so far failed to reach a consensus. Thus, a certain amount of uncertainty remains about how to categorize OCD. Unfortunately, people with OCD typically crave certainty.

Therefore, we've combed through the literature and distilled a pretty comprehensive list of OCD subtypes. Although not every expert would fully agree that our list is definitive, we think you're likely to find the most common types of OCD listed and even a few that are rather rare:

✔ Checking and doubting

✔ Fearing contamination

✔ Hoarding

✔ Having inappropriate thoughts — religious, sexual, and aggressive

✔ Heeding superstitions

✔ Needing symmetry

Each subtype of OCD can occur by itself or in concert with other categories of obsessions and compulsions. It is not unusual to have a mix of symptoms or for OCD to morph and change over time. Having a mix of symptoms can make treatment a little more challenging, but certainly not impossible.

Doubts, fears, and uncertainties

Doubt and uncertainty plague the minds of those with the "checking" form of OCD. Some experts even call OCD a "disease of doubt." When doubts show up, the person goes back to check over and over again. A slight amount of uncertainty always remains even after checking, so the person does it yet again. Sometimes it takes an awful lot of rechecking before the person is able to stop. Doubts involve the following types of concerns:

✔ Forgetting to do important tasks like:

• Closing doors, windows, and blinds correctly

• Turning appliances off

• Locking doors

• Turning the water off

✔ Fear of making mistakes, such as:

• Forgetting appointments

• Turning in imperfect school or work assignments

• Balancing your checkbook incorrectly

✔ Needing reassurance that:

• Loved ones are safe

• Loved ones still care

• Your appearance is okay

• Your home is safe

Each time people with this problem check on a concern, they feel momentary relief. That relief is short-lived as uncertainty begins to creep in again. Some people with obsessions and compulsions regarding checking spend hours each day worrying and futilely checking and rechecking. See Chapter 13 for more information about this form of OCD and its treatment.

Contamination, germs, and dirt

Obsessions about contamination, germs, and dirt plague more sufferers with OCD than any other issue. Some worry about getting ill from dirt or germs; others believe they may become contaminated and sickened by chemicals, radiation, asbestos, insects, sticky substances, animals, bodily waste or secretions, or pesticides.

The OCD mind greatly exaggerates real risks. Although it's possible to catch a cold from shaking someone's hand, people with OCD worry excessively each time they shake hands with someone. These fears lead to immediate, vigorous hand-washing in order to avoid coming down with a serious, dreaded cold or something even worse. The exaggerated fears about germs and contamination often lead to one or more of the following:

✔ Avoiding items that have touched other items imagined to be contaminated

✔ Avoiding people or places thought to be contaminated

✔ Avoiding public restrooms

✔ Hours of daily cleaning with harsh disinfectants and chemicals

✔ Hours of hand-washing every day causing raw, bleeding skin

✔ An inability to eat outside of the home

✔ Throwing away clothes imagined to be contaminated

✔ Washing dishes in a particular order and manner — a ritual which must be repeated if not done "properly."

✔ Wearing face masks in public

Because contamination issues represent the most common type of OCD, we provide more details and focus on its treatment in Chapters 8, 9, and 10. Those chapters also feature more variations and extreme manifestations of this particular type of OCD. The other categories of OCD that follow are covered in more depth in their own short chapters in Part III.

Collecting and hoarding

Children begin "hoarding" hobbies at young ages. Kids like to collect coins, bottle caps, and pine cones. Collections are a normal developmental process — unless the collecting goes awry and spirals out of control. Hoarders start with a normal amount of stuff, but evolve into perpetual, driven squirrels. They find themselves collecting a wider and wider variety of things. Eventually, some hoarders discover that they can't throw out much of anything.

Over the years, hoarding can lead to isolation from others, sanitation problems, fire hazards, and serious health consequences. The homes of hoarders often become choked with "stuff" from ceiling to floor. This fascinating phenomena is covered in Chapter 16, along with treatment strategies.

A number of researchers now believe that Hoarding OCD is a slightly different category of problem than the other types of OCD. We explain this issue in detail in Chapter 16.

Shame, embarrassment, and inappropriate thoughts and behaviors

This type of OCD involves a host of concerns about the possibility of doing something humiliating or grossly inappropriate. As with most categories of OCD, the specifics of these concerns can vary greatly from one person to the next. Following, you find a multitude of flavors.

Religious obsessions and compulsions (Scrupulosity)

Scrupulosity describes someone's over-concern with sin and morality as well as fears about offending God. The word scrupulosity comes from the Latin word "scrupulus" and means sharp stone — suggesting the feeling of stabbing pain that results from acts against the conscience. People with this type of OCD have extreme concerns about not pleasing God or dread that they will be dammed and rejected. They often spend hours praying or performing complicated rituals.

Religious obsessions can come in the form of blasphemous thoughts. Some people with OCD worry that they might shout out swear words during a religious ceremony. Others have repeated sexual images of contemporary spiritual leaders or even historical religious figures. Some have repeated phrases, such as "god damn," popping into their thoughts throughout the day. These obsessions are accompanied by feelings of profound dread and shame. The person tries to neutralize or undo the feelings of intense guilt by resorting to compulsive prayers or rituals.

The compulsions that follow religious obsessions don't always make logical sense. The example of Cade below illustrates how illogical these compulsive rituals can be.

> **Cade** finds himself obsessing about displeasing God. He constantly worries when profane words come into his mind because he believes that having such thoughts greatly offends God. In order to deal with his distress, he has developed a compulsion designed to undo the obsession.
>
> His compulsion involves walking a few blocks to his church, day or night. Then he climbs the stairs and stands by the door. He counts to 45, and then says 45 prayers. If he is interrupted or distracted, he must start the routine over until it feels just right. Cade's compulsion may seem strange and silly to others, but Cade believes that he must do this in order to show God that he is worthy. When he's finished, he feels better for a while, but the obsessions and compulsions always return.

As you can see, Cade's counting and praying compulsions don't make a great deal of sense. Nonetheless, he believes that they somehow rectify his standing with God.

Sexual and aggressive obsessions and compulsions

People with these types of OCD dwell on the possibility, no matter how slight, that they might harm others or engage in sexual acts that they feel would be abhorrent and repugnant. See Chapter 14 for more information about sexual and aggressive forms of OCD, as well as treatment strategies for dealing with them. There, you will also see that those with this type of OCD *almost never* do the things they gravely fear they'll do.

A fairly common variant of sexual obsessions has to do with believing that one is gay. Often these folks are not especially "homophobic" and they don't have particular biases against people who are gay. But they are repelled by the idea that they might actually be gay. Another sexual obsession concerns worry that one might be a pedophiliac (someone who sexually abuses children).

Other people with OCD become concerned that they will harm or hurt someone. Here are a couple of common obsessions and compulsions with this theme:

- ✔ While walking on a busy sidewalk, a man worries that he may push someone next to him into oncoming traffic. He is abhorred by this image and tries to block it by repeating "God, save me" 17 times in his head.

- ✔ A young mother has intrusive thoughts and images (in other words, obsessions) of harming her baby daughter in some horrific way. Her beliefs cause her to put away all the knives on the counter, and she feels unable to bathe her baby for fear that she will drown her.

Sometimes OCD in one category can easily overlap with OCD themes from another category. Thus, those with sexual and aggressive OCD obsessions and compulsions commonly have concerns about the religiously inappropriate nature of their thoughts.

Superstitions and rituals

Superstitions involve beliefs that various events, circumstances, and happenings have extraordinary significance with ominous implications. The ultimate concern of most superstitions involves fear of death. Thus, one with Superstitious OCD may attach great meaning to the power of:

- **Numbers:** Those with Superstitious OCD may feel they must do everything in sets of five or some other special number or something horrific will occur. Hotels typically skip the 13th floor because so many people feel it's unlucky. However, folks with that concern only have Superstitious OCD if they spend lots of time worrying excessively about certain numbers.

- **Anything related to death:** Here, special significance is attached to having passed a hearse, cemetery, or funeral home. Sometimes these obsessions and compulsions have only a superficial, subtle connection to death. For example, a woman with this type of OCD may avoid sitting in a chair previously owned by a now-dead person.

- **Words:** Sometimes the superstitions concern the special power and meaning of specific words. For example, a man with this type of OCD may feel compelled to say "Bingo!" whenever he ends a sentence because he fears that someone will die if he doesn't.

Again, these categories of OCD are somewhat arbitrary. Superstitions permeate many of the earlier categories of OCD.

Symmetry and perfectionism

A driven need for symmetry, slowness, and precision are common themes in an OCD category we've chosen to call the "just so" or the "just right" type of OCD. As with most OCD categories, "Just So" OCD frequently accompanies other types of OCD. Some examples include:

- Feeling compelled to order books alphabetically by the second word in the title and align them exactly one-half inch from the bookshelf's edge

- Spending hours each day making sure the fringe on floor rugs is lined up perfectly

- A teenager rewriting class notes in perfect calligraphy each day

Joey is a 10-year-old child who worries about his parents' safety. His story illustrates OCD with a checking component along with a need for his rituals to be "just so."

> **Joey** gets up several times each night to check on his parents. He also believes that he must follow a special bedtime routine involving reading a special story, putting his pajamas on in a certain way, smoothing out his bed perfectly, placing his pillow diagonally from the left bedpost, and demanding that both of his parents say "I love you" three times. Otherwise, he believes that his parents will die during the night. He spends hours on these routines until he gets a feeling that he's done everything "just right."

Joey's story demonstrates how "Just So" OCD has no real logic to it. People with this form of OCD believe that the feeling of "just so" has some kind of special importance and significance. See Chapter 15 for more information, illustrations, and treatment strategies for this type of OCD.

Separating OCD from Normal Worries

Are you obsessively wondering whether you have OCD? Table 2-1 is a simple little quiz that can help you gain some insight on the matter. Check the appropriate "Yes" or "No" box next to each question (each question is representative of a symptom of OCD).

Table 2-1		**Could You Have OCD?**
Yes	**No**	**Have you . . .**
		Counted the stairs as you walk up them?
		Carried a lucky charm?
		Knocked on wood?
		Had a horrible image of hurting someone you care about?
		Felt a need to clean your house more than usual?
		Gone back to recheck the locks in your house?
		Had a bad feeling you may have left the coffeepot on?
		Wondered whether you might be gay?
		Avoided stepping on cracks?
		Worried that your house might burn down?
		Struggled to throw out things you don't need?
		Had an inappropriate, unwanted sexual image in your mind?

(continued)

Table 2-1 *(continued)*		
Yes	**No**	**Have you . . .**
		Worried that you may have committed a sin?
		Worried that you may have offended someone?
		Had a minor physical symptom that your mind blew up into a serious illness?
		Felt dirty for no good reason and had a strong urge to wash your hands?

Did you check "yes" to two or more items in Table 2-1? You did? Good! That means you answered honestly. But no matter how many items you checked yes or no, this quiz doesn't say much at all about whether you suffer from OCD.

Studies tell us that almost everyone has *occasional* unwanted thoughts (obsessions) or engages in a *few* actions designed to reduce tension or distress (compulsions) just like the ones in Table 2-1. Yet the "symptoms" in Table 2-1 look pretty much like the obsessions and compulsions that make up OCD. The operative words are *occasional* and *few*.

Over 90 percent of people report occasionally experiencing some of the *exact same kinds* of obsessive thoughts, urges, and images that someone with OCD may have (and we wonder if the other 10 percent are telling the truth!). For example, most people have occasionally imagined physically hurting someone in a terrible way. Maybe you've walked by the knife holder and had a brief disturbing image of pulling one out and stabbing your child. You are not alone! Occasional imaginings like this are neither rare, nor an indication you have OCD.

Someone with OCD, on the other hand, *frequently* experiences unsettling images, truly worries about acting out those images, and feels *enormously upset* by them.

Getting to a Diagnosis of OCD

To be officially diagnosed as having OCD, three factors must be present:

- ✔ The person must frequently experience either obsessions, compulsions, or both.

- ✔ Except for children, at one time or another the person must at least *partially* recognize that the symptoms are illogical or unreasonable.

- ✔ Dealing with the symptoms must take up lots of time and interfere with life in a significant way.

Insight or awareness of the "unreasonable" nature of OCD varies widely from person to person. If you talk with most adults who suffer from OCD, usually they know at some level that their obsessions and compulsions don't make a whole lot of sense. For example, people who fear becoming contaminated by touching telephones probably know that their fear is overblown. But ask a man with this fear to touch a telephone and you'll encounter surprising resistance and emotional upset at the very thought.

Children sometimes have almost no insight or awareness that their OCD is irrational. They sometimes think that their rituals or obsessive thoughts are quite plausible and necessary. For example, a child may truly believe that she must repeat "Thank you God for my family" 20 times in order to keep everyone safe — and if she doesn't say it just right, she must keep repeating the phrase or someone in her family will die.

Sometimes people with OCD even worry that they're losing their minds. OCD takes over so much of their lives that they feel totally helpless and incapacitated. At its worst, OCD can take many hours of a person's time every single day. OCD interferes with jobs, relationships, school, achievements, and everyday household chores.

Although OCD can be quite serious, the problem is definitely treatable. If you or someone you care about has OCD-like symptoms, seek help. See Chapter 7 for more on finding appropriate treatment for OCD.

OCD takes away joy, productivity, time, and relationships while giving back anxiety, doubt, uncertainty and misery. If you spend an hour each day worrying about and trying to solve your financial problems while teetering on the edge of bankruptcy, that's not OCD. That's realistic concern. But if you're sitting on a six-million-dollar stash of cash and worrying for hours each day whether you'll have enough to retire, you just may be showing signs of OCD.

Avoiding self-diagnosis

Please do not attempt to diagnose OCD in yourself or others. We give you general guidelines so that you can know enough to get any such concerns checked out by a professional. OCD is complex and should be evaluated by a professional who is experienced with this disorder. See Chapter 7 for information on finding qualified professionals who can diagnose and help you.

Avoiding misdiagnosis

OCD is often missed or misdiagnosed by doctors and counselors. Quite a few people go from professional to professional before receiving a correct evaluation. According to the Obsessive Compulsive Foundation, people with OCD take up to 9 years to obtain an accurate diagnosis and an average of 17 years to receive appropriate treatment. One of the reasons it can take so long is that many of those with OCD keep their symptoms secret, especially the more bizarre symptoms. So be open with your mental-health professional and be sure you go to someone well-qualified in diagnosing OCD.

Chapter 3

Meeting the Relatives and Associates of OCD

....

In This Chapter

▶ Exploring the OCD family tree

▶ Getting to know the family

▶ Hanging out with the friends of OCD

....

*O*bsessive-compulsive disorder (OCD) has many relatives and lots of associates. Relatives are disorders that look very much like OCD, but are not necessarily OCD. These related disorders all involve difficult-to-repress, *repetitive* urges, thoughts, images, impulses, and/or behaviors. These impulses are very difficult to control, even though people find them quite disturbing and disruptive to their lives.

Associates of OCD are disorders or emotional problems that often accompany OCD, but are not thought to be directly related to the disorder. They don't always show up, but OCD sufferers are usually at greater risk of succumbing to them.

In this chapter, we briefly describe the relatives of OCD, and what their relationships to OCD are like. Some of these relatives are almost indistinguishable from OCD and there's some controversy as to whether there should be a distinction. We also tell you about the associates of OCD so you'll recognize them if they come knocking.

Meeting the Relatives of OCD

A rainbow contains a spectrum of colors. Although each color is distinct, the colors are all formed by reflected sunlight within the same rainbow. Okay, we know we're mixing metaphors now, but our point is that scientists continue to engage in robust arguments about whether or not OCD can be thought of as a spectrum of closely related disorders sharing certain common features as opposed to a single distinct disorder. And recent studies on the neurobiology of OCD-related disorders suggest that they have some common genetic and biological roots (see Chapter 4 for more information about the biological aspects of OCD and its relatives).

In OCD, *compulsions* are primarily driven by the need to decrease a feeling of dread or distress. In other words, compulsions are actions that decrease anxiety or avoid risk (see Chapter 2 for more information about compulsions). By contrast, some of the related disorders involve repetitive urges or *impulsions* driven by a need to maximize stimulation or pleasure. Impulsions are stimulating and done with little thought about safety or risk. Both impulsions and compulsions are repetitive and difficult to control or inhibit.

The following sections describe most of these related disorders and what makes them like and unlike OCD. We include a table at the end of each section that summarizes these similarities and differences. See Chapter 19 for an overview of ideas about how to deal with these relatives of OCD. And see Appendix A for additional information and resources.

Body dysmorphic disorder (BDD): A seriously distorted self-image

Probably everyone has at least one thing they don't like about their appearance or body, but it's ultimately no big deal. On the other hand, people with body dysmorphic disorder (BDD) believe something is horribly wrong with their appearance or bodies. They obsess about minor flaws in their appearance and engage in compulsive actions to reduce the discomfort they feel. BDD often occurs in people with a diagnosis of OCD and shares many of the same features. Common obsessive thoughts associated with BDD include worries about having:

- A complexion with mild discoloration
- A crooked nose
- A head that's too big or too small for the body
- A small facial scar
- A thin mouth

> ✔ A weak jaw
>
> ✔ Bumps on the face
>
> ✔ Eyes that are too small
>
> ✔ Hair that's too curly or too thin, or too much hair
>
> ✔ Mild acne
>
> ✔ Protruding ears
>
> ✔ Wrinkles

Other concerns involve the size of the sex organs or other body parts. The list is endless. The defects that concern people with BDD are greatly exaggerated and *rarely* (if ever) noticed by others.

The concerns of those with BDD may change from one aspect of the sufferer's appearance to another. Symptoms may ease up for awhile and then get worse.

BDD involves much more than normal preoccupation about one's looks. People with BDD feel that they are deformed, ugly, and defective. In order to feel better, BDD sufferers engage in compulsive behaviors, such as:

> ✔ Asking for frequent reassurance from others
>
> ✔ Becoming housebound because of embarrassment
>
> ✔ Checking themselves constantly in the mirror
>
> ✔ Digging or picking at imagined deformities (causing infections, skin irritations, and scars)
>
> ✔ Washing or shaving excessively
>
> ✔ Visiting dermatologists frequently
>
> ✔ Having extensive cosmetic surgery
>
> ✔ Keeping the head down or combing hair across the face
>
> ✔ Wearing excessive make-up to hide the perceived flaw
>
> ✔ Wearing hats or clothes to camouflage the imagined defects

One could make the argument that BDD is actually a specific type of OCD, one that has an exclusive focus on the issue of appearance. On the other hand, BDD is a little different from the usual OCD in that behaviors like getting plastic surgery or wearing a wig don't occur repeatedly throughout each day like compulsions associated with most OCD (see Chapter 2 for more information about OCD and compulsions). Table 3-1 summarizes how BDD is like and unlike OCD.

BDD can result in severely disabling depression, isolation, and even suicide. If you or someone you know has symptoms of BDD, have an evaluation by a professional experienced with this disorder and get help.

Table 3-1	How BDD is Like and Unlike OCD
Like OCD	*Unlike OCD*
Consumes a significant amount of time	More likely to seek plastic surgery
Causes great distress	More likely to have depression
Checking is difficult to repress	Often occurs with less insight than OCD
Reassurance often sought from others	Some of the compulsive-like behaviors (such as plastic surgery) occur much less often than most compulsions associated with OCD

Hypochondriasis: "I think I'm really sick"

People with hypochondriasis have deep fears and are preoccupied with the idea that they suffer from a serious illness. These fears are usually based on misinterpretations of vague bodily sensations, and they persist even after medical evaluations confirm that nothing is wrong. Often those who suffer from this disorder have had multiple medical tests, made frequent trips to the doctor's office, and repeatedly changed medical professionals. Hypochondriasis significantly interferes with vocational and interpersonal functioning.

Vague physical symptoms can be signs of real, treatable illnesses. If you or someone you care about experiences pain or new, undiagnosed symptoms, see your primary care doctor or other medical expert for an evaluation. If you receive a diagnosis of hypochondriasis, it will be important for your mental-health provider and your healthcare provider to communicate closely with one another.

What makes hypochondriasis similar to OCD? First, the over-concern and attention to physical complaints are obsessional. These worries are in the mind of the sufferer. People with hypochondriasis ask for repeated reassurance from caregivers and family. Second, they engage in repetitive checking for bodily symptoms, like unusual coloration or consistency of their stool and minor aches and pains. Normal results of lab tests are typically doubted and they ask for tests to be repeated. Table 3-2 shows how hypochondriasis is similar to OCD, as well as how it differs.

It is, of course, *possible* that someone exhibiting symptoms of hypochondriasis suffers from a real, undiagnosed illness and that a doctor will eventually discover the problem. However, people with hypochondriasis and OCD of other types function better if they can learn to live with a certain degree of uncertainty.

Table 3-2	How Hypochondriasis is Like and Unlike OCD
Like OCD	*Unlike OCD*
Many thoughts that appear obsessional and difficult to stop	Generally a greater emphasis on bodily symptoms
Repeated checking	More distorted thoughts, especially in relation to illness
Reassurance often sought	More frequent, repeated medical tests
	Possibly a greater incidence of panic disorder

Trichotillomania: Pulling your hair out

Trichotillomania is repetitively pulling hair out of one's body and sometimes eating the hair. The hair can be pulled from anywhere on the body — the scalp, the eyebrows, other parts of the face, the underarms, the stomach, or even the pubic area. Hair-pulling can occur sporadically and briefly throughout the day, or it can go on for hours. In order to have this diagnosis, a person must exhibit noticeable hair loss.

Besides hair loss, other effects of trichotillomania can include skin infections, social isolation, tendonitis, muscle strains (from repetitive movements of the wrist, head, or neck), and even gastrointestinal problems from ingesting hair. Some hair-pullers stroke pulled hairs, inspect them, or slide them between their teeth (causing wear of tooth enamel). People who have this disorder often go to great lengths to disguise their problem by combing over, using cosmetics, wearing wigs, or pulling hair from areas usually covered by clothing.

Some people with trichotillomania report feeling pleasure when they pull hair. Others report feeling an overwhelming urge to pull out hair, followed by a reduction of the urge and tension after they have pulled their hair for a while. While anxiety can increase hair-pulling, anxiety seems to play a less important role in trichotillomania than it does in OCD.

Like OCD, impulses or urges are repetitive. Rituals or compulsions can be involved with the hair-pulling. Hairs are sometimes chosen because they feel just right, are a particular color, or are in a certain location. After hairs are pulled, they can be eaten, placed or preserved in ritualistic ways, or brushed against the face.

Table 3-3 lists some ways in which trichotillomania resembles OCD and other ways in which it differs from OCD. See Chapter 19 for a brief overview of treatment strategies for trichotillomania and Appendix A for additional resources for this problem.

Obsessive-compulsive dogs

Studies suggest that OCD may exist in the animal kingdom as well as in humans. Acral canine lick is a skin disorder in dogs that involves repetitive licking, scratching, or grooming. Dogs who are bored, left alone, or suffer from separation anxiety begin excessively licking an area, resulting in irritation and hair loss. This behavior may temporarily reduce tension but usually results in discomfort, infection, and sometimes nerve damage. The similarity to OCD and other impulse control disorders is that the behavior is repetitive, impulsive, and probably originally intended by the dog to decrease anxiety or distress. That's why many veterinarians consider Acral canine lick to be the OCD of dogs. Interestingly, the same class of antidepressant medication that has been found to be helpful in treating OCD and trichotillomania has helped dogs with this disorder. But, please, don't ever give any of your medication to your pets. Take them to the vet to get their own dosage prescribed.

Table 3-3	How Trichotillomania is Like and Unlike OCD
Like OCD	**Unlike OCD**
Repetitive, frequent behaviors that are difficult to suppress	Sometimes involves a pleasurable sensation
Causes considerable distress	Anxiety less prominent
Sometimes includes a need for "just right" feelings	Symptoms more often worse at night or at times of boredom and low arousal

Tics and Tourette's syndrome: Involuntary sounds and movements

Everyone demonstrates a few behaviors from time to time that can look a lot like tics. For example, who hasn't drummed fingers, tapped a pencil, or experienced a sudden body jerk? However, those behaviors don't quite qualify as tics. That's because tic disorder involves movements or sounds that occur against a person's will, suddenly, repeatedly, and irresistibly. Tourette's syndrome includes multiple movements with sounds.

If you or someone you care about has signs of tics or Tourette's syndrome, obtaining a complete neurological examination is important. Other types of neurological conditions can mimic tics and/or Tourette's syndrome. Such conditions include *Sydenham's chorea,* which is related to rheumatic fever; *autism,* which is a complex developmental disorder; and *pediatric autoimmune neuropsychiatric disorders* associated with streptococcal infections (also known as PANDAS). These other conditions may require different treatment approaches.

Tic disorders

Simply put, tics are rapid, repetitive movements or vocalizations that a person can only temporarily suppress. Tics usually get worse when someone is under stress and improve when the person is completely absorbed by an activity (such as video games, playing the piano, giving a lecture, or even performing surgery). Tics usually abate during sleep. Common motor tics (involving body movements) include:

- Blinking
- Facial gestures
- Facial grimacing
- Grooming
- Hand gestures
- Jumping
- Shoulder-shrugging
- Sniffing
- Stamping
- Touching something

Common vocal tics (involving noise) include:

- Barking
- Clicks with the tongue or teeth
- Grunting
- Making screeching sounds
- Repeating words
- Snorting
- Throat-clearing

Tics show up in young children as early as the age of two. Often the sounds or gestures can be rather subtle and almost unnoticeable. Other times, they can appear dramatic and disruptive to others. Tic symptoms usually worsen between the ages of nine and fifteen. Over time, symptoms wax, wane, and shift from one type of tic to another.

Tourette's syndrome

The diagnosis of Tourette's syndrome (TS) is given when a person exhibits multiple motor tics along with at least one vocal tic. This distinction between tics and TS seems somewhat arbitrary. For example, someone with many motor tics would not receive the diagnosis of Tourette's syndrome, but someone else with two motor tics and one mild vocal tic would be deemed as suffering from TS.

Good news. No one knows why for sure, but many people with either tic disorders or TS discover that their symptoms significantly improve over the years. And even if the symptoms don't improve, there are treatments that can help (see Chapter 19 for information about treating tic disorders and TS).

So how are tic disorders and TS like OCD? Tics feel irrepressible and uncontrollable just like compulsions feel for most people with OCD. And after a tic has been carried out, sometimes people report feeling slightly better for a while. Compulsions in OCD have an explicit intent to reduce anxiety or distress. By contrast, no clear goals are associated with tics and they seem automatic and reflexive. Table 3-4 points out the similarities and differences between OCD and tics and TS.

Although tics, TS, and OCD appear to be a little different from each other, it is common to suffer from both tics and OCD at the same time. Scientists theorize that tics, TS, and OCD have genetic links.

Table 3-4	How Tics and Tourette's Are Like and Unlike OCD
Like OCD	*Unlike OCD*
Repetitive and difficult to suppress	Not as clearly designed to reduce anxiety and distress
Causes great distress	More often can entail socially inappropriate behaviors
Runs in families	Obsessional thoughts and worries do not appear to precede tics
	More often triggered by boredom and situations involving low arousal (though high arousal also triggers it, as in OCD)

Skin-picking and nail-biting

Almost everyone occasionally picks at the skin on their hands or face to a limited degree at one time or another. This behavior is especially common when a scab forms, a rough patch of skin appears, or some other minor anomaly emerges on the scalp, nails, or skin. However, for some people, nail-biting and skin-picking evolve into a serious disorder that causes scarring, bleeding, sores, infections, and considerable tissue destruction.

Skin-picking and nail-biting are surprisingly common. Although precise statistics are not available, some researchers have reported as many as 5 percent of a sample of college students picked at their skin for over an hour per day. Those with this problem report great shame and worry about reactions from other people.

When Tourette's syndrome is misunderstood

Tourette's syndrome is often confused or miscategorized by the public and media who are familiar with one of Tourette's more noticeable sub-types, coprolalia. Those with the misfortune of having this type of verbal tic find themselves uncontrollably shouting out obscenities. Sometimes teachers, coaches, and friends think that this symptom is under the sufferers' control and incorrectly blame them for their seemingly inappropriate behavior.

Interestingly, some people with OCD (see Chapters 2 and 14 for information about inappropriate thoughts and OCD) greatly fear that they will shout out obscenities in public. However, they almost never actually do what they fear. Those with coprolalia unfortunately do experience uncontrolled shouting and swearing.

Fortunately, most people with Tourette's syndrome do not experience the symptom of coprolalia. Estimates vary, but experts contend that only about 10 to 15 percent of those with Tourette's syndrome have coprolalia. Furthermore, many of those with tic disorder or TS have fairly mild tics that often go undiagnosed for many years. Getting a diagnosis can be useful because then treatment can be sought for the disorder (and tics and TS are treatable). However, some people's symptoms are sufficiently mild that they do not greatly interfere with their lives and treatment may seem unnecessary. See Chapter 19 for a brief overview of treatment for these problems and Appendix A for more resources.

Typically, skin-picking and nail-biting seem to be driven by strong urges and a sense of temporary relief once the act is completed. Anxiety may not play quite as large of a role with skin-picking as it usually does with OCD, but skin-picking shares the repetitive, difficult-to-control aspects of OCD. Furthermore, those who skin-pick have higher than average rates of OCD.

 Skin-picking and nail-biting sometimes occur because a person has body dysmorphic disorder (see the section on BDD earlier in this chapter). Thus, a woman with BDD may perceive a slight imperfection on her face and pick at the area in an attempt to remove the imperfection. Unfortunately, the skin-picking and nail-biting associated with BDD usually start with an attempt to improve appearance and end up making things worse — sometimes much worse.

Table 3-5 notes how skin-picking and nail-biting resemble OCD and how they differ from it. See Chapter 19 for a brief overview of treatment ideas for skin-picking and nail-biting and Appendix A for additional resources for this problem.

Table 3-5	How Skin-Picking and Nail-Biting Are Like and Unlike OCD	
Like OCD	**Unlike OCD**	
Repetitive and difficult to suppress	Though unclear, anxiety may not play as large of a role as in OCD	
Causes great distress	Performed during times of boredom and low arousal	
	Obsessional thoughts apparently not as prominent	

Eating disorders: Intense fear of fat

Most eating disorders share the issue of obsessive concern with appearance found in those with body dysmorphic disorder (BDD; see earlier section). In addition, research has shown that roughly 20 to 30 percent of those who have eating disorders also have OCD. Table 3-6 points out the main similarities and differences between OCD and eating disorders.

Eating disorders occur in various forms, but share an obsessional concern about weight. Sufferers intensely fear gaining weight and frequently have a distorted view of their body and shape. People with eating disorders sometimes:

✔ Exercise to excess in order to lose weight

✔ Have highly restricted diets

✔ Overuse laxatives as a weight-loss strategy

✔ Self-induce vomiting to purge their bodies of calories consumed

✔ Use diuretics and enemas to lose weight

Eating disorders can result in brain damage, loss of tooth enamel, erosion of the esophagus, malnutrition, abnormal heart rhythms, hormonal imbalances, and even death. If you or someone you care about exhibits any of the symptoms of an eating disorder, please see a specialist in eating disorders to receive an appropriate diagnosis and treatment plan. You may also want to check out *Eating Disorders For Dummies* by Susan Schulherr (Wiley).

Table 3-6	How Eating Disorders Are Like and Unlike OCD	
Like OCD	**Unlike OCD**
Involve repetitive, obsessional thoughts	More often highly threatening to health or even life
Logic and evidence frequently disbelieved	Treatment more complex
Reassurance frequently sought	Compulsive behaviors less often reduce distress immediately
Cause great distress	

Impulse control disorders: Unstoppable bad habits

Impulse control disorders share the concept of repetitive urges found in OCD. However, with impulse control disorders, the urges are not as clearly about needing to reduce distress or anxiety. Rather, the impulses seem more related to increasing a sense of pleasure or excitement. Table 3-7 notes some of the ways in which impulse control disorders resemble and differ from OCD. Impulse control disorders include

- **Kleptomania:** Kleptomaniacs can't resist the impulse to steal things that they don't even really need. They feel tense before stealing and experience pleasure and excitement following the act.

- **Compulsive buying:** Compulsive shoppers have problems similar to kleptomaniacs in the sense that they can't resist things they don't need. But in this case, they at least pay for the items. Their compulsive shopping frequently leads to serious financial problems.

- **Gambling:** Those with this problem often get themselves into serious trouble with finances, relationships, and even illegal behavior. They have recurrent, obsessive thoughts about gambling. Logically, they have some insight into the futility of their pursuits, but they cannot stop themselves from going after the next big win.

- **Paraphilias:** People with paraphilias are drawn to sexually arousing fantasies and various sexual activities that are typically considered unacceptable or deviant (see the sidebar "Sexual obsession versus acting out").

- **Pyromania:** People with pyromania are fascinated and obsessed by fires. They feel tension prior to setting fires and excitement following the act. They do not set fires for financial gain or revenge. Nonetheless, their behavior often lands them in jail.

Sexual obsession versus acting out

Paraphilias are quite different from sexual obsessions experienced by some who have OCD (see Chapter 2). Sexual obsessions associated with OCD are deemed to be *highly inappropriate* by the person who experiences them. Those with OCD sexual obsessions obsess about whether they might have a paraphilia, but they actually do not. Thus, those with OCD sexual obsessions almost *never* act out their obsessions.

On the other hand, those with paraphilias derive considerable pleasure from their fantasies and often act them out. Just a few paraphiliac fantasies and activities include:

✔ **Exhibitionism:** Exposing one's genitals to strangers

✔ **Fetishism:** Using various non-living objects, such as underwear or shoes, to stimulate masturbation

✔ **Frotteurism:** Touching or rubbing against a non-consenting person

✔ **Pedophilia:** Sexual activity with underage children

Table 3-7	How Impulse Control Disorders Are Like and Unlike OCD
Like OCD	*Unlike OCD*
Repetitive and difficult to repress	Often do not cause distress except or until legal problems encountered
Can cause significant impairment	Anxiety appears to play little or no role
	Pleasure frequently reported from the behaviors

Recognizing Associates of OCD

OCD associates are the emotional problems that often occur along with OCD but are not considered part of the OCD spectrum. Thus, they do not involve the same repetitive, irresistible obsessions and compulsions found in OCD. Those with OCD are at higher risk of having these emotional disturbances than those without OCD. In fact, OCD commonly is accompanied by one or more of these or other emotional disorders. We discuss the five most common types of emotional disorders that crop up alongside OCD.

Mood disorders

Studies suggest that at least a quarter of people diagnosed with OCD also have a disturbance of mood. Mood disorders come in two major types: depression and mania.

- **Depression:** Depression involves intense, prolonged feelings of sadness and low mood. Symptoms can include a lack of interest in things, insomnia, poor or excessive appetite, feelings of worthlessness, problems concentrating, and fatigue.

- **Mania:** Mania involves inflated self-esteem, decreased need for sleep, distractibility, rapid speech, increased energy, excessive indulgences in high-risk behaviors (such as foolish business endeavors), and lack of judgment. Although some with mania report extremely high moods, most people with mania do things that are not in their best interests. And they usually crash at some point. Bipolar disorder involves alternations between manic and depressive states.

If you experience symptoms of a mood disorder, you should get them checked out. Left untreated, mood disorders can lead to serious problems. For a more thorough review of mood disorders, see *Depression For Dummies* by yours truly and *Bipolar Disorder For Dummies* by Candida Fink (both published by Wiley).

Anxiety disorders

In Chapter 2, we note that OCD has traditionally been considered an anxiety disorder. So it shouldn't be surprising to know that those with OCD are at higher risk than other people for also having additional anxiety disorders. Symptoms of anxiety disorders include:

- Avoidance of people and places
- Excessive worry
- Fears of losing control
- Feelings of impending doom
- Hyper alertness
- Intense fears
- Panic attacks
- Tension

If you experience symptoms of an anxiety disorder, you should get them checked out. Left untreated, anxiety disorders can lead to problems with health, relationships, and work. For a more thorough review of anxiety disorders, see our book *Overcoming Anxiety For Dummies* (Wiley).

Attention deficit disorders (ADD)

The various attention deficit disorders involve problems with attention, impulsivity, and/or hyperactivity. Attentional problems include trouble staying focused, making careless errors, losing everyday items, forgetfulness, and distractibility. Little kids with hyperactivity can't stay in their seats at school whereas adults with hyperactivity may remain seated, but look physically restless and have problems staying with a single activity. People with impulsivity talk before they think, have trouble waiting in line, and often interrupt others.

People diagnosed with OCD frequently receive an additional diagnosis of one of the attention deficit disorders. And undoubtedly, sometimes this diagnosis is accurate. However, clinically we see people whose obsessions and compulsions have interfered with their ability to focus, perform their jobs, or complete assignments. In other words, OCD consumes lots of attentional resources. In some of those folks, treating the OCD is likely to greatly alleviate what appears to be ADD.

Substance abuse

People with OCD suffer a lot of distress. It's no surprise that some of them may turn to substance abuse (alcohol, prescription drugs, illegal substances, and so forth) as a way of coping with their worries. In general, when substance abuse accompanies OCD, treatment becomes a little more complicated. However, excellent interventions exist for both problems and should be considered when they occur together.

Sometimes shame holds people back from seeking the help they need. Mental-health and medical specialists are accustomed to dealing with issues like substance abuse and OCD. They view them as problems to be solved rather than character weaknesses. Please don't let embarrassment prevent you from getting help.

Personality disorders

People with healthy personalities have satisfying relationships and live meaningful lives. They can handle stress effectively and solve most problems of daily living. For the most part, they understand their feelings and those of others. They tend to be resilient and flexible.

On the other hand, people with personality disorders demonstrate a wide variety of longstanding, rigid patterns of behavior and problems relating to others. These patterns interfere with living, relationships, work, and play. These problems are quite wide-ranging and most people with a personality disorder have only some of them. But in order to give you a sense of the personality disorders, here are a few of the types of problems associated with them:

✔ A paranoid distrust of others

✔ A pervasive sense of inferiority

✔ A sense of inner emptiness and meaninglessness

✔ An exaggerated sense of entitlement

✔ Excessive need for attention

✔ Excessively intense emotional reactions to events

✔ Intense fears of abandonment

✔ Preoccupation with self-glorification

✔ Seeing people as either all good or totally evil

✔ Stubbornly needing to be right

✔ Taking pleasure in manipulating other people

OCD versus OCPD

There's a particular personality disorder known as obsessive-compulsive personality disorder (OCPD). You may assume that most of those with OCD would also suffer from OCPD. Although those with OCD do have an elevated risk of OCPD, most people with OCD do not also have OCPD.

People with OCPD tend to:

✔ Be excessively dedicated to work and productivity

✔ Be perfectionists

✔ Be preoccupied with control

✔ Be self-righteous

✔ Demonstrate excessive frugality and fear of spending money

✔ Exhibit rigid, rule-bound thinking

✔ Have a reduced need for friendships and leisure versus work

✔ Have an excessive need for orderliness and rules

✔ See recreation as serious work

In other words, OCPD has a plodding, chronic pattern of general rigidity, orderliness, righteousness, and perfectionism. Although this list of OCPD tendencies may seem a little like OCD, OCPD does not include specific obsessions or compulsions (see Chapter 2 for more information about obsessions and compulsions).

Chapter 4

Blaming the Brain for OCD

. . . .

. . . .

*J*ust a few hundred years ago, many people believed that obsessive-compulsive disorder (OCD) symptoms were signs of demonic possession. People prayed over, exorcised, or scorned OCD sufferers. Life for those with OCD improved only slightly when Sigmund Freud came along and blamed OCD on hidden desires or early traumatic experiences. Neither approach was very helpful.

Today, OCD is considered a disorder involving brain function, emotions, and behavior; there may even be a link between OCD and infections. What all this means is that OCD can appear in well-adjusted, smart, normal people without a history of trauma or deep-seated emotional problems. In this chapter, we discuss how the brain plays a critical role in the development of OCD.

Looking at the Brain's Role in OCD

The brain governs perception, thinking, memory, behaviors, and emotions. Thus, the brain plays a major role in all emotional disorders, including OCD. But saying the brain is heavily involved with OCD isn't quite the same as saying that OCD is a brain disease and nothing more. In actuality, you can't really separate the brain, behavior, thoughts, and the environment. All of these contributors interact in intricate ways — and they can't be considered as operating in isolation, independently from one another.

In other words, every single thought that you have is generated by neurons communicating inside some portion of your brain. Medications that change the way the brain functions also change the way people think. Alternatively, therapies designed to change the way people think have been shown to change the way the brain functions as well.

To date, no one can point to specific biological processes that *directly cause* OCD (infections are an exception — see the sidebar "PANDAS: Part of the puzzle," later in this chapter). However, brain circuitry appears to work a little differently in those with OCD versus those who do not have OCD. No one knows for sure whether biological processes, learning, genetics, or environmental events contribute the most to that circuitry going awry.

Connecting genetics with OCD

Biological and genetic factors that impact the brain clearly assume some of the blame for OCD, as these factors significantly increase the risk of developing the disorder. Many studies support a genetic predisposition for OCD, that is, the idea that OCD runs in families. If several members of your family have OCD, you run a risk of developing symptoms. If you have an identical twin with OCD, your risk is even higher. However, the particular way the disorder is inherited is not yet clear.

OCD has many faces, and the face shown by OCD in the parent may differ from that seen in the child. For example, a mother who has the kind of OCD in which she checks door locks can give birth to a son who is obsessed about germs and a daughter with no signs of OCD.

OCD seems to be biologically or genetically linked to Tourette's syndrome (tics involving sudden movements such as grimacing, eye-blinking, grunts, or throat-clearing). OCD sufferers are much more likely to develop tics, and people with tics are more likely to develop OCD. This holds true for families as well as individuals. Families in which OCD is prevalent are more likely to also have family members with tic disorder (for more information on tics, see Chapter 3).

Getting inside your head

Knowledge of the brain — its structures, functions, and biochemical processes — has accumulated rapidly since the 1980s. In part, that's because we now have highly sophisticated, safe ways of observing the brain at work. These imaging assessment methods have allowed scientists to increasingly understand the ways in which the OCD brain works both before and after treatment. At this time, OCD is not diagnosed via brain scans, but they do enable us to see how treatments affect the brain. Some of these modern methods for viewing the brain in action are

✔ **Positron Emission Tomography (PET) scans:** PET scans involve inject-ing a small quantity of radioactive glucose into the bloodstream. Brain cells use glucose as fuel to perform their jobs. The PET scan observes these cells as they work and metabolize the injected glucose. On PET scans, the most active brain areas show up in different colors than less active regions. PET scans are not typically used to examine children's brains because small amounts of radiation exposure are involved.

✔ **Computerized Axial Tomography (CAT or CT) Scan:** The CAT scan uses multiple X-ray images to produce 3-D pictures of the brain (and other body organs). It can reveal brain damage and brain activity. The CAT scan is often used to evaluate injuries to the brain. Studies of brain injuries have provided some pieces of the OCD/brain puzzle.

✔ **Magnetic Resonance Imaging (MRI):** The MRI produces a huge magnetic field that reveals detailed images of the brain. Unlike the PET scan, MRIs do not use radioactive material. The MRI is best at viewing brain struc-tures rather than their activity. The MRI can show minor changes to the brain following stroke or injury.

✔ **Functional Magnetic Resonance Imaging (fMRI):** The fMRI is a type of MRI. It can view blood flow in the brain, which changes according to what the brain is doing. Therefore, it can show brain activity while a person performs various tasks, including thinking, looking, touching, problem solving, or focusing on various emotions.

✔ **Magnetic Resonance Spectroscopy (MRS):** The MRS is another form of an MRI. This amazing technique can actually reveal neurotransmitters in the brain at work.

✔ **Single Photon Emission Computed Tomography (SPECT):** The SPECT technique takes images from multiple angles and constructs a 3-D pic-ture. This technology may ultimately allow diagnosis of dementias in their early stages.

Knowledge gleaned from these sophisticated imaging techniques has enabled scientists to increase their understanding of the relationship between the brain and OCD.

In the following sections, we take a close look at how the brain functions in relation to OCD. We look at

✔ The areas of the brain

✔ The circuitry of the brain

✔ The transmitters of the brain

Feel free to skip this material if you're a brain surgeon (we're guessing you already know this stuff). Or you can skip it if you're a regular person who simply doesn't like anatomy and physiology.

Exploring Four Regions of the Brain

The brain is an amazing collection of cells and connections intertwined with a vast network of blood vessels. The average adult brain weighs around 3 pounds. Within those 3 pounds are two types of cells — neurons and glia.

- ✔ **Neurons:** The brain has about 100 billion neurons (give or take). Neurons are the cells that communicate with one another. They order muscles to move and generate thoughts. They congregate in groups. Each group communicates within itself as well as with other neuronal groups in the brain.

- ✔ **Glia:** Your brain has about ten times as many glia cells as it does neurons. Glia cells help out by protecting and nourishing the neurons as well as keeping the house clean by removing waste and dead neurons.

Neurons and glia come in many specific forms depending upon the type of work they are called upon to do. They form the basic structures of the brain described in the next four sections.

The anatomy of the brain has been studied for thousands of years. Various scientists have labeled brain structures using Latin words, Greek words, numbers, and letters. Some areas are even named for the people who first described them. Maybe some of them are named after favorite dogs or lovers. Who knows? Needless to say, the language of brain anatomy can be daunting. Making matters even more complex, various areas of the brain have been given different labels over time, and brain structures are sometimes combined in different ways.

We provide an overview of one of the many ways in which the brain can be divided into global regions. In the sections that follow, we explore the four regions known as the hindbrain, the midbrain, the diencephalon, and the forebrain.

Hold your fist straight up. Think of your forearm as your spinal cord and hind brain. Your wrist represents your midbrain. Your fist is analogous to the diencephalon. Now, imagine putting on a boxing glove. The boxing glove is the equivalent of your forebrain, the largest part of the human brain. Or, if you're not good at imagining your fist as your brain, take a look at Figure 4-1 for an illustration of the four major regions of the brain.

Hiding out with the hindbrain

The hindbrain contains structures that have to do with breathing, swallowing, heartbeat, gagging, muscle tone, wakefulness, and arousal. Pretty basic stuff. A serious blow to the hindbrain can mean lights out. The cerebellum, within the hindbrain, is thought to help coordinate posture and motor control. At this time, there doesn't appear to be much of a relationship between OCD and the hindbrain.

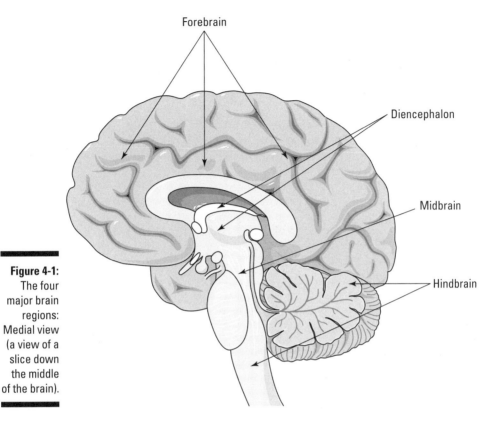

Figure 4-1:
The four
major brain
regions:
Medial view
(a view of a
slice down
the middle
of the brain).

Forebrain

Diencephalon

Midbrain

Hindbrain

Minding the midbrain

The midbrain coordinates auditory and visual information. The midbrain is essential for awareness of your surroundings as it orients you to sights, sounds, and sensations. For example, if your ears hear a shout behind you, your midbrain tells you to turn around and look for the source. If you feel a burning sensation in your foot, your midbrain directs you to pick up your foot and see what's going on. If your eyes then tell you that you're walking on hot coals, you know to jump.

Preliminary studies suggest that the midbrain may play a role in OCD. Neurotransmitters such as serotonin (see the section "Singling out serotonin and dopamine," later in this chapter) apparently are less available in this brain region among those who suffer from OCD. This reduced availability of serotonin may cause problems with attention and aggravate OCD.

Deciphering the diencephalon

The diencephalon consists of two major parts — the thalamus and the hypothalamus. Both of these are thought to be involved in OCD.

The thalamus

The thalamus receives, interprets, and integrates information from multiple sites in the brain, including those involved with hearing, seeing, touching, tasting, and smelling. The thalamus sends this information on to other regions in the forebrain.

The thalamus has been shown to be overly active and even larger in size in some studies of OCD sufferers. Other studies have demonstrated that the thalamus appears to normalize after treatment with either medication (see Chapter 11) or Cognitive-Behavioral Therapy (see Chapters 8, 9, and 10).

The hypothalamus

Less direct information is known about the role of the hypothalamus in OCD. The hypothalamus is a highly complex structure that functions to keep these bodily processes in balance:

- Body temperature
- Circadian rhythm
- Fatigue
- Hunger
- Sexual behavior
- Thirst

The hypothalamus also coordinates a variety of hormones and endocrines. Some studies suggest that the hypothalamus is involved in OCD. This seems highly likely, given its critical role in overall brain functioning.

Finding the forebrain

The forebrain is the largest region of the human brain. It includes the cerebral cortex, the basal ganglia, and the limbic system. From an evolutionary standpoint, the forebrain was the most recent portion of the brain to develop. In a global sense, the forebrain is responsible for advanced planning, judgment, and integrating sensory information with logic.

The cerebral cortex

The *cerebral cortex* is an area of the forebrain. It makes up the wrinkled outside layer of the brain. The cerebral cortex governs reasoning, abstract thinking, planning, organizing, and bringing us sensations from the outside world to form what we know as reality. The cerebral cortex can be divided into two hemispheres: right and left. It can also be subdivided into four lobes: frontal, temporal, parietal, and occipital.

The *orbital frontal cortex* (a part of the frontal lobe lying above the eyeballs) appears to be especially important in OCD. The orbital frontal cortex regulates planning, decision-making, and how one processes consequences. The orbital frontal cortex also helps detect errors. It is closely connected with the emotional centers of the brain. Those with OCD report trouble with decision-making, planning, and over-interpreting danger and peril.

The basal ganglia

The *basal ganglia,* sometimes referred to as the striatum, are nuclei in the forebrain that primarily function to control movement. The basal ganglia turn thoughts into actions (for example, translating the idea of walking into actual walking, or going from thinking about picking up a chocolate bar to the act of putting the bar into your mouth). The basal ganglia serve as a relay station among the thalamus, the cerebral cortex, and the hindbrain. The basal ganglia as a whole appear to help with the ability to *inhibit* responses. As we discuss in Chapter 3, irrepressible impulses represent a problem for many who have OCD.

The basal ganglia are most affected by Parkinson's disease. People with this disorder are not able to get their bodies to move in the way their brains want them to (that is, they can't translate thoughts into actions). They have trouble initiating movement and switching from one task to another.

Many books on OCD refer to various structures within the basal ganglia. Research has shown that these structures have a link with OCD, but don't get hung up on the jargon. Just know that when you see the following terms, they are referring to some part of the basal ganglia:

- Putamen
- Caudate nucleus
- Globus Pallidus
- Substantia nigra (associated with the basal ganglia, but actually located in the midbrain)

The limbic system

The limbic system takes on critical jobs having to do with human motivation, emotion, and memory. Three main structures in the limbic system include:

- **The amygdala:** This structure processes emotional information, which just happens to be most of what makes life feel fulfilling and meaningful. The amygdala also sounds an alarm when threatening events occur — even before you consciously know what's going on. People who suffer damage to the amygdala lose much of the ability to process emotions — good or bad — along with the early warning system.

  The amygdala is the seat of memories that stir the emotions — everything from love to fear. That's why you remember emotionally meaningful events like where you were when you first heard about 9-11 as opposed to what you did on 9-10 (unless that's your birthday). The amygdala is more active in those with OCD when they encounter situations that relate to their particular type of OCD — like contamination, checking, or superstitions.

- **The hippocampus:** This part of the limbic system is critical for forming new memories and learning. The hippocampus also stores information about where you are and how to get to the places you want to go. People with damage to the hippocampus become disoriented and have severe memory problems. Those with Alzheimer's or severe alcohol-related brain damage usually have a damaged hippocampus. The role of the hippocampus in OCD is probably somewhat less significant than the roles of the other limbic structures.

- **The cingulate gyrus:** This structure influences what you pay attention to. The cingulate gyrus receives emotional information and regulates responses to pain and aggression. This part of the limbic system is responsible for feelings of intense dread. Those with OCD often report fear and dread concerning what will happen if they don't carry out their compulsions. And studies have demonstrated that the cingulate gyrus goes into overdrive among those who have symptoms of OCD, as opposed to those without such symptoms.

Tracing the Brain's Circuitry

Think of the brain as an orchestra with a variety of sections coordinating their parts to produce a pleasant-sounding symphony. If the sections of the orchestra don't communicate well because the conductor isn't doing a good job, the entire performance collapses. The OCD orchestra is conducted by the orbital frontal cortex (see the preceding section, "Finding the forebrain"), and trouble arises when groups of uncooperative musicians in the brain ignore or overwhelm the conductor.

We describe some of the basic neurobiological processes as they appear to operate with many types of OCD. However, certain subtypes of OCD (such as hoarding; see Chapters 2 and 16), and certain relatives of OCD (see Chapter 3), probably work differently. Many of the same brain structures are likely involved, but less is known about the precise ways in which these structures impact these other subtypes of OCD or related disorders.

In OCD, several sections of the brain play too loudly or out of rhythm with other sections, disrupting the melodic flow of the brain. Jeffrey Schwartz, M.D., from the University of California at Los Angeles, presented what he called *brain lock*. He described the brains of people with OCD as stuck in a circuit of activation that feeds the obsessions and compulsions of OCD.

The worry circuit starts with the orbital frontal cortex, which is overly active and transmits false alarms. The alarms are sent to part of the basal ganglia (especially the caudate nucleus), part of the limbic system (particularly the cingulate gyrus), and the thalamus. These sections are more active in the brains of people with OCD.

The normal brain puts out a few false alarms too, but manages to detect and repress the response to them. An OCD brain lacks the ability to inhibit or put brakes on the reaction to false alarms. The following two stories about Ben and Brad illustrate the normal brain's response to false alarms versus the response of the OCD brain.

> **Ben** wakes up at 3 a.m. and thinks, "I think I left the stove on; maybe I need to go check. I'd hate to burn the house down." His orbital frontal cortex sends a mild signal of alarm throughout the worry circuit. However, Ben's worry circuit doesn't go into high gear. Various parts of his brain process the information and he concludes, "Well, it's pretty darn unlikely that I left the stove on. I never have before. I'm pretty comfortable right now; it doesn't seem worth getting up. Besides, I have smoke detectors." Ben turns over and goes back to sleep.

> **Brad** wakes up at 3 a.m. and has the same thought as Ben, "Gosh, I think I might have left the stove on; maybe I need to go check. I'd hate to burn the house down." Brad has OCD and his orbital frontal lobe screams a message to the rest of his worry circuit. Brad's heart races and his entire body fills with dread. He jumps out of bed to check the stove. He feels relief when he sees that it's turned off. He returns to bed. Then he thinks, "Maybe I didn't really check the stove carefully enough. Did I check all the burners?" The worry circuit reactivates and sends Brad scrambling to check the stove again. The entire process is repeated many times before Ben can settle down and go back to sleep.

The contrasting stories of Ben and Brad illustrate how the brain circuitry in people with OCD differs from that of non-sufferers. They both experienced a worrisome thought, but Ben's brain responded in a realistic manner, whereas Brad's OCD brain made him feel that the house was in imminent danger.

Additional evidence supporting the idea that these brain structures and the ways they communicate are involved with OCD can be found in the fact that injury to any of these areas sometimes results in OCD-like symptoms. Even more intriguing is the fact that surgery designed to cut the connections between some of these brain structures appears to improve OCD symptoms. As we discuss in Chapter 11, this approach to OCD is reserved for extremely severe cases that have repeatedly failed to respond to numerous other treatments — not something to be tried at home.

Transmitting Thoughts between Brain Cells

Brain neurons communicate with each other through a sophisticated system that involves both energy and chemistry. Neurons have a cell body and projections that assist in communication. Axons are the projections that transmit information from the cell body toward the next cell. Dendrites are the projections that collect information from other cells. Axons and dendrites transmit their information across something known as a *synaptic cleft*. The cleft is a small space between axons and dendrites.

Using electricity and chemicals to communicate

Communication among brain neurons starts with an electrical impulse in the cell body that is transmitted down the axon toward another cell. Once the impulse arrives at the presynaptic ending (or terminal), substances known as neurotransmitters are released. These neurotransmitters function as chemical messengers between cells.

Neurotransmitters are released from one neuron and travel across the synaptic cleft. There, most are vacuumed up by a receiving neuron at the postsynaptic receptor site. From the postsynaptic receptor site, an electrical impulse travels down the dendrite toward the receiving cell body. Some of the neurotransmitters don't make it to the receiving cell and return to the sending cell. See Figure 4-2 for an illustration of how this process works.

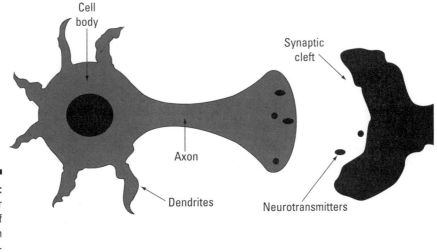

Figure 4-2:
The cellular
method of
carrying on
a conversa-
tion.

PRESYNAPTIC NERVE   POSTSYNAPTIC NERVE

Singling out serotonin and dopamine

Scientists continue to discover new types of neurotransmitters. Currently, two transmitters — serotonin and dopamine — seem to be particularly related to the brain functioning of people with OCD. These transmitters follow circuits through different regions of the brain and are thought to be central to mood, energy level, and behavior. Serotonin and dopamine form the basis of the serotonergic system and the dopaminergic system, respectively. Although much remains to be determined about how and why these systems cause problems in the brain, the following has been discovered:

✔ **Serotonergic System:** This system is involved in wakefulness and mood. Disruptions in serotonin are related to OCD, anxiety, depressed moods, eating disorders, tics, aggression, and impulsivity.

Medications that increase the availability of serotonin have been found to help most people with OCD. Some report that they continue to have obsessive thoughts, but are able to cope with their feelings without acting on compulsions (see Chapter 2 for more about obsessions and compulsions).

✔ **Dopaminergic System:** This area is involved in maintaining smooth movement. It is also involved in the reward system of the brain and seems to be related to addictions. Parkinson's disease, a condition in which people experience tremors and muscle rigidity, is associated with decreased availability of dopamine. Schizophrenia, a disorder that involves disorganized thinking, is related to too much dopamine. OCD and Tourette's syndrome (see Chapter 3) also appear to involve disruption in the dopaminergic system.

Drugs that block dopamine have been found to be effective in treating tics as well as repetitive behaviors. Drugs that increase dopamine can induce tics and symptoms of OCD. See Chapter 11 for more information about medication and OCD.

People check the oil level in their cars by using a dipstick to see if more is needed. No dipstick equivalent exists to check the levels of neurotransmission in the brain. That's why sometimes multiple medications that target these areas need to be tried before the right one is found (see Chapter 11 for more information about medication).

PANDAS: Part of the puzzle

So, what do Chinese bears that eat bamboo have to do with OCD? Nothing, really. PANDAS is the abbreviation for Pediatric Autoimmune Neuropsychiatric Disorders Associated with Streptococcal Infection. Whew. No wonder they're called PANDAS.

PANDAS describe children or teens who suddenly develop OCD symptoms or tics (see Chapter 3 for more on tics and Tourette's syndrome) following a strep throat. Other infections, such as a complication of rheumatic fever called Sydenham's Chorea and some types of encephalitis, also can result in these or similar symptoms. Symptoms develop rapidly, almost overnight. Kids usually have tics, obsessions, compulsions, and lots of irritability. This sudden onset of symptoms gradually improves unless another strep throat comes along.

Researchers believe that PANDAS occur when the body produces antibodies to combat the strep infection. These antibodies do a good job of fighting off the infection. However, sometimes, in some kids, the good guys (antibodies) go after the wrong bad guy. In PANDAS, the antibodies attack the basal ganglia in the brain, which in turn leads to OCD and/or tics.

The use of antibiotics for the treatment of PANDAS is currently being investigated and shows some promise. If antibiotics work, they will do so quickly; otherwise, treatment of PANDAS is conducted in the same way as for other types of OCD and has about the same effectiveness. Refer to Chapters 20 and 21 for more on OCD and kids.

Chapter 5

Developing and Reinforcing OCD

In This Chapter

▶ Looking at how OCD begins

▶ Rewarding OCD inadvertently

▶ Reviewing faulty reasoning

*H*ow does obsessive-compulsive disorder (OCD) begin and why does it develop in some people and not others? OCD symptoms often start in childhood and get worse without treatment. But the disorder can also manifest in adults. In Chapter 4, we discuss the biological basis for OCD. But biology and the brain are not the only culprits in its development. The environment, experiences, and thinking styles are also important in the genesis and maintenance of OCD.

OCD can become more entrenched through the innocent reinforcement of others. It can also worsen because of the wrong thinking patterns exhibited by OCD sufferers.

In this chapter, we reveal the childhood experiences that may contribute to the development of OCD. Next, we describe how OCD is maintained and reinforced by giving in to its demands. Finally, we run down the problems worsened by the way the OCD mind thinks.

An obsession is an intrusive thought, urge, or image. Compulsions are repetitive mental acts or behaviors. Both obsessions and compulsions cause mental distress because they are unwanted, time-consuming, and feel completely unacceptable to the sufferer.

Developing OCD as a Child or Adult

More often than for other emotional disorders, such as anxiety and depression, the origins of OCD can be traced to childhood where both nature and nurture play roles. Parents are usually quite well-intentioned, but sometimes their efforts to protect or teach their kids go too far and provide fertile ground for the development of OCD.

But OCD can also crop up in adulthood for a number of reasons. In most instances, OCD occurs in adults who have shown some predisposition or symptoms of OCD in childhood. However, OCD can also occur in adults who have no such obvious predispositions but who have suffered a serious infection, head injury, trauma, or major life change. In this section, we examine potential roots of OCD in childhood, as well as look at some of the likely triggers for adult-onset OCD.

Developing OCD early

Have you ever observed the bedtime routines of typical 2-year-old children? Many have elaborate rituals that they insist their parents follow. These patterns of behavior are rigid and serve to ease children into sleep.

Most children have some anxiety over separating from their mothers or fathers at nighttime. Having rituals helps young children make that separation from awake during the day to asleep at night more securely. In the following example, Alaina illustrates a normal, albeit time-consuming, bedtime routine.

Two-year-old **Alaina's** mom starts the process shortly after dinner. "Time for your bath; let's pick up your toys," she tells her. Alaina insists on lining up all of her stuffed animals and dolls on a bench in her room. She places each one carefully in an order only she understands. If her mom moves one, she gets upset and rearranges them so that they're just right.

Other toys are tossed into a toy chest. Next is the bath. Again, she has certain toys for the water. She allows her mom to wash her, but is busy in a pattern of play, singing a song, and carefully arranging her water toys in order on the edge of the tub. After the bath and getting into her pajamas, Alaina chooses three books. Her mother must read them in a certain order.

Then to bed. The comforter must be placed with a certain pattern showing. She has a blanket that she holds onto and three stuffed bears that sleep next to her. The closet door must be completely closed and the blinds up one inch so that a little light from the street shines through. A family picture sits on the night stand, angled so that Alaina can see it from her bed. Alaina likes to have her mom sit with her for a couple of minutes. Then there's a short prayer, a kiss, and mom says "Good-night, I love you forever."

Alaina's story, which is cute and perfectly normal, shows how rituals and conventions can help a child feel cozy and secure. However, these rituals can also point to the first signs of impending OCD. The change from normal to OCD is thought to happen due to unknown mixtures of biology and early experiences (nature and nurture).

Childhood experiences can involve well-intentioned but misguided parenting, trauma, stress, or other negative events. They can also involve a child modeling or adopting the behaviors of a parent who suffers from OCD.

If family members have OCD, the probability of a child having OCD is higher. This increased probability could be a result of children learning OCD behaviors from their parents. But this increased risk could also be a result of genetics. See Chapter 4 for more info on genetics and biological causes of OCD. In fact, in one person, OCD may be entirely the result of genetics, while in another it may be entirely the result of the environment, while in a third it may be due to a combination of the two. Pinning down the cause of OCD in any individual case is pretty much impossible.

Good intentions; bad results

Early childhood experiences shape personalities and can set the stage for the development of later emotional difficulties, such as OCD. Parents have tremendous influence over their children. They generally mean well and want only what's best for their kids. The concepts they may introduce their children to are intended to have a positive effect. If taken too far, however, these intentions may boomerang and contribute to a child's OCD.

Misguided or bad parenting is not the primary cause of OCD. OCD is a complicated disorder that involves the brain as well as learning. However, experiences do influence the occurrence of OCD symptoms and how severe OCD becomes. See Chapters 20 and 21 for more information about OCD in children.

Giving too much information

Good parents warn their children about dangers. But sometimes children are exposed to information that they're not ready to handle. For example, sternly warning 3-year-olds to stay away from strangers because people they don't know might kidnap them won't keep 3-year-olds safe. A 3-year-old who hears this information may develop intense fear of any unknown person. This fear can lead to obsessional thinking about various dangers in the world. Making sure 3-year-old children are never left unsupervised is better than frightening them.

Modeling misguided thinking

Parents want to teach their kids appropriate behavior. But in doing so, sometimes parents inadvertently teach their children that having bad thoughts means they're bad people. The story about Tom that follows illustrates how such teaching can foster OCD thinking (see the section "Worsening OCD with Bad Thinking," later in this chapter).

> Five-year-old **Tom** loves to play with his Legos. He builds castles and towers. When Tom's 3-year-old sister Michelle knocks over his tower, Tom pushes her and shouts, "Get out of my room, you creep; I hate you!" Tom's father overhears the ruckus and tells Tom, "You should *always* love your sister; God punishes kids who have thoughts like that!"

Tom's father may have gone overboard and frightened his son. Though his intentions were honorable (wanting Tom to love his sister), he used a scare tactic that can lead to OCD-like thinking. In particular, Tom's dad suggested that merely having bad thoughts equates with being a bad person — a style of thinking quite common in OCD. Thinking is not the same as doing, but kids can be convinced that they're bad people if they have greedy, mean, or even illogical thoughts. What starts as a random thought can become an obsession.

Seeking perfection

Parents naturally want children to put their best effort into everything they do, but parents can scare their children by telling them they must do things perfectly or not at all. The saying, "If it's worth doing, it's worth doing right," can be pushed too far. Children who feel they must do everything perfectly sometimes stop trying altogether because they're afraid of making mistakes. (See the section "Needing everything perfect," later in this chapter, for more on the role of perfectionism in OCD.)

Overprotecting

Parents are right in thinking that it's their job to protect their children, but they may contribute to the development of OCD if they become *over*protective and never allow their children to goof up or assume any responsibility. Parents who fall into this trap end up sending a message to their kids that they're not capable of dealing with the world. These kids sometimes grow up believing that the world is a dangerous place and that they have little control.

When bad things happen

Bad things happen to children and their families. When these experiences occur, they can start a pattern of worry and fear. These initial fears can contribute to the development of OCD in children who are susceptible.

Illness

Children who suffer from a serious illness or have close family members who are sick often believe that the illness could have been prevented. For example, a child may be told that if he doesn't wash his hands he'll get sick. He then actually does get very sick and believes that it's his fault because he didn't wash his hands. Thereafter, he spends more and more time washing his hands. Or a girl whose grandmother gets cancer believes it happened because her grandmother didn't pray at night. She may start performing rituals to protect herself and other family members.

Accidents

Accidents happen every day. Children, their friends, or family members are often involved in car accidents. Children are exposed to other accidents by overhearing adult conversations, reading the newspaper, or hearing the news on television. Because accidents are frightening and difficult for children to understand, kids often invent ways to protect themselves by using magical chants, rituals, or avoidance. The story below about 8-year-old Austin illustrates how a ritual may emerge after an accident.

> **Austin** returns home from a visit at his cousin's house. On the way, his parents' car is rear-ended by a drunk driver. His brother is seriously injured. Luckily, no one else in the car is hurt. Austin thinks he hears someone ask about the seat belts. Austin jumps to the conclusion that his brother did not correctly fasten his seat belt. In the ensuing weeks, Austin starts checking to see whether his belt is fastened "just right." At first, he buckles and unbuckles it several times before allowing his mother to pull out of the driveway. This activity gradually develops into a complex pattern — including locking and unlocking the car doors, positioning himself "just so" in the seat, and fastening and unfastening his seat belt until the click sounds "just right." This ritual must be performed every time he gets into the family car. His ritual starts consuming a lot of time, and then he starts other "protective" rituals. Austin develops a full-blown case of OCD.

Austin's story shows how easily children can develop OCD from their attempts to understand and cope with traumatic events. The symptoms sometimes start out making a little bit of sense (such as Austin carefully checking his seat belt), but evolve into activities that have little to do with anything that could realistically serve to protect.

Stress

When children are exposed to lots of stress, symptoms of OCD become worse. No study has directly linked a stressful event to the start of OCD; however, plenty of evidence suggests that stress leads to an increase in distorted thinking, which is characteristic of OCD.

Children may have a bad thought, such as wanting a younger sibling to be hurt. In rare cases, the sibling actually gets hurt sometime later. Children who experience bad thoughts that happen to come true may believe that their thoughts cause bad things to happen.

For example, a girl wishes that her father would stop yelling at her mother. Sometimes she has thoughts of hating her father when he yells. Later, her parents get a divorce and her father moves out. She believes that her thoughts of hating her father and wishing that he'd stop yelling caused him to leave. Thinking that thoughts cause events to happen is typical of OCD thinking. For more on this, see the later section, "Worsening OCD with Bad Thinking."

Stress can also develop from giving children too much responsibility before they're developmentally ready. For example, an older child who has to assume care for younger siblings can become overwhelmed by the responsibility. The older child worries about somehow hurting the younger ones. The child in charge of his siblings develops an OCD style of thinking that we discuss further in the section, "Being too responsible."

Trauma

Unfortunately, many children experience abuse or trauma. These events trigger worry and fear. Some children react with anger or depression. Others develop symptoms of OCD. For example, a boy who is at a bank with his father when it's robbed starts to worry about making sure the doors and windows at his house are locked. His daily checking routine starts each evening and involves both of his parents. He also frequently asks his parents to check throughout the house before he goes to bed.

Learning by seeing

Children learn from watching their parents. Thus, parents who exhibit OCD can inadvertently teach or model OCD to their children. The following example of Jane demonstrates how a parent with OCD can pass it along without intending to do so.

> **Jane** (a mother with OCD) worries about contamination. She obsesses about germs and the possibility of her or her family coming down with a serious illness. In order to protect everyone, Jane compulsively cleans the house with bleach for hours every day. She warns her children about all the dangers from germs. She makes her kids take baths every morning and before bed — as well as when they return home from school or play outside. Her children listen and accept their mother's fears as being reasonable. Therefore, they begin to fear getting contaminated themselves.

Jane shows how a mother with OCD can model and teach her children to develop the disorder, quite possibly whether they have a genetic predisposition or not. However, not every child with a parent like Jane will develop OCD. Some kids may be more resistant or resilient, whether due to genes or some other unknown factor.

Developing OCD as an adult

Sometimes adults develop OCD even though they did not suffer from it as children. Major life changes such as divorce, loss of loved ones, natural disasters, and significant financial setbacks, all can trigger the emergence of OCD in an adult. OCD symptoms can start gradually or have a sudden onset. Trauma would be particularly likely to cause a sudden onset of OCD. OCD is especially likely to occur in adults who tend to be anxious and/or have a genetic predisposition for developing OCD.

Trauma and PTSD versus OCD

Traumatic events frequently cause severe emotional pain. One of the more common reactions to severe trauma is known as post-traumatic stress disorder (or PTSD). PTSD involves recurrent thoughts or images of the event and avoidance of reminders of the trauma. For example, a soldier may have repeated images of a bomb exploding and avoid driving near construction sites and congested traffic because loud noises trigger the images.

Less often, trauma may trigger the onset of OCD. But distinguishing between OCD and PTSD can be tricky. If the obsessions and compulsions closely relate to the traumatic event in some way, then PTSD is usually diagnosed as the only emotional disorder. However, in the case of the soldier, if he only obsessed about cleanliness and avoided public restrooms, he would be deemed as suffering from OCD that was triggered by trauma. Finally, if the soldier had repeated images of the bomb exploding, avoided driving in noisy areas, and then began to obsess about cleanliness, he would be suffering from both PTSD and OCD.

Reinforcing OCD with Positives and Negatives

If left alone and untreated, OCD usually gets worse. One reason that OCD becomes more time-consuming and more distressing is because of what psychologists call reinforcement. Before we explain how reinforcement works specifically for OCD, here is the basic premise: *Reinforcement increases the likelihood of something occurring.* Reinforcement can be positive, negative, or both negative and positive.

Supporting OCD with positive reinforcement

Most people don't go to work without getting a paycheck. The paycheck increases the likelihood of working and is therefore a positive reinforcement. Dogs are trained to associate getting a reward for sitting. Dogs will sit for their owners when they expect to get a treat. Even when they don't get a treat, they still have hope. Dog treats positively reward dog sitting.

Positive reinforcement can be found in encouraging words, a pat on the back, an ice cream cone, or a hug. Praise can also be a powerful form of positive reinforcement.

Friends and family can fall into a trap of positively reinforcing those with OCD. When people you care about suffer from obsessional worries, the most natural thing in the world is to tell them that everything will be okay. Saying that everything will be alright is also known as "providing reassurance to the sufferer."

Supporting OCD with negative reinforcement

Negative reinforcement happens when a behavior gets rid of a distressing, unpleasant event or feeling. Like positive reinforcement, negative reinforcement increases the likelihood of a behavior occurring in the future. The behavior becomes more frequent because it reduces distress.

Our dog Murphy is a master at negative reinforcement. Murphy loves to be petted. When Murphy wants a pat, she finds any human who's sitting down and purposely begins scratching that human's kneecap. The feeling is never pleasant, and sometimes it's downright painful. Murphy stops scratching as soon as she is petted. She knows that most people figure out quite quickly what she wants. So, people increase their petting because Murphy has negatively reinforced them for doing so.

Between sleeping in a sunny spot, occasionally stretching, eating, and going outside to . . . well, you know, Murphy spends her day going back and forth scratching people. Sometimes she doesn't even have to scratch them before they start petting her — she has trained them that well with negative reinforcement.

The negative reinforcement process is a little more complex when applied to OCD. Negative reinforcement comes into play when people with OCD experience an obsession and try to deal with it through either avoidance or compulsion. The process goes like this:

1. **Obsession:** The OCD sufferer experiences an unpleasant, distressing, obsessive thought, urge, or image that creates anxiety.

2. **Avoidance or compulsion:** The sufferer attempts to cope with the obsession by avoiding it or engaging in a compulsion.

   • *Avoidance* is an attempt to suppress the obsession by avoiding potential causes, such as staying away from things that may be contaminated or not driving due to fear of hitting someone.

   • *Compulsions* are acts intended to neutralize the obsession, such as hand-washing or frequently stopping the car to see whether someone was hurt.

In both instances, the sufferer's anxiety is temporarily relieved.

3. **Negative Reinforcement:** Both avoidance and compulsions become more frequent because they succeed in temporarily reducing anxiety and distress. In other words, anxiety and distress are unpleasant. Negative reinforcement involves a behavior that succeeds in reducing this unpleasantness. People tend to do things more often when they are negatively reinforced by having their distress reduced.

The temporary relief that people with OCD get when they try to avoid an obsession or act out a compulsion makes these strategies seem like they're working. So, people repeat them and the cycle becomes more ingrained and compelling. The following example clarifies the concept.

Bert worries about dirt and germs. He particularly hates touching other people's hands. When someone attempts to shake hands with him, he imagines filthy bathrooms and disease-carrying germs. Along with the image, he feels a surge of anxiety. Whenever possible, Bert avoids shaking hands. When he successfully avoids a handshake, Bert feels a huge sense of relief (his anxiety goes down sharply). Therefore, not shaking hands is negatively reinforced.

If Bert is forced to shake hands, his anxiety and distress increase. He limply puts out his hand and withdraws it quickly. He then excuses himself and washes or disinfects his hands. After this act, he feels a bit better. So the next time he feels distress, he's more likely to wash and disinfect his hands. Washing and disinfecting become more frequent because they've been negatively reinforced.

Bert's behaviors interfere with his work and his interactions with friends and family. Without treatment, his OCD is likely to intensify. Bert is a typical example of how OCD grows and intensifies over time.

Combining positive and negative reinforcement: A double whammy

People with OCD ask for reassurance as a way of getting both positive and negative reinforcement. Positive reinforcement comes from the care and understanding the person receives. Negative reinforcement happens because the reassurance temporarily removes the feelings of worry and distress.

So, what happens when something is both positively and negatively reinforced? In short, it becomes more frequent. People with OCD who ask for reassurance do so with increasing frequency as time goes on. Yet the more often they ask, the more insecure they feel. A few quick examples can help clarify how the reassurance cycle works.

Arthur has obsessive thoughts about having sex with children. He is appalled by those thoughts and has never even come close to acting them out. He goes to confession every day. On bad days he goes to more than one church so that he can confess more than once. He asks each priest for reassurance that he will not go to hell for having bad thoughts. Every priest has patiently answered that thoughts are not the same as acts. Arthur feels momentarily better after the confession. The care and concern of the priest both positively and negatively reinforce Arthur because his anxiety is temporarily decreased and he enjoys receiving the concern.

Brenda believes that she has left the stove or other appliances on. She is often late for work because she returns home to check. She also calls her husband and asks him if he thinks she may have left the stove on. Brenda's husband reassures her that he's she turned it off. Five minutes later, she may call him again and ask the same question. Sometimes she asks about the coffeepot. Brenda's husband loves his wife and puts up with frequent interruptions during his workday.

Colin lives alone. He is obsessed with order and cleanliness. His house is spotless. He arranges the food in his cupboards alphabetically. He spends hours each day arranging and rearranging his belongings. When something is amiss, he gets very upset. Colin seeks reassurance by calling his mother 4 or 5 times a day. He asks her whether she loves him and whether he is a good person. His mother worries about Colin, but is always there for him.

Family members, counselors, and friends can unknowingly contribute to OCD by giving reassurance. See Chapters 21 and 22 for information about how to handle reassurance-seeking in children, family, or friends with OCD.

Worsening OCD with Bad Thinking

The thinking styles of those with OCD make OCD worse. These ways of thinking likely originate from early experiences and are perpetuated by reinforcement, as discussed in earlier sections. As these ways of thinking become engrained, they deepen and intensify OCD. Even when peoples' OCD originates in adulthood, it is quite possible that they developed styles of thinking consistent with OCD during childhood. These styles of thinking likely increase the risk of acquiring OCD later in life.

Everyone's brain fills with weird thoughts, impulses, or urges once in a while. Having strange or scary thoughts is perfectly normal. For example:

✔ You're walking down stairs carrying an infant, and you fear you might drop the baby.

✔ Standing on a balcony, you have an impulse to jump.

✔ You hear someone coughing and you think you might get sick and die.

✔ You feel like taking all of your clothes off.

✔ You find a certain minister very attractive, so you must be a sinner.

Those thoughts can be pretty uncomfortable. But if you don't have OCD, you may dismiss them as odd or a bit disgusting. However, people with OCD misinterpret their thoughts as overly important or dangerous. They try to stop thinking the thoughts or do something to prevent the thoughts from occurring.

Various types of OCD thinking often work in concert with each other. Thus, most obsessions or compulsions involve more than one type of distorted thoughts. The story of Diane shows you how this collusion works.

> **Diane** believes that in order to protect her children, she must repeat the number 3 all day long in her mind and do everything in sets of three. Thus, she washes the dishes three times and she flushes the toilets three times. As you can imagine, Diane has trouble getting things done.

Diane's story illustrates how many types of OCD thinking gang up to ruin her life. Although her obsessions and compulsions all revolve around the number 3, you can see how these thought distortions overlap. Diane's thinking includes:

✔ Being too responsible

✔ Controlling thoughts

✔ Exaggerating risk

✔ Thinking magically and illogically

✔ Viewing thoughts as real

But all is not lost for Diane or for you. We show you how to untangle OCD thinking in Chapters 8 and 9.

The next sections explain the most common OCD thinking errors. In Chapters 8 and 9, we spell out how to combat OCD thinking.

Exaggerating risk

People with OCD tend to believe that bad things happen all the time, and that bad things have horrible consequences. For example, no one likes to be around people who are coughing and sneezing and not covering their mouths. Have you ever been on an airplane seated next to someone with a bad cold? Yuck. OCD turns that unpleasant feeling into panic about getting sick. The OCD mind imagines that catching the cold will result in bronchitis, pneumonia, or even death. OCD thinking exaggerates the likelihood of catching something as well as the consequences of getting ill.

The thinking of those with OCD tends to rate the likelihood of almost all types of obsessional fears actually occurring as much higher than logic would dictate. For example, a woman with scrupulosity OCD (see Chapters 2 and 14 for more information) has obsessions about screaming out profanities in church. She worries about doing so at each and every service. In actuality, she has never in her life even said an obscenity out loud in front of anyone. But when asked by her therapist, she rates the likelihood that someday she'll lose control in church at around 80 percent.

Not accepting uncertainty

Life does not come with guarantees. But those who suffer from OCD attempt to eliminate uncertainty of all kinds. Unfortunately, this creates greater misery than you might imagine. The following example of Ed shows how intolerance of uncertainty becomes a never-ending, nerve-wracking quest.

> **Ed** suffers from a type of OCD in which he greatly fears that he is a *pedophile,* one who sexually abuses children (see Chapters 2 and 14 for more information). He has never abused a child, and he really doesn't have sexual desires for children. However, he worries constantly about the possibility, no matter how remote, that he might one day actually attack a child sexually. His relatives are puzzled as to why he never attends their gatherings — but that's because children attend those events. He spends hours each day reading about pedophiles to assure himself that he isn't like them. This reading reduces his worries for a little while, but the uncertainty always returns. He believes that he must stay away from children at all costs — at least until he's finally able to achieve 100 percent certainty that he is not a pedophile.

Ed's story shows how desperately those with OCD crave certainty. Unfortunately, living without some degree of uncertainty is impossible.

Needing everything perfect

OCD thinking drives its sufferers to seek perfection. Perfectionists believe that perfection is actually possible and they should strive for it. Perfectionistic thinking dictates that everything should be arranged "just so" and completed without errors. This thinking often prevents people with OCD from finishing important work due to fear of making mistakes. Even miniscule mistakes are viewed with loathing and fear — if errors do occur, this thinking greatly magnifies their significance. You can probably see why perfectionism leads to avoidance and procrastination.

Controlling thoughts

Typically, people don't spend a whole lot of time thinking about their thinking. Once in a while, a strange or disturbing thought may pop into people's minds and they usually dismiss the odd thought as unimportant. For example, Melinda may have the thought that she could let her car drift into an oncoming lane of traffic. But she quickly realizes that the thought is pretty silly and lets it go. Her attention returns to driving and listening to the radio.

However, those with OCD believe that thoughts are very important. They believe they should exert mental control by not allowing disturbing thoughts to occur in the first place. They think that controlling one's thoughts is both possible and essential. If Sam, who has OCD, has a thought about driving into an oncoming lane of traffic, he believes that having that thought is a sign of poor mental health or even insanity. Ironically, Sam finds himself focusing on his fearful thought for a long time.

Being too responsible

Those with OCD believe that they must be vigilant and do everything possible to protect others from harm. And if a bad outcome does occur, they think they probably could and should have done something to prevent it. Sometimes this thinking gets pretty bent out of shape. The story of Ellen demonstrates this inflated sense of responsibility run amok.

> **Ellen** believes that she must never fall ill out of concern for making others around her sick. She wears a face mask throughout the cold season and washes her hands every hour. She believes that her compulsions protect those around her from contracting any germs — which she feels she carries even if she isn't sick. If one of her family members catches a cold, she obsesses over what she did to cause the illness. She firmly believes that there must have been something she could have done to prevent the cold.

Like many who have OCD, Ellen starts with an idea that sounds almost reasonable — she wants to avoid making others sick. But the OCD throws the sense of responsibility into hyper-drive. She enormously inflates the extent to which she influences events and blames herself for things she has little or no control over.

Viewing thoughts as real

The OCD mind tends to view thoughts way too seriously — so much so that it blurs the distinction between thoughts and actions. This distinction can be blurred in three ways:

- ✔ **Bad thoughts = bad deeds.** This way of blurring thoughts and actions involves thinking that having a bad thought is the same thing as actually carrying out a bad deed. Thus, someone who has a thought of robbing a bank may conclude that he is as immoral as if he'd actually robbed the bank.

- ✔ **Thoughts are always true.** For example, if someone with OCD has a thought that the wallpaper is contaminated, she concludes that it must actually *be* contaminated.

- ✔ **Thoughts cause events.** Another way of thinking about thoughts as real is by making the assumption that thoughts can actually *cause* events in the world to occur. Thus, some people with OCD think that if they experience a thought about a loved one dying, the thought itself may cause the person to die.

Thinking magically and illogically

OCD thinking usually has a magical, illogical quality to it. Thus, those with OCD often imbue numbers with magical properties. For example, some numbers are thought to be either safe or dangerous, good or bad. Some with OCD feel a compulsion to repeat actions a certain number of times in order to prevent a catastrophe from occurring.

Superstitions lack logic as well. In OCD, superstitions can look particularly bizarre. For example, someone with superstitious OCD (see Chapters 2 and 17 for more information) may feel driven to wear certain colors in order to feel safe from harm. Someone else may avoid driving on streets that start with the letter C out of a conviction that C is an unlucky letter.

Lots of people have a few superstitious beliefs and even a little magical thinking — especially kids. It's not OCD thinking until the beliefs start interfering with a person's life. So if you don't like the number 13 or the color black, so what? But if you spend hours each day consumed with thoughts about numbers and colors, you may have a problem.

Part II
Starting Down the Treatment Path

The 5th Wave   By Rich Tennant

"My hunch, Mr. Pesko, is that you're still making mountains out of molehills."

In this part . . .

In this part, we cover the issues you need to know before starting treatment for OCD. Many people with OCD never get help due to fears about treatment. We show you ways to overcome these fears. We also help you understand who is qualified to provide OCD treatment and how to know whether you've found the right person for you.

Chapter 6

Overcoming OCD Obstacles to Change

In This Chapter

▶ Understanding resistance to change

▶ Figuring out why people defeat themselves

▶ Running through the roadblocks

The process of change often stirs up a deep-seated, almost primal fear. Change for anyone can be uncomfortable. Fear of change leads many people to choose to live with the devil they know rather than the one they don't. Other times people say and believe that they want to change, but they end up engaging in self-defeating behaviors without even knowing why.

The nature of OCD makes change even more challenging for those in its throes, and resistance is more multifaceted. In this chapter, we help you understand the nature and frequency of resisting effective treatment for OCD. We lay out how people defeat themselves before they even start. Then we discuss why engaging in such resistance is so understandable. Most importantly, we show you what can be done to turn from self-defeat to self-success.

Realizing Resistance is Futile

People who are trying to overcome OCD rarely succeed without first putting up a really good fight — against themselves. As odd as it may seem, their first instinct is often to resist necessary change and remain stuck exactly where they are.

Does this mean that people *want* to hold onto their problems such as OCD? We don't think that's the case. Nobody prefers to have OCD. Why would they? OCD consumes large chunks of time, causes distress, and creates misery for those affected.

People resist and avoid treatment of their OCD for various reasons. These roadblocks to change fall into three major categories:

✔ Specific fears and myths about OCD treatment

✔ Self-handicapping and fear of shame

✔ Self-beliefs that make change seem out of reach

We discuss each of these three change-blockers and provide a few hints for dealing with them as we go.

Fearing treatment

Most people don't understand mental-health issues particularly well. Because OCD comes in highly varied forms (see Chapters 2 and 3 for information about the types of OCD and its relatives), it is even less understood than other mental-health problems, such as depression or anxiety. And lack of knowledge provides fertile ground for fears and myths to grow like weeds.

In the following sections, we discuss some of the most common fears and myths sufferers experience related to OCD and its treatment. Often, they're the reasons people stop seeking treatment.

Going crazy

Some people are afraid that not being allowed to perform the compulsions that define their disorder may literally drive them crazy. This fear stems from the fact that compulsions often feel *absolutely necessary* to the person who performs them. OCD sufferers have described the desire to act on a compulsion as being as strong as the need to breathe.

The distress that OCD brings is very frightening, and carrying out compulsions provides a temporary sense of reduction in anxiety or distress. Thus, it feels better to:

✔ Arrange items perfectly in the closet for someone with symmetry concerns

✔ Check the locks 25 times for someone with checking and doubting worries

✔ Stop the car to check whether someone has been hit for someone with Hit-and-Run OCD

✔ Wash hands repeatedly for someone with contamination worries

We've never seen or heard of anyone going crazy by not carrying out a compulsion, but it's an understandable and legitimate fear nonetheless. Getting over this fear means learning to trust in the advice you're given and slowly acting on that trust.

ERP for OCD

Estimates vary widely, but it appears that at least 25 to 50 percent of people who are offered treatment for their OCD either refuse treatment entirely, drop out early, or fail to comply with treatment fully. Although many people refuse treatments such as medication, refusal may also come in relation to a specific type of treatment. This is particularly common with what's known as *exposure and response prevention* (ERP) treatment (see Chapter 10 for more information about ERP). This refusal is quite unfortunate because ERP may be the most effective treatment currently available for OCD.

Briefly, ERP involves asking people to expose themselves to the very things that tend to trigger their obsessions and compulsions. While doing so, they must work very hard to resist engaging in the compulsions that they feel desperate to perform. For example, people with fears of contamination may be asked to touch doorknobs, dirt, and motor oil while their therapists instruct them to avoid washing their hands for a period of time. As you may imagine, ERP is not an especially easy or comfortable procedure, especially if you have OCD. So it isn't surprising that many people who might benefit from ERP refuse to carry it out.

Although ERP *may* be the most effective treatment for OCD, the edge it holds over other approaches is modest. Alternatives do exist that are quite effective and that may arouse less fear (see especially Chapters 8, 9, and 11 for information on Cognitive-Behavioral Therapy, mindfulness, and medications).

Treatments for OCD work (see Chapters 8 through 18 for lots of information about the types of treatment for OCD and its subtypes). In fact, they work pretty well — especially when people can be persuaded to stick with their treatment.

Resisting risk

People with OCD hate nothing more than uncertainty and risk. Many OCD thoughts and behaviors are specifically designed to insulate against risk of any kind. And the OCD mind continuously conjures up all kinds of possible dangers and potential disasters.

That's why some people with OCD check things over and over again — just to be sure. Some repeatedly wash their hands to be absolutely certain of eliminating all germs. Still others engage in various rituals designed to protect the ones they love — all in the name of reducing risk.

Life comes with a degree of uncertainty, and when all is said and done, nothing can truly eliminate it. Review Chapters 8 and 9 for ideas on coping with risk.

Being wary of inconsistency

Psychologists have known for a long time that people try to remain largely consistent in the behaviors, beliefs, and attitudes they exhibit. Being consistent simplifies life and makes everything feel a little more predictable. You may not like your OCD thoughts or behaviors, but at least they're familiar and predictable. Fear of inconsistency and the discomfort that accompanies breaking old routines and replacing them with new ones may keep you from following through on treatment that demands change.

At first, shaking old habits creates an uncomfortable shift from what you've come to know. Embracing new patterns of thoughts isn't easy, but sticking with the treatment is crucial for success. With time and practice, you and your world will settle into a new consistency. Life will seem no less predictable than before treatment if you have a little patience.

Missing OCD

People with OCD come to believe that their thoughts or behaviors keep bad things from happening. Because they've become so accustomed to using compulsions to manage their obsessions, they often worry that eliminating their OCD will leave them without any tools for coping with distress.

If you have this concern, remind yourself that out of all the patients we've successfully treated for OCD, no one has ever begged to have their OCD back! We suspect such an outcome would be very rare, but if you were indeed to discover yourself missing your OCD, you could always go back to it if you wanted to (which you won't).

Getting sick or worse

People starting OCD treatment worry that they might really get sick and die if they move ahead with treatment. For example, those who consider trying ERP treatment (see the previous sidebar and Chapter 10), frequently fear that exposure of certain types may result in death. Someone with contamination concerns is almost certain to greatly fear exposure to dirt and surfaces that other people have touched.

The risk of getting sick cannot be 100 percent eliminated. That's because a very small degree of risk does indeed exist with exposure treatment. It's conceivable, though exquisitely unlikely, that you could pick up a virus, get sick, and even die from touching a doorknob. Mind you, we've never heard of anyone undergoing ERP and dying in this manner, but *anything* is possible. Part of overcoming OCD involves finding ways to overcome the exaggerated fears of uncertainty and risk that accompany it. These fears can be overcome by taking a slow, gradual approach — but you can never fully eliminate risk.

Hurting someone else

People with a type of OCD known as Doubting and Checking OCD sometimes fear hurting others. They develop elaborate ways of ensuring that they won't carry out these feared acts, especially against a loved one. They truly fear that terrible things will happen if they don't listen to what their OCD tells them to do. Parents often have fears of hurting their children. The following story about Valerie shows how one mother resists treatment for her OCD due to fear that her obsessional worries may come true.

> **Valerie**, a mother with OCD, believes she needs to count each step she takes up to the number six, over and over, or her children will get seriously injured. Throughout the day, she spends so much time counting that she can't get the basic chores of everyday living completed. She loves her children and doesn't want to chance hurting them. She feels terrified when a therapist tells her that in order to treat her problems she needs to stop counting. She worries that in spite of what the therapist says, there may be truth to her obsession and her kids might get hurt. No wonder following the therapist's advice is so hard to do.
>
> Valerie's OCD controls her mind. She leaves therapy because of her intense fears. Her therapist may have pushed her a little too far too fast. However, six months later, she returns to therapy and works out a plan with her therapist to take a slower, more gradual approach.

Valerie's story is not uncommon. Many OCD obsessions seem quite real to the person who has them. That's what makes fighting them so difficult.

Another common OCD fear is the fear of losing control and hurting or abusing someone as a result. Once again, this fear is exaggerated, as those with this type of OCD concern are actually at lower risk of harming others than most people. But in order to deal with this OCD-related fear, one must once again be willing to deal with a very small degree of uncertainty. Building up sufficient trust to work on this issue takes time.

Doing things against your will

People with OCD worry that their mental-health professional will make them do things that they don't want to do. However, no competent, ethical therapist will ever insist that you engage in anything that you say you simply cannot do. Therapists may try to help you see the advantages in following a treatment plan, but they will not force you to do so.

Being unable to stand the treatment

Some people are so afraid that the distress associated with OCD treatment may overwhelm them that they can't even contemplate treatment. If you fear discomfort greatly, you may benefit from reading Chapter 8 to gear yourself up to seek treatment.

Thinking therapy doesn't work

Some people have heard that therapy is ineffective, expensive, and takes an extraordinary amount of time to work. In reality, OCD treatments of various types do work, and they usually improve symptoms significantly in months rather than years (though treatment for complicated OCD and OCD along with other problems can take much longer).

The outcomes for Cognitive-Behavioral Therapy, mindfulness, ERP, and medication are reviewed in Chapters 8, 9, 10, and 11, respectively. These treatments are considered very successful. Just one catch . . . you have to show up and participate actively in the treatments for them to work.

Handicapping against treatment success

Many of those with OCD fear working hard on their issues, so they engage in *self-handicapping* instead. What is self-handicapping? Essentially, it amounts to anything you do to limit yourself or your efforts in ways that provide an excuse for not making progress. It's like engaging in a wrestling match with one arm tied behind your back. If you lose the match, you can always say, "But I had one arm tied behind my back!"

You may wonder why anyone would do this. The answer is actually quite simple: Self-handicapping avoids a loss of face and the resulting shame you might otherwise feel if you were to work very hard and still fail. It also allows you to save face if you succeed for a little while, but then fail later.

No one likes feeling ashamed. Yet those with OCD often feel ashamed of their symptoms and fear seeking treatment because they fear being judged negatively. They think the therapist will see them as crazy; after all, some of the symptoms of OCD can look very strange indeed. But therapists are very good at being nonjudgmental. They don't see you as a defective human being just because of your OCD. On the contrary, they know that OCD is a complicated problem and almost everyone engages in behavior that's a little OCD-like from time to time.

So what does self-handicapping look like? It comes in a fascinating array of colors, shapes, and sizes. In the following sections, we discuss some of the ways people self-handicap their efforts. Head to the later section "Seeing that Resistance Can Be Overcome and Change Is Good" to find out how you can recognize and deal with your own self-handicapping behaviors.

Waiting until you're "ready"

By delaying therapy until you feel really ready, you avoid failure by never really starting. In other words, you're waiting for the *perfect* time. The problem, of course, is that the perfect time doesn't exist — except for the time you actually begin therapy.

Reducing effort

If you don't try very hard, you're giving yourself a built-in excuse for failure: "Well, I would have done rather well if I had actually made the effort." Missing sessions and showing up late can be ways of reducing effort. This self-handicapping strategy fits the earlier example of tying one hand behind your back while wrestling.

Raising the bar

Sometimes people self-handicap by declaring that they can only succeed if they're 100 percent perfect in their attempts to change. Anything less is unacceptable. Thus, attaining a 65 percent reduction in OCD symptoms does not represent success. Although this strategy avoids declaring success, it indirectly avoids failure. People who raise the bar in this way know that failing to achieve perfection isn't really failing because no one can be perfect anyway.

Giving up early

Some folks will make a run at improving their lot, but abandon the effort prematurely. Thus, they may try a few sessions of therapy, but quit well before treatment has had a chance to succeed. At the first moment that therapy gets difficult or feels scary, they jump ship. That's because doing so avoids the chance of failure.

Seeing yourself as hopeless

If you're already hopeless, it's pretty hard to fail, isn't it? Hopelessness is a little like the "reducing effort" form of self-handicapping, but taken to the extreme. If you're hopeless, why even bother to try?

Blaming others

One way to limit yourself is to totally blame others for your problems. If you blame your parents, your therapist, or even your friends for not doing enough for you, then you don't have to put forth your own efforts to change. If you don't make an effort, you effectively prevent failure (unfortunately, you prevent success as well).

Reporting symptoms dishonestly

Sometimes those with OCD feel such shame about their symptoms that they lie or fail to tell their therapists the nature of their problems. In fact, we believe that OCD is an underreported epidemic because so many people are intensely embarrassed and ashamed of their symptoms.

Criticizing yourself harshly

Harsh self-criticism robs you of motivation and thus reduces your ability to keep putting forth effort. People engage in harsh criticism because they think that by doing so they'll beat everyone else to the punch. But like all self-handicapping strategies, it simply prevents success.

Arguing with the therapist

One way people avoid dealing with their problems is by going into therapy and then constantly disagreeing with the therapist. Thus, the focus of the discussion is about how wrong the therapist is rather than on the work that's necessary in order to get better. Others avoid working by questioning the competence or skills of the therapist or dismissing therapy as nonsense.

Although arguing for the purpose of avoiding treatment is never a good idea, there are times when disagreeing with a therapist is actually very appropriate. Some practitioners are not well-trained or may not be a good match for you. If this is true in your case, you need to change therapists. See Chapter 7 for more information about getting professional help and knowing whether you've found a good match.

Passive acceptance

While arguing excessively with your therapist isn't a good idea, passive acceptance isn't good either. Some people enter therapy and sit quietly waiting for the therapist to change them. That doesn't work. Getting better takes active involvement and cooperation.

Presenting distractions

Most people with OCD find it difficult to talk about their symptoms. A common way to avoid dealing with difficult subjects is through distraction. Clients want to talk about another problem at work or a difficult relationship. Sometimes their pressing concerns are really just ways of staying away from doing the hard work of therapy.

Waiting for the guarantee

Some people with OCD want an absolute guarantee that if they're going to make the effort to try a difficult treatment like ERP, it will work. Of course, no such guarantee is possible. The outcome data is highly promising, but no one can provide absolute assurance that it will work.

Denying improvement

Another way to self-handicap and avoid failure is to deny success. We've seen clients improve a great deal on a wide variety of indicators of their OCD severity. Yet they insist that they're doing no better. Denying improvement provides a buffer — just in case things take a turn for the worse. However, denying real improvements when they occur can also rob you of the motivation needed for continuing with difficult treatments.

Putting too much blame on biology

In Chapter 4, we point out that the brain is heavily involved in OCD. Problems with the way the brain functions clearly contribute to the development of the disorder. But other factors also enter in. And as we discuss in Chapter 4, when you change your thinking and your behavior, studies have shown you can literally affect the way your brain functions, for the better. But if you completely chalk up your OCD to a brain disease, you may be less willing to engage in some of these other effective, albeit a little challenging, strategies. You probably just want to take medication. Although medicines do play a role in treating OCD, you can limit your success by not considering the alternatives.

Believing the worst about yourself

All people hold certain beliefs about themselves. Some of these beliefs are positive, while others may hold you back. Negative beliefs — seeing yourself as inadequate, dependent, undeserving, and/or blameworthy, for example — can have a very negative impact on your ability to deal with your OCD. The following sections explain the most common types of self-beliefs that can get in the way of dealing with your OCD.

Believing you are inadequate

OCD can make people lose confidence in their ability to handle the everyday stresses in the world. No wonder many who suffer from OCD start to feel that they can't solve their problems. Feelings of inadequacy go hand in hand with OCD. The belief that you can't do something (like change or get better) stops you from trying.

Inadequacy often leads to dependency. Because people with OCD feel that they're inadequate, they often seek some outside help. They often become dependent on friends or partners, asking for frequent reassurance. Unfortunately, getting reassurance may give temporary relief, but doubt quickly returns (see Chapter 5 for more on the dangers of reassurance).

Believing you are guilty

Some people with OCD believe they're 100 percent to blame for having the disorder. Feeling guilty about something takes a lot of mental energy. If people with OCD feel guilty, they may also feel that somehow they deserve to suffer, and therefore they deserve the pain of OCD.

Guilt is focused on the past. In order to get better, you need to move past the guilt and go forward. If you feel guilty and ashamed about having OCD, ponder these questions:

> ✔ Do I remember ever having wanted to get OCD?
>
> ✔ Does feeling guilty about my OCD help me get better?
>
> ✔ If I had friends with OCD, would I tell them they were to blame for having it?
>
> ✔ Is it possible that if I stop feeling guilty about having OCD, I might actually have more energy to devote toward recovery?
>
> ✔ Is it possible that my OCD is largely a result of genetics, my early development, and other experiences (such as stress and trauma) I encountered over the years?

Use your answers to these questions to help you find self-acceptance. Once you can accept yourself where you are right now, you will find it much easier to move forward.

Believing you are undeserving

Those who believe that they're undeserving don't feel that they're worthy of getting better. Typically, they received those messages in childhood. They feel uncomfortable when others are kind to them. They often wallow in their own misery sincerely convinced that happiness is meant for others, and that they don't deserve the relief that treatment can bring.

Friends and family may find that those who feel undeserving can be rather frustrating because they resist help. Such friends and family may want to read Chapter 22 for ideas about how to help without making themselves miserable in the process.

Believing you are a victim

As discussed in Chapter 5, OCD is sometimes triggered or worsened by traumatic events. When terrible things happen to people, their views of the world and themselves change. More often than not, they shift from viewing themselves as independent, competent, and capable to dependent, incompetent, and incapable. This is a completely natural and understandable reaction to the horrible event. Victims often focus on unfairness and injustice. They feel angry about what's happened, but fail to see their responsibility for taking positive action in order to recover. Victims tend to believe that their fate and emotional well-being are largely controlled by outside forces.

At the same time, some who suffer from OCD unrelated to trauma also feel like victims — of their OCD. Their reactions are also understandable because OCD is a terrible affliction. However, in order to progress, victims must learn to let go of these views of themselves and shift to the perspective of those who've found ways to cope. Those who cope have also had something bad happen to them, but they've managed to focus on what they can do to recover. Theirs is a more active, involved stance.

Seeing that Resistance Can Be Overcome and Change Is Good

The preceding sections help you understand that resistance to treatment is both common and understandable. At the same time, fighting or refusing treatment doesn't help you overcome OCD. Realizing that you did nothing to ask for your OCD is important. And as much as you may resist treatment, you probably hate having OCD just as much.

The way out of this mess is to stop blaming yourself and stop seeing yourself as a victim. You just need to take responsibility for doing something about your problem.

Embracing the process of change

Change of almost any type frequently requires multiple attempts. Psychologists and researchers, Drs. James Prochaska, John Norcross, and Carlo DiClemente have studied the process of change and discovered that it typically involves six phases — whether you're talking about OCD, stopping smoking, losing weight, or overcoming depression. Understanding these phases and how they work can help you stay on the right path. The phases are

1. **Precontemplation:** In this phase, people haven't even started to ponder doing anything about their problem. Sometimes in this stage people deny that they have a problem at all. The good news here is that if you have OCD and you're reading this book, you've no doubt moved past this stage.

2. **Contemplation:** This phase is where people start giving serious thought to doing something about their problem. Sometimes they feel that their problem is a little overwhelming, so they remain on the sidelines for a while until they can see a light at the end of the tunnel that doesn't look like an oncoming train. This chapter is designed to help you with this phase.

3. **Preparation:** At this point, people usually feel there is something they can do to get better. So they design a plan for how they can attack their problem. Chapters 8, 9, 10, and 11 help you with ideas for this stage and the next one — taking action.

4. **Action:** This is where the rubber meets the road. In this phase, people carry out the plan that they've designed.

5. **Maintenance:** This phase is one that people often don't think about ahead of time. It's when you've gotten better, but then discover that maintaining those gains requires a little more effort than you thought it would. You, however, will be ready because we prepare you for this phase beforehand. We give you lots of information about avoiding relapse and maintaining your gains in Chapter 12.

6. **Termination:** Some people manage to reach a phase where their change is so complete and ingrained that they no longer have to put much effort into holding onto their gains. Not everyone reaches this phase, and it isn't realistic for most of those who have OCD to expect a virtually complete cure with no further effort required. However, people with OCD can improve greatly and, with continued maintenance strategies, manage to live very fulfilling lives that are far less weighed down with OCD than when they had not yet contemplated change.

You may think that these phases occur sequentially, one through six. And sometimes they do. However, it's more common to jump around these stages a number of times. For example, some people leap into action without having made much of a plan. Then when the action fails, they bounce back to the precontemplation phase and don't consider changing for a while.

Jenny's story is a typical example of someone who vacillates from one phase of change to another. Though it takes her several years to successfully tackle her OCD, she eventually makes great strides.

Jenny, an X-ray technician working for a major hospital, suffers from *Contamination OCD* (see Chapter 2). Of course, hospitals stress the criticalness of clean hands, which makes things worse for Jenny. Her co-workers make comments about her compulsive hand-washing. At first, Jenny denies she has a problem and keeps her hands hidden from others by wearing gloves much of the day. However, her supervisor talks with her about the issue one day when he sees that Jenny's hands are raw and oozing from her excessive washing.

At this point, Jenny is in the precontemplation stage. After her conversation with her supervisor, she moves to the preparation stage by entering treatment. She immediately starts ERP therapy and tries very hard to stay the course for five days. In Jenny's case, she still must wash her hands more than most people due to her hospital- and patient-related work. However, she no longer washes for an hour each morning and evening.

Unfortunately, after five days, Jenny's OCD overwhelms her and she gives up — returning once again to the precontemplation phase. Jenny's supervisor recommends that Jenny try a different treatment approach that may feel less intense and threatening. He even suggests that she read *Obsessive-Compulsive Disorder For Dummies* before she starts treatment so she can take her time and carefully contemplate what changes and treatments she may want to try.

Jenny ultimately selects cognitive therapy (see Chapter 8) as something that sounds a little easier. She also talks to her physician about medication (see Chapter 11). A few months later, Jenny's symptoms have improved greatly. At this point, she's in the maintenance phase.

A year later, she experiences a relapse and her symptoms return full-blown. She needs to regroup and moves into the contemplation phase. Finally, she selects mindfulness (see Chapter 9) and a little ERP (see Chapter 10). These strategies work very well for her. In the ensuing four years, she experiences minimal trouble with her OCD, although she needs to remain vigilant and continues in the maintenance phase.

Jenny's story shows you that change isn't always smooth, even, and easy. Most people make progress and have slip-ups. But each time Jenny struggled, she gained something from the process.

People who succeed at improving their OCD (or anything else) take a number of runs at their problems. Just because you've made a few attempts only to slide back does *not* mean that you won't ultimately succeed. The fact is, each time you make a solid attempt, you discover things that will help you in your next go-round.

Defeating self-handicapping

Self-handicapping occurs whenever you do anything that interferes with making progress. People with OCD are especially vulnerable to the self-handicapping trap because the treatments can be so challenging. If you have OCD and are starting treatment, we suggest that you monitor your own behavior for any signs of self-handicapping. When you see the self-handicapping occurring, try to respond to it by recognizing how self-defeating this behavior can be. Talk back to the self-handicapping part of your OCD mind.

In the example below, Art had started treatment for his OCD six weeks earlier and had been struggling to get on track. Art's story shows how self-handicapping can interfere with treatment until you start attacking it.

Art suffers from what's sometimes called *Hit-and-Run OCD* (see Chapters 2 and 13 for more information). Whenever he drives, it isn't long before he feels some type of bump in the road — usually from a pothole, running over a speed bump, an out-of-balance tire, or going over a rock. When he feels the bump, he instantly imagines that he's run over a person. His body floods with adrenaline and fear as his heart races and his shirt becomes soaked with sweat.

He pulls over to the side of the road and looks back. At that moment, he's quite certain that he will find a body. He never does. Sometimes Art inspects his car looking for signs of blood or dents from the impact. He also returns to the scene multiple times just to be sure that nothing has happened. Needless to say, it takes Art an awfully long time to get where he's going.

At his wife's insistence, Art seeks therapy for his problem. Art encounters a lot of difficulty getting started with his treatment. Therefore, his therapist suggests that he monitor his self-handicapping, recognize it for what it is, and respond to it. Table 6-1 shows what Art came up with.

Table 6-1	Art's Monitoring of Self-Handicapping	
Day	**Self-Handicapping**	**Response**
Monday	I didn't read the material my psychologist suggested.	When I don't do these things, I'm handicapping myself. OK, this reading will take 15 minutes; I'm not going to let my OCD mind defeat me!
Tuesday	I was 20 minutes late for my appointment.	Sure, I was busy, but in truth, I think I was self-handicapping again. At least I caught you in action, OCD mind.
Wednesday	Today, I stopped my car and looked for a body on the road. My therapist has asked me to not do that. Maybe I'm hopeless.	I'm defeating myself again. I knew I didn't have to cave in. But I also don't have to see myself as hopeless. Next time, I'll be on the lookout for this.
Thursday	I had a partial success today in that I resisted going back to the scene, but I did look into my rearview mirror. I must not be doing any of this right.	I am self-handicapping when I view actual progress as a failure. I need to pat myself on the back whenever I take a step in the right direction.

Day	Self-Handicapping	Response
Friday	I had a thought that this treatment is too difficult. Why should I do all this when I've read that OCD is all biological anyway? Maybe I should just take some medication and be done with it.	My therapist talked with me about medication and he pointed out that it is an option, but this treatment will probably work better in the long run. I'm just handicapping myself when I see it as entirely biological.
Saturday	I've gone two days now without stopping my car. I understand this approach now, so I think I can quit therapy.	Wow, that's a great way to snatch defeat from the jaws of victory. I have so many other issues, and I'm pretty sure there's more to be done with my Hit-and-Run OCD. I'm just kidding myself by thinking it's gone just because I've done well for two days.
Sunday	Today I found myself getting really mad at my mother. She's the cause of my OCD — what with the way she used to clean the house all the time and warn us constantly about every imaginable danger. When I learned to drive, all she would do is yell at me.	OK, perhaps she did contribute to my OCD. But if I focus only on blaming her, I won't get any-where myself. I need to let my anger go.

My Reflections: I can see that my OCD mind has lots of ways of handicapping my efforts. I'm going to have to be very vigilant and recognize when I'm starting to defeat myself. I can win this war, but only if I stay alert.

Art's story illustrates how easy it is to self-handicap. When you start your treatment for OCD, be on the lookout for things like missing appointments, blaming others, not wanting to carry out assignments between sessions, and so on. We urge you to also track your self-handicapping on the "Monitoring Self-Handicapping" form, which you can find in Appendix B.

Here's how to go about monitoring and responding to your self-handicapping tendencies:

1. In either a notebook or on a copy of the form from Appendix B, write down the date that you are monitoring your self-handicapping.

2. To the right of that, indicate what behaviors or thoughts you've had that indicate some type of self-handicapping.

3. Respond to your self-handicapping by talking back to that part of your OCD mind. Formulate a reason to not engage in that type of self-handicapping.

4. After you've recorded your self-handicapping for at least a week, write down what you've discovered from the exercise.

 Although you don't have to explicitly label your self-handicapping, you may find it useful to review the list of ways people engage in self-handicapping. Refer to the earlier section, "Handicapping against treatment success."

Dismantling change-blocking beliefs

Recognizing that you may be holding onto negative beliefs about yourself (such as feeling guilty, inadequate, undeserving, or a victim) is the first step toward pushing them out of your way. The second step involves analyzing those beliefs in order to help you see how badly they interfere with your desire to change.

For that step, we recommend that you carry out a cost/benefit analysis. A cost/benefit analysis is a simple, but highly effective, technique. It helps you focus on the problem and develop a sensible alternative. Although most beliefs at least *seem* to confer a few benefits or advantages, close scrutiny usually reveals that those advantages are far outweighed by the costs.

Here's an example of how Roberto carries out a cost/benefit analysis of his success-busting belief about himself:

> **Roberto** is an engineer in his late twenties. Other than work, he lives a very solitary life. He has always felt different from others and avoided making friends because he assumes others won't like him. Roberto suffers from *Hoarding OCD* (see Chapter 16). He feels driven to collect an unimaginable array of useless junk. He has newspapers from the last several years. Junk mail, catalogs, rubber bands, paper clips, pencils, nuts, bolts, tools, wires, and nails overflow his garage and have overtaken many of his other living spaces. He stopped inviting anyone over months ago out of shame.

> But he feels inadequate to the task of cleaning up his house. He can't even seem to get any part of his collections organized. He feels overwhelmed by the task and incapable of making changes. However, Roberto contemplates taking a shot at his OCD. He realizes that his success-busting belief of inadequacy stands in his way. So he carries out a cost/benefit analysis of this belief, as shown in Table 6-2.

Table 6-2   Cost/Benefit Analysis of Roberto's Inadequacy Belief

Goal, problematic thought, belief, or decision: I believe I am inadequate.

Benefits	*Costs*
If I feel inadequate, I don't have to work hard to make changes.	If I feel inadequate, I may not have to work at making changes, but I won't make any changes!
Maybe I can get my mother to help me with this problem if I feel inadequate to do it myself.	Feeling inadequate invites my mother to keep controlling my life. She makes me feel even more stupid when she takes over.
I won't have to tackle my problem and then fail.	If I continue feeling inadequate, I won't make changes. And if I don't do something, the fire department will be called.
	By holding onto my belief in my inadequacy, I ruin any chance I'd ever have of meeting someone.
	Believing in my inadequacy feels awful.

My Reflections: Now I can see how much my belief in inadequacy has been hurting me. I need to be on the lookout for that belief. This weekend, I vow to take two garbage bags' worth of stuff out, and I'll call that psychologist who specializes in OCD.

After Roberto reviews his cost/benefit analysis of his success-busting belief, he decides to act as if he were actually adequate. He realizes that staying stuck will enable his OCD to keep him down. He grabs the phone book and makes an appointment to see a psychologist (see Chapter 7 for ideas about finding professional help).

You can find a blank copy of the cost/benefit analysis form in Appendix B. Here's how to design a cost/benefit analysis of your problematic beliefs:

1. Either in a notebook or in the form in Appendix B, write down a success-busting belief that you think applies to you.

2. Underneath the heading "Benefits," write all the imaginable advantages or ways in which your belief feels useful to you.

3. Under "Costs," write down all the ways that your belief may be holding you back, costing you, or causing you harm.

4. Beneath your table, write "My Reflections" and summarize what you've discovered from your cost/benefit analysis.

You can use a cost/benefit analysis to change a belief, make a decision, rethink your perspective, decide about goals, and motivate your efforts. It helps you move past contemplating changes and actually start moving forward.

If you discover that your cost/benefit analysis results in more benefits or advantages for retaining your core belief about yourself, you will likely benefit from professional help for continuing your work.

Taking one step at a time

You may think that you're sick of your OCD and you want to change it and change it now. Great! But, be careful. Successful change requires careful contemplation, planning, and work. Thinking you can just jump right into eliminating your OCD sets you up to have unrealistic expectations. Those expectations can cause you to crash quite suddenly if and when your attempts falter.

We suggest a slow and steady strategy for tackling OCD. For example, if you're trying ERP therapy (see Chapter 10) to help rid you of your fears of contamination, starting out by rubbing the inside of a dumpster with your hand probably isn't a good idea. But you might be able to tackle touching a doorknob.

The same advice holds for how you approach this book. We hope the 380 or so pages don't overwhelm you. We want to be sure that almost anything anyone would want to know about OCD is covered in these pages. But you don't have to read every single chapter, and you certainly don't need to carry out every single exercise. Furthermore, you should take it at your own pace.

Resistance to change is not a good option. But taking reasonable risks and accepting occasional setbacks in your therapy are good options that can help keep you on track to overcoming OCD.

Chapter 7

Getting Help for OCD

In This Chapter
▶ Knowing the types of help available
▶ Collaborating with your mental-health professional
▶ Deciding whether you've made the right choice

Many people who have obsessive-compulsive disorder (OCD) never seek help for their problem. Those who suffer often fail to get help because they feel ashamed of their obsessions and compulsions. Unlike the worries associated with anxiety or the sadness that comes with depression, the thoughts and behaviors of OCD can appear quite bizarre to others. People with OCD fear that their disorder will make them look crazy, so they work hard to hide their symptoms. But OCD can worsen over time if treatment is not sought.

In this chapter, we tell you about the kinds of help available for treating OCD. If your symptoms are quite mild, you may want to select one of the various types of self-help for your OCD. However, most people with OCD benefit more if they also receive some type of professional help. In any case, educating yourself about OCD should be part of your treatment plan.

We introduce you to the cast of characters in the mental-health field. More importantly, we tell you how to find the right person and what to expect when you make an appointment. Finally, we help you evaluate whether your choice was a good one for you.

Going After the Types of Help You Need

If your brakes fail, you take your car in to a garage and let the mechanic do the repair job. If you have an ear infection, you go to a medical provider and get some antibiotics. You can pretty much leave the fixing to the experts. You have to cooperate — that is, pay the bill or take the pill — but little personal effort is required.

Taking on OCD is different, however. When you fight OCD, you have to go into the boxing ring yourself and engage in the battle. You may have someone in your corner coaching you, but you're the one who has to throw the punches and bob and weave to avoid getting hit.

If you or someone you care about has OCD, you probably wish the solution could be quick and easy. Unfortunately, there are no quick fixes for OCD. But don't despair — highly effective treatments are available.

OCD can be severe and is sometimes accompanied by depression (see Chapter 3). If you have thoughts of hopelessness or suicidal thoughts, please seek immediate help from a health professional. Furthermore, if OCD is making it nearly impossible to get to work, sleep, eat, or get along with others, you should get professional help without delay.

Educating yourself about OCD

Self-help is a necessary part of any successful OCD treatment, and a huge chunk of that self-help is becoming educated about OCD causes and treatments. You may seek professional help in addition to self-help for guidance, support, and motivation (see Chapter 6 on overcoming obstacles and resistance to change), or you may be ready to jump-start treatment on your own. Either way, you need to actively participate in your treatment program, and self-help motivates you to do so.

You can help yourself in two ways — by finding out all you can about OCD and by getting support from family, friends, and others. In this section, we discuss the education aspect of self-help. (Skip ahead to the next section for more on enlisting support.)

Obtaining information about what you're up against prepares you for the battle ahead. Prior to the Super Bowl, the coaches try to find out all they can about the opposing team so they're prepared to make the right moves at the right time. In the same way, educating yourself about OCD can help you come up with a winning game plan. You can turn to any of the following sources for information about OCD:

- ✔ **Audio CDs:** You may find it helpful to use the time spent in your car driving to and from work to listen to audio CDs. If you can focus on the road at the same time, CDs can be a great way to learn about OCD. If you ride the subway, you can listen to audio books or podcasts on your portable media player. However, not everyone easily retains information this way. Last summer, for instance, we tried to learn Spanish while driving. It didn't work very well. Qué lástima (what a pity).

- ✔ **Books:** We love books. Books are great for self-help, and, of course, we hope this book is especially useful. Books are fairly inexpensive, especially if you buy them used. Owning books about OCD is nice because you can refer to them over and over again. If you enjoy reading, try to read more than one book about OCD. Repetition helps you retain information.

✔ **Television and movies:** Because entertainment is usually the purpose of television and movies, you have to be cautious about believing everything you see. However, as part of our preparation for this book, we watched the entire first four seasons of the television show *Monk*. We were impressed with the skill of the actor who played the main character, Tony Shalhoub, and his portrayal of OCD. We really enjoyed watching the show. Sitting in front of the TV is sure easier than writing books. You may also enjoy various movies that portray characters who suffer from OCD, such as *As Good as It Gets* with Jack Nicholson and Helen Hunt.

✔ **Web sites:** Nowadays, you can access virtually unlimited information on the Internet. But, be careful about what you find there. Both amateurs and professionals alike can offer advice, and it's often hard to differentiate between the two. Be even more cautious if you come across anyone trying to sell quick-fix services or products. A good place to start is with the OCD Foundation at `www.ocfoundation.org`.

See Appendix A for our other top selections of books and other media sources of good information about OCD.

Whether you choose books, CDs, or search the Web, check out the credentials of the author or publisher. Buyer beware — especially if the product promises quick and easy solutions.

Getting support from family, friends, and others

People with OCD are often isolated. Obsessions and compulsions take up time and energy. Many people with OCD can barely make it through the day, let alone have time to socialize. Yet, getting support can be an integral part of getting better. One OCD treatment in particular, exposure and response prevention (ERP — see Chapter 10), may involve getting together with a buddy or partner to carry out some of the assignments. Social support can come in the form of:

✔ **Friends and family:** If you have an understanding family or friends, they may be willing to pitch in and help. First, they'll need to become educated about the ins and outs of OCD — this book can be a great start for them. Once educated, they can serve as assistants to ERP. Typically, their assistance should be guided by a professional whom you are seeing for your OCD. Friends and family can also serve as gentle coaches giving you needed encouragement (see Chapter 22 for more information about the role played by family and friends).

✔ **Online support:** Online chat rooms, forums, and other support groups related to OCD allow you to be anonymous, and many people benefit from sharing with others online. The good online groups abide by codes of conduct — offensive, inappropriate, and unrelated comments are discouraged. Some of these groups even have moderators who edit and delete prohibited messages. Other groups provide a specific community with related news, updates, and a chance to talk with others through e-mails only. A few groups even involve professionals who volunteer their time to the online community.

✔ **Support groups:** Groups for people with OCD can provide compassionate support. Some groups involve a mental-health professional who leads the discussion, provides education, and offers suggestions. Other groups consist of people with OCD and function mainly as places to talk about experiences, solve problems, and offer empathy.

Be careful about who you share personal information with, and don't buy into what anyone trying to sell you quick-cure products may tell you.

Choosing a professional to help you

Not every mental-health professional is well acquainted with OCD. That's because at one time, OCD was thought to be extremely difficult to treat and quite rare. Now we know that these ideas are not true at all — OCD is both treatable and fairly common. The bottom line is that you need to ask your mental-health professional about his or her experience and training with OCD. A qualified person will have received training and education about OCD and treated OCD fairly frequently.

Anyone you choose should be familiar with the major therapeutic approaches to OCD, such as Cognitive-Behavioral Therapy (CBT), mindfulness, a specific type of CBT known as exposure and response prevention (ERP), and medications (see Chapters 8, 9, 10, and 11, respectively).

Picking the right professional

You may have to seek services from more than one professional. Although all of them should be familiar with the treatment approaches to OCD, not everyone administers all the OCD treatments. For example, you could obtain ERP training from a psychologist and medication from a psychiatrist. Here are the types of professionals who sometimes work with OCD sufferers:

✔ **Coaches:** Coaches or life coaches are fairly new in the area of mental-health treatment. Some coaches have good skills (and are also trained counselors or psychologists). However, at this time no licensing requirements exist for this class of professionals. And coaching doesn't have a lot of science backing it up. We think coaching can be great for setting goals and increasing motivation in your personal or business life, but we recommend sticking to a licensed practitioner for OCD.

✔ **Counselors:** Counselors have graduate training in counseling, education, theology, or psychology. They obtain a master's degree and are licensed to practice in their state of residence. The backgrounds of counselors vary widely and you need to check on the specific training of the counselor that you choose. Many counselors are very well trained and have expertise in treating OCD.

✔ **Psychiatrists:** Psychiatrists attend medical school and obtain an MD degree. They follow the attainment of this degree with additional training in the diagnosis and treatment of emotional disorders. Psychiatrists are experts in prescribing medications for OCD. Most psychiatric practices emphasize biological treatments for emotional disorders and do not typically engage in psychotherapy treatments for OCD, such as ERP, mindfulness, and CBT.

✔ **Psychoanalysts:** A psychoanalyst usually starts out as a psychiatrist, psychologist, or other therapist and gets additional training. This approach looks at deep-seated childhood issues. Treatment usually requires several sessions a week for many years and no research that we know of has been conducted on its use with OCD. Effective OCD treatment targets symptoms directly and usually brings at least some relief within a few months or less. Psychoanalysis is not a good fit for someone with OCD.

✔ **Psychologists:** This group of professionals is most likely to have extensive training in the various psychotherapies specific to OCD. Psychologists have doctoral degrees (PhD or PsyD) in psychology and are licensed by the state in which they practice. The psychotherapies they deliver have been scientifically proven to be effective. Although most psychologists do not prescribe medication for OCD, a few states now allow prescription privileges for psychologists who obtain additional training in that area.

✔ **Social workers:** Social workers attend graduate school and obtain a master's degree in social work. Many social workers also obtain supervision and training in psychotherapy, including techniques for treating OCD. They are licensed by the state in which they practice. Social workers also have training and expertise in case management and helping people obtain needed social or governmental services.

You may hear the word *therapist* or *psychotherapist* used to describe a mental-health professional. "Therapist" is a general word used to describe someone who does therapy. Sometimes the word "psychotherapist" is used to describe a person who does psychotherapy. A therapist may be a social worker, counselor, or psychologist.

Avoiding the wrong pseudo-professional

Lots of people hang shingles on their door proclaiming their expertise in various healing arts. They provide a range of services, such as chiropractic healing, massage, and acupuncture. A few of these approaches work for pain or other disorders, but they have not demonstrated effectiveness for OCD.

In addition, some individuals have strings of letters after their names (designating something, but we have no idea what) and may not have a license to practice anything. They may advertise services such as:

- Ear candling
- Exposure to low-level magnetic fields
- Listening to special sounds while lying on a vibrating table
- Past-life regression

We live in New Mexico — trust us, we see lots of interesting alternative health practices. By the way, we heard of one guy who listed CCG after his name. What the heck is that, we asked? Certified Crystal Gazer.

Asking the important questions

When you decide to call the office of a professional, there are some things you'll probably want to know before making your first appointment. Some of these questions can be answered by the office manager or secretary, if there is one. These questions include:

- **How soon can I be seen?** If the answer is in several months, you may want to keep checking around.

- **What are the fees, and do you take my insurance plan?** Not all practitioners accept all insurance plans, and some do not accept any. You need to know the fee schedule upfront.

- **What are your practice hours?** If you require evening or weekend appointments, you need to see whether these are available.

- **Does this person hold a license to practice in this state?** If not, we recommend you seek services elsewhere. You can verify this information on the Internet in most cases.

With all the complex ins and outs of insurance these days, we strongly advise you to call your health insurance plan; that is, assuming you can get through to a real, live person! Ask about how many sessions your policy allows, how frequently those sessions can occur, and at what rate your policy will reimburse for OCD treatment. If your provider does not accept insurance, inquire as to whether your insurance carrier will consider reimbursing you for sessions with a receipt from the provider.

You may also want to consider the convenience of the professional's office in relation to where you live. However, convenience is relatively less important than the person's experience and skill in working with OCD.

You'll want to ask the mental-health professional a few questions directly. These only require about five or ten minutes of time, and most professionals will be willing to answer them on the phone prior to you making your first appointment. These questions include:

- **Do you ever consider administering treatment outside of your office for OCD?** Although most professionals do not conduct treatment outside of their offices for most problems, OCD treatment sometimes calls for flexibility.

- **Do you teach your OCD clients how to administer ERP for themselves?** A good therapist not only guides you through ERP, but also teaches you how to apply it for yourself. See Chapter 10 for information about ERP.

- **Do you treat and/or evaluate OCD?** Not everyone does, so be sure to ask. You may not know for sure whether you have OCD, but if you suspect that you do, you need a good evaluation.

- **Do you treat OCD regularly?** You want to hear that the professional either regularly treats OCD or will get supervision from someone who does.

- **Do you use scientifically validated therapies for OCD?** You certainly want a treatment that has been proven effective in the treatment of OCD. The professional should mention at least one of the following therapies: CBT, ERP, mindfulness, or medications.

Billions of bucks couldn't save Howard Hughes

Billionaire Howard Hughes, famous airplane designer, pilot, movie maker, and womanizer, lived from 1905 to 1976. It is well-known that he also happened to suffer from OCD. He had various symptoms, including intense fears of contamination along with elaborate rituals for handling all sorts of objects. His symptoms worsened over time, and he disappeared from public view in his later years. In those last years, he spent his days and nights lying naked in bed in darkened hotel rooms — as a way of creating what he considered to be a germ-free zone. He even burned his clothes if someone near him was stricken ill.

Unfortunately, little was known about the treatment of OCD in Howard Hughes' day. It wasn't until the 1970s that ERP was studied and found to be an effective treatment for OCD. Furthermore, effective medication options for OCD weren't available. Today, Howard Hughes could be treated with a good expectation of success. You can, too, and you don't even need billions of dollars.

✔ **Is your treatment for OCD confined to single, one-hour sessions each week?** Sometimes effective OCD treatment calls for more frequent and longer sessions. These may or may not be covered by your insurance, so you may want to ask about that as well. Your provider may be able to facilitate obtaining coverage for OCD treatment that exceeds usual policy coverage. That's because the treatments that really work for OCD often require more than one standard, 50-minute session per week.

If you receive the answers you hoped to hear, ask yourself how talking with that person felt. Were you comfortable? Did you feel rushed? Did the person sound interested in treating your problem? If your answers are positive, make an appointment! If you talk to someone who doesn't have a lot of experience with OCD, ask for a recommendation — many professionals who don't treat OCD themselves know of others who do.

Understanding What to Expect in Therapy

When the door closes and the first session begins, feeling a bit nervous is normal. Whether you're going to a psychologist, psychiatrist, social worker, or counselor, generally the initial session is one in which you are asked a lot of questions. The questions are the start of the assessment process. Your therapist is trying to understand you and your symptoms in order to come up with a treatment plan. Therapists have different approaches, but generally the following areas are covered in the first session:

✔ **Problems:** What are your current symptoms? How severe are they? How often do they occur? Do certain situations make them worse? Do you avoid people, places, or situations? Do your obsessions or compulsions interfere with your life? How are your moods? How do you handle anger? How do you sleep? Has your appetite changed lately? Do you have trouble making decisions or concentrating? Do you ever have trouble thinking clearly?

✔ **Daily responsibilities:** Do you work in or out of the home? How are you handling your responsibilities? Have there been any recent changes in your job, family, or finances? Do you have trouble following through on important tasks?

✔ **Safety:** Have you ever thought about hurting yourself? Have you ever attempted suicide? Do you feel hopeless? Have you ever worried about hurting anyone else? Have there been times in your life when you have lost control and hurt someone?

✔ **History:** When did you first notice these problems? Have there been times when the symptoms have decreased or increased? Have you had other emotional problems in the past? Have members of your family had emotional or behavioral problems?

✔ **History of treatment:** Have you ever seen a therapist before? What was your experience like? Did you learn anything useful? Do you have any complaints about your past therapy?

✔ **Health:** Are you healthy? Have you ever had significant health problems? Serious injuries? Are you taking any medications? Have you ever taken medication for an emotional problem in the past? If so, was it effective? Do you smoke or drink? How much and how often? Do you use any other drugs?

✔ **Trauma:** Have you ever been abused? Are you afraid of someone hurting you? Have you ever been exposed to traumatic events? Has anyone close to you experienced trauma?

✔ **Anything else:** Is there anything else that you would like to mention during this session?

Don't expect the first session to be primarily focused on the symptoms of OCD. That's because critical areas like safety, health, and functioning must be considered before treating OCD. For example, if you're feeling suicidal, that danger must be addressed immediately. Or there could be significant substance abuse that may have to be dealt with before OCD treatment can be effective. Furthermore, your therapist may discover that you're not actually suffering from OCD, but something else entirely — or that you have OCD in addition to one or more other problems.

The first session is also a time for you to assess how comfortable you are talking about your problems. Ask yourself whether you were able to communicate your concerns and leave the session with hope.

Keeping your therapy private

Maybe you've heard the saying, "What happens in Vegas, stays in Vegas." The implication is that whatever you choose to do in Las Vegas, no one else ever has to know about it. The therapeutic relationship is like this saying in that what you say in therapy, stays in therapy.

The relationship that you have with your therapist is unique because of the practice of confidentiality — the promise that what you say will not be disclosed to others. Without that promise (backed by law), therapy would not feel safe, nor would it be very effective. There are only a few exceptions to this confidentiality rule, such as:

✔ **Abuse:** If you tell your therapist that you are abusing someone, your therapist may have to inform authorities.

✔ **Dangerousness:** If your therapist feels that you pose an imminent danger to yourself or others, authorities may have to be informed.

Having intense worry that you may hurt someone else (but finding the thought abhorrent) is not usually considered a sign of dangerousness. In fact, it's more likely a sign of a particular type of OCD (see Chapter 2 and 14). Those people are generally at lower risk than most people of actually hurting someone, so your therapist won't be calling authorities if that's the case for you.

Finally, your therapist could be subpoenaed if you are involved in litigation. This issue should be discussed prior to beginning therapy if it is potentially relevant to you. Exceptions such as these are rather rare, and you should be sure to talk about them in detail with your therapist if you have any concerns. Overall, you can rest assured that what you say in therapy will remain in confidence with your therapist.

Digging deep into an OCD diagnosis

Sometimes diagnosing OCD can be pretty difficult. After the first interview, the doctor or therapist will often use a more formal checklist, test, or interview to better understand your symptoms. Common instruments include:

- **Obsessive Compulsive Inventory:** This is a questionnaire that assesses a broad range of obsessions and compulsions and evaluates the severity of the symptoms.

- **Structured Clinical Interview for the DSM-IV (SCID):** This is a comprehensive, time-consuming interview that is usually used in research studies. The questions pertain to a very wide range of symptoms.

- **The Padua Inventory:** This 60-item questionnaire was first developed in Italy and is used to assess the level of distress a person with OCD symptoms is experiencing.

- **The Yale-Brown Obsessive Compulsive Scale (Y-BOCS):** This is probably the most commonly used interview to nail down the specifics of OCD. The Y-BOCS asks about obsessions and compulsions that have to do with contamination fears, hoarding, religion, symmetry, sexual obsessions, aggressive obsessions, worries about illness, superstitious thoughts, rituals, and checking (of locks, appliances, and so on). There are several forms of Y-BOCS, including a clinician interview, a self-report, and a children's form.

Not all practitioners use all of these instruments, but your therapist is likely to ask many questions specific to a wide variety of OCD types. Your therapist will also want to know about the triggers that set your OCD off. Be patient; the evaluation and assessment process can take up to two or three sessions. But that time will pay off by allowing your therapist to know what symptoms to target and in what order.

Speaking the truth to your therapist

Lots of people believe that psychologists or psychiatrists have special powers and can read the minds of the people they treat. Oh, if only it were true. Our job sure would be a lot easier. Although our training and experience provide us with the ability to understand, diagnose, and treat emotional disorders — and we are usually pretty good at understanding our clients — we can be fooled.

Most people who step into a therapist's office want to be helped. But some-times they're embarrassed to discuss their deepest fears, worries, weak-nesses, or thoughts. It's human nature to try and present a good front. And the thoughts and worries that the OCD brain gives you can feel disturbing.

Nonetheless, we urge you to dig down deep and open up with your mental-health professional. Believe it or not, there are very few symptoms that professionals experienced in treating OCD haven't heard about. As you read other chapters in this book, you may see that at least a number of your symp-toms show up. It may help to know you're not the only person in the world to experience troubles like yours.

Evaluating your therapist

After you've been to two or three sessions, the evaluation phase is usually complete. Soon thereafter, you need to start an evaluation of your own. Does your therapist seem like a good fit for you? Does there seem to be a reason-able game plan for your therapy?

Getting to know you

The relationship between you and your therapist matters. Considerable research tells us that the quality of that relationship contributes a lot to the amount of progress you're likely to make. So, what makes a good relationship with a therapist? Here are some questions to ask yourself:

- ✔ **Do I feel comfortable telling my therapist almost anything?** If the answer is no, that's something you should discuss. If you still feel uncomfortable after that discussion, you may not have the right therapist. On the other hand, if your own shame is what keeps you from discussing your thoughts or feelings with your therapist, that difficulty can also be discussed.

- ✔ **Do I feel judged or criticized?** Good therapists are experts at not judg-ing or criticizing their clients. Your therapist may not think what you're doing is a great idea (such as checking the stove 40 times each hour), but you shouldn't feel put down for that. If you do feel criticized or judged, that's something to discuss.

✔ **Does my therapist seem to really listen?** If your therapist is playing a video game during your session, that's really not a good sign! But seriously, you need to feel truly heard. Signs of being listened to include eye contact, head nods, expressions of concern or empathy, and being provided with brief summaries of what you've said.

✔ **Does my therapist speak to me in language I can understand?** Occasionally therapists use professional jargon. However, most of them try to communicate clearly and only use technical words when they must. You should feel comfortable asking for clarification of any idea or word your therapist uses.

✔ **How do I feel talking with my therapist?** You should feel that your therapist cares about you and wants to help. Therapy is a professional relationship and not the same as a friendship. However, like a friend, a therapist should be reasonably warm and understanding.

The treatment of OCD will likely involve times of discomfort and some struggle. Having the support of a therapist who has a good connection with you is important. But you also need a good game plan.

Reviewing the game plan

Therapy for OCD involves more than a good relationship, as important as that is. In addition, your therapist needs to help you devise a set of goals and come up with a plan to reach them. By the third or fourth session, you should know whether you have OCD. You should also know whether you have problems above and beyond OCD.

You and your therapist should discuss how you plan to address the problems. Your therapist should be using one or more of the therapies discussed in Chapters 8, 9, 10, and 11. You should have some idea of which problems are to be tackled, in what order, and with what strategies. If you're unclear about the game plan, ask. Both of you should have some idea of what progress will look like as well.

Occasionally, therapists and clients find that they are not a good match. For example, you may feel you're not being heard or supported, and your attempts to discuss the issue don't improve things. Or you may find that your therapist's training in OCD is lacking and goals are not made clear to you. Or maybe your therapist looks exactly like your ex-spouse or mother — possibly taking your attention away from a collaborative relationship. In any event, if you feel things aren't working, first discuss the issue with your therapist. If that doesn't work, look for a new therapist.

Part III
Overcoming OCD

The 5th Wave   By Rich Tennant

"OCD has really limited my ability to perform the simplest activities. I can't leap a tall building in a single bound anymore without counting the windows."

In this part . . .

In this part we bring you good news. Whereas OCD was considered almost untreatable a few decades ago, today you have several good options for getting real help. These treatments are now backed by solid scientific research. In this section, we discuss Cognitive-Behavioral Therapy (CBT) as well as mindfulness, exposure and response prevention (ERP), and medications. The vast majority of people who have OCD will find one or more of these approaches quite helpful. We illustrate these treatments with examples primarily related to Contamination OCD because it is the most common type of OCD.

Chapter 8

Cleaning Up OCD Thinking with a CBT Reality Check

. . . .

In This Chapter

▶ Seeing how your thoughts may diverge from reality

▶ Freeing yourself of distorted ways of thinking

▶ Writing your own OCD stories

▶ Giving your stories happier endings

. . . .

Cognitive-Behavioral Therapy (CBT) is based on the relationship between your thoughts and the way you feel. The premise is that the way you interpret situations (what you think) determines your emotional response (what you feel). Hundreds of studies have shown that learning to change the way you think can improve the way you feel.

If you have OCD, you tend to misinterpret aspects of your reality in various ways. This leads to a sort of misalignment between how you feel about what's going on around you and the actual reality of the situation.

Researchers have identified a number of ways that people with OCD tend to interpret or think about situations related to their OCD that are particularly problematic. In this chapter, we present seven ways that OCD sufferers misinterpret events and provide various CBT-based methods for changing them. Modifying these misinterpretations allows you to develop more balanced ways of thinking that reduce your OCD and the distress that goes along with it.

Because contamination fears are the most common type of OCD, many of the examples in this chapter (as well as Chapters 9 and 10) focus on this particular type of OCD. Never fear; the material we provide here can be readily applied to other types of OCD, and specific chapters are devoted to other types of OCD as well.

Realigning Interpretations with Reality

While people with OCD interpret many events in their lives rationally, in the same way that most people do, they interpret *portions* of their lives in highly distorted ways. The distorted interpretations primarily occur in response to events that have something to do with *that person's* OCD. So someone with Contamination OCD perceives a dirty towel as dangerous, but probably does not obsess about running people over on the way to work. And someone with symmetry OCD looks at disorder with shock and dismay, but isn't likely to worry about dirty towels.

Seeing common types of OCD distortions

These seven ways of misinterpreting reality show you how the thinking of those with OCD is distorted. Regardless of the specific type of OCD one has, these misinterpretations are quite common:

- Doubting
- Exaggerating risk
- Viewing thoughts as real
- Confusing facts and feelings
- Needing perfection
- Needing to control thoughts
- Being excessively responsible

See Chapter 5 for more information about how these types of thinking interact with and aggravate OCD. Although a few of these types of distorted perceptions show up in other emotional disorders as well, they appear especially troublesome for those with OCD.

Using CBT to correct distorted thinking

CBT applies techniques that aim to improve well-being by bringing about specific changes in the way you think and behave (see Chapters 9 and 10 for more strategies based on CBT). CBT, when applied to these distorted OCD interpretations, helps you more accurately align your feelings with reality.

In this section, we look at seven ways of misinterpreting reality commonly associated with OCD (see the preceding section for a list). We also show you how CBT can be employed to realign these types of distorted thinking.

CBT: Changing thoughts versus changing behaviors

The first highly successful treatment for OCD was developed in the late 1960s and was a specific cognitive behavioral technique called exposure and response prevention (ERP). See Chapter 10 for more information about ERP. Subsequent research over several decades has consistently demonstrated that ERP works very well. There's just one problem — many people refuse ERP and/or drop out of the treatment before they complete it.

Why do people drop out of or even refuse ERP altogether? Well, it's icky, yucky, and sometimes downright disgusting. For example, people with worries about dirt and germs may find themselves instructed by their therapists to touch dirt, doorknobs, toilet seats, urine, and maybe even the inside of a dumpster. People who fear hurting somebody may be asked to talk about stabbing loved ones, pick up knives, and carry babies they fear they may harm. As you can imagine, not exactly everybody is willing to do those things — even with the guidance of a trusted, competent therapist.

Because of these concerns, behavioral scientists have searched for other ways to treat OCD. Early research findings support the idea that Cognitive-Behavioral Therapy (CBT) techniques primarily aimed at improving thinking are effective for OCD, and for some may be as effective as the specific CBT strategy known as ERP. CBT thinking techniques are often combined with ERP as well.

Defeating unreasonable doubts

The doubts that plague those with OCD are not based on reality, direct evidence, or the actual here and now, but rather on imagined scenarios that are concocted in the sufferer's mind. What all these OCD doubts have in common is that they're not tied to experience and information from the body's senses, that is, sight, touch, sound, smell, and taste. For example, the obsession about whether one closed the windows in the house before leaving is not connected to not having felt the windows actually click shut. Similarly, those imagined microbes emanating from the microwave cannot be seen, felt, or touched.

People with OCD accept a reasonable degree of uncertainty and doubt in some areas of their lives. For example, they may assume that the sun will rise and set each day, even knowing there could be a slight possibility that it won't. But when the OCD mind takes control over a particular topic or concern (for example, contamination, harming others, and so forth) doubt permeates, creating a haze that makes seeing reality almost impossible. Even though they usually know their thoughts are going against their own common sense and gut feelings, OCD sufferers repeatedly lose out to the "what if" mentality. In other words, they distrust their own senses and perceptions. So they ask themselves:

- What if I don't scrub the counters with bleach?
- What if I left the windows unlocked?

✔ What if I lose control and shove that person I am walking behind?

✔ What if I take that knife out and stab my dog?

✔ What if that microwave is emitting radioactive microbes?

Obsessive thoughts that cause distress are usually based on a premise that something really bad may happen. Doubt lurks behind almost all obsessions. *Maybe, just maybe* the obsession will come true if action is not taken to prevent it.

Distinguishing doubts from what's real

Most true dangers have elements that can be directly sensed. Natural gas comes with an added smell of rotten eggs to serve as a warning. And if something is burning on your stove, you can see or smell smoke coming from the kitchen.

Of course, some dangers are not easily detectable by the average person's senses. In many of these cases, warning signs are posted, such as, "Danger: High Voltage," "Danger: Radioactive Materials," or "Warning: Non-Potable Water." Or a loud siren may be sounded to warn of tornados in the area. Those warning signs are put there by people who are knowledgeable about the risks and whose senses (often aided by scientific instruments) enable them to assess specific risks that others might not be aware of. The signs themselves, though, are directly observable by *your* senses.

The OCD mind creates warning signs based entirely on made-up, fanciful material. The story of doubt becomes grabbing and compelling because it can't be disconfirmed absolutely. But as the story departs from that which can be confirmed by your senses, it also drifts far from any likely reality.

Dismissing unrealistic doubts

The first step toward changing the way you think is becoming aware of the basis for your thoughts. If you're plagued by OCD doubts, ask yourself the following questions to help you realize that these doubts are not realistic:

✔ Are your doubts based on direct information from your senses (sight, sound, smell, taste, or touch)?

✔ Does your doubt seem to have a life of its own and keep coming back, even without new evidence to support it?

✔ Is there anything about your doubt that other people would see as illogical?

✔ Is there anything that would convince you that your doubt is likely false?

Realistic doubts are based on evidence from the senses, they don't keep returning without new supporting evidence, other people see them as reasonable, and they can be disproved or proved. Realistic doubts keep you safe from danger, but OCD doubts only keep you upset.

The following story about Pam and Debbie shows you how realistic doubts and OCD doubts are as different as night and day.

Pam and **Debbie** are sales representatives for a large pharmaceutical company. Their jobs require weekly travel. A few months earlier, they both came down with a case of food poisoning after eating hamburgers in a messy airport restaurant. Pam happens to have OCD and Debbie does not. Since the illness, Pam's OCD goes into hyper-drive whenever she travels. She no longer eats at restaurants, opting to carry her own food wherever she goes.

At a sales conference, Pam and Debbie are seated at the same table for a company luncheon. They reminisce about their previous bad experience at the restaurant together. Debbie tells Pam that she had a few qualms and doubts for a little while about eating in airport restaurants, and tends to avoid ordering rare hamburgers now; plus she checks the place out for general cleanliness.

Pam says, "That doesn't do it for me. I haven't gone into a restaurant ever since that happened." She then pulls out her can of liquid meal replacement for her lunch while she wipes the table top with a bleach towelette.

Debbie asks, "Are you on a diet?"

Pam says, "No, but this place is crawling with germs. You never know what the waiters have touched. Lots of times they don't even wash their hands after going to the bathroom."

Debbie responds, "It looks pristine and clean to me. What are you talking about?"

"You can't see the microbes on the glasses, but I know they're there. You should know too; we both got sick that way once. Some waiters carry hepatitis C. Do you know how horrible that is? You can catch it from unclean plates. That's not going to happen to me — ever!"

An important point to take away from Pam and Debbie's story is that sometimes OCD fears do come true. However, Debbie's doubts are realistic and based on evidence from her senses. She now takes precautions to avoid undercooked meat and messy-looking restaurants. Pam, on the other hand, has interpreted events related to food and restaurants with extreme, non–reality-based doubts and a refusal to accept any uncertainty. She avoids all restaurants and imagines microbes and diseases that cannot be seen.

How can you tell the difference between the two types of doubt? Filtering doubts through the series of questions we present earlier in this section can help you determine whether your doubts are reasonable or not. We do this with Debbie's and Pam's doubts in Table 8-1.

Table 8-1	Distinguishing Debbie's Doubts from Pam's	
Question	**Debbie**	**Pam**
Are your doubts based on direct information from your senses (sight, sound, smell, taste, or touch)?	Yes. She ate an undercooked, bad hamburger in a messy restaurant.	Yes. She ate an undercooked hamburger in a messy restaurant. But *now* her fears are not based on her senses. She cannot see the microbes she imagines and cannot tell whether her waiters have diseases.
Does your doubt seem to have a life of its own and keep coming back even without new evidence to support it?	No. Debbie has an occasional qualm, but those have gotten much better with time.	Yes. The more Pam thinks about her doubts, the more they seem to grow. She does more and more things to avoid possible contamination.
Is there anything about your doubt that other people would see as illogical?	No. It is reasonable to avoid unclean restaurants and undercooked meat.	Yes. Most people know that eating in restaurants carries a slight risk, but they don't make assumptions about unseen microbes and diseases.
Is there anything that would convince you that your doubt is likely false?	Debbie uses evidence about how restaurants look and cook their meat. She only had food poisoning once in her life and knows it could happen again, but probably not for a long time.	Because she can't see the imagined microbes and diseases, *nothing* can convince Pam that restaurants are essentially safe.

The answers to the questions in Table 8-1 illustrate how OCD doubts are not based on reality that is observable. And when doubts are not based on solid evidence and logic, the quest to disconfirm them never ends — because they simply cannot be totally disconfirmed. In fact, if you try to disprove OCD doubts, they only intensify because they can't be absolutely proven as false.

The OCD mind directs you to eliminate *all* doubts and uncertainty, especially in areas related to your OCD (such as contamination, imagined catastrophes, harming others, and symmetry). But doubt and uncertainty can never be fully eliminated and must be accepted as an inherent part of life.

Ending exaggerating risk

When thinking about their OCD-related concerns, OCD sufferers inflate the risks. And should any of those worries actually come true, the OCD mind substantially exaggerates the degree of suffering that is likely to result. This way of interpreting the world keeps anxiety and distress levels high.

Most people without OCD know that touching a doorknob could conceivably allow a cold virus to infect them. However, they proceed to touch many doorknobs each day knowing that the actual risk they incur each time is rather small. And they know that catching a cold is hardly catastrophic.

However, for someone with OCD contamination obsessions, each and every doorknob is crawling with millions of highly contagious viruses of all kinds — flu, HIV, colds, tuberculosis, SARS, you name it. A touch of a doorknob sets off emergency warning sirens in the OCD mind. These sirens urge the person to take immediate action to eliminate the viruses and avoid illness. Even the possibility of a cold becomes greatly feared because there's at least *some* chance that a cold could turn into pneumonia and ultimately result in death.

Doubting Thomas

The term *doubting Thomas* refers to a skeptic — one who is not easily convinced. The expression "doubting Thomas" comes from the biblical account of a disciple of Jesus. After Jesus was crucified, Thomas did not believe that Jesus had risen from the dead. Although other disciples told Thomas that Jesus had appeared to them, he wanted evidence. The following week, Jesus appeared to Thomas and allowed him to touch his wounds. After that, Thomas became a believer. He was able to see and touch Jesus. People with OCD have doubts as well. However, they don't look to real evidence to check out their doubts.

Religious practices are largely based on faith rather than direct evidence from one's senses. Faith is known to be extremely helpful for billions of people worldwide. However, faith and OCD don't mix. OCD does not enhance people's lives. So if you want to act on faith, do it with respect to spirituality, not to deal with obsessions and compulsions.

One way to deal with the tendency of OCD to exaggerate risks is to check the evidence and logic of one's obsessive fears. You may find that this helps you reevaluate the exaggerated risks that your OCD mind is fooling you with. Working with a therapist can greatly facilitate this process. Consider answering these questions:

✔ Do I have any direct evidence that is contrary to my fears?

✔ Do I have any direct evidence to confirm my fears?

✔ How often have my fears of this risk come true (versus not coming true) in the past?

✔ Is there anything about the risks I'm imagining that other people would likely see as illogical?

The following story of Blair illustrates how OCD can exaggerate risks and how her therapist helps her.

Blair is a 39-year-old CPA. She has struggled with OCD that's focused on contamination and germs for years. Blair worries about contamination that may emanate from health-care facilities. There is a clinic near her workplace, and she walks several blocks out of her way in order to avoid coming close to the clinic.

Her therapist asks her to estimate the probability that serious, potentially lethal contaminates could be picked up simply by walking near the clinic. She tells him the risk is about 10 percent — not exactly a certainty, but rather troubling for the likelihood of contracting a serious, life-threatening infection. Her therapist guides her to a reexamination of her estimated risks. He asks her to search for any evidence or logic she can think of that might change her estimated risks. She comes up with the following evidence and logic:

✔ If the real risk was 10 percent, that would mean that a full 10 percent of those who walk by the clinic would die. Hard to imagine that someone wouldn't have noticed that.

✔ If walking by a clinic incurs a 10 percent risk, then working there would probably kill off half of the employees within a short time. Blair assumes that's not happening.

✔ Blair figures that she's probably walked by hundreds, if not thousands, of doctors' offices, hospitals, and clinics without even realizing it. If her estimate was real, she'd be dead by now.

Blair's new evidence allows her to re-estimate her risks as far less than 1 percent. She is more ready to try her therapist's next suggestion of walking by feared places like health clinics (ERP therapy; see Chapter 10 for more information).

After you have scrutinized your OCD mind's ways of misinterpreting risk, re-rate that risk once, and only once, for any given thought. *Do not* keep returning to this exercise. If you do, the technique can actually become a compulsion that you are using to reassure yourself (see Chapter 5 for the problem with reassurance with OCD). Used once, and only once, for any particular OCD thought, this strategy can help you see that risks are much smaller than you think and allow you to work on accepting a certain amount of uncertainty in your life.

Rethinking the idea that thoughts have real power

If you have OCD, you may give thoughts far more importance than they merit. Just because you think something weird, strange, immoral, or cruel, does not mean that you are bad, crazy, or mean. *All* people have weird thoughts once in a while. That's perfectly normal. When that happens to most people, the thoughts are quickly dismissed or forgotten. Not so in OCD. The OCD mind takes thoughts way too seriously, thereby causing anxiety, guilt, shame, and revulsion.

Calculating real probabilities

About 5,000 people die each year from food poisoning in the United States. No wonder concern about contaminated food is common among those with OCD — nothing seems illogical about that. However, let's turn to a little basic math to see how dangerous our food supply is. At last count, over 304 million people lived in the United States. Most of those people eat three meals a day, 365 times each year. So take 304 million × 3 × 365, and you get 332,880,000,000 (a little more than 332 billion) meals consumed each year. Five thousand of these meals kill someone. Thus, your odds of dying from any given meal are about one in 6,657,600. Even over a lifetime that risk only climbs to about one in 85,353. So relax, and take another bite out of that medium-rare hamburger.

By contrast, only a minority of those with OCD focus on fears of dying from heart disease, diabetes, respiratory disease, or stroke. However,

you have almost a 40 percent chance of dying from one of those causes.

People are often more concerned about food poisoning than these far more likely causes of death because the media headlines each and every outbreak of salmonella and such every time one occurs. By contrast, they do not blare announcements about Joe Blow's heart attack.

Obviously, you want to avoid buying tomatoes or spinach when there is a sudden, known outbreak. And you should wash your vegetables thoroughly and avoid leaving your mayonnaise out on the counter for three hours.

The bottom line: OCD tells you to spend *serious* amounts of time attempting to prevent relatively improbable events. Consider spending less time on OCD and more time on improving your health through exercise and diet.

Just because you think something doesn't make it true. Imagine that you have an obnoxious manager at work. After a frustrating day, you think, "I wish I could wave a magic wand and make him disappear."

Pretend that the offensive manager just happens to run away to Tahiti with his secretary the very next day (leaving his job, wife, and children). You celebrate, throw a party. But someone with OCD may think that the thought of wanting someone to disappear caused the occurrence. The OCD mind may say, "I had a bad thought; therefore, I am a horrible person. My thought caused my manager to run away. I have ruined the lives of his poor wife and seven children."

An obsession is an unwanted, intrusive thought. Everyone has obsessive thoughts once in a while. Say you don't have OCD and you think, "Wow, it's really hot in my office today. I feel like taking off all my clothes!" Do you worry that you might start stripping? Probably not. In fact, you may not think about the thought at all and go get yourself a cold drink instead.

But if you have OCD and you have the same thought, your OCD mind may say something like this: "Oh my, I am really a weirdo. I wonder how many other people in the office know what I'm thinking? People must think I'm loony. What if I can't control myself, and I actually rip off my clothes? How can I stop myself? I better start counting the ceiling tiles to distract myself from that horrible thought. I'm starting to sweat. People will know. I better go home. I hope I can make it to the car without losing it completely."

If your OCD mind tricks you into thinking that thoughts are very important, try this experiment to help you understand that thoughts don't equal action:

1. Put a glass of water next to this book on a table.

2. Stare at the water.

3. Now say to yourself, "I think I am going to spill the water on top of this book with my thoughts alone."

4. Say it again.

5. Think really hard.

6. Did you spill the water?

We would safely bet that most readers did not spill the water. You can't make things happen just by thinking them. And if you did spill the water just by thinking about it, a visit to Las Vegas may be in order. Be sure to invite us to join you.

Think up some other experiments to help you remember that bad thoughts are not the same as bad actions — that thinking about something does not cause it to happen. Be creative. If you're working with a therapist, this may be a very good activity to bring up in a session. Here are a few examples of other experiments designed to show you that thoughts don't cause events:

✔ Take out a ten-dollar bill and stare at it. Try to turn it into a 100-dollar bill. Command it to change. (***Note:*** It doesn't count if an unexpected check shows up in your mailbox in a few days — that's just a random happening).

✔ Stare at your car and command it to change color. If it's white, try turning it to black. Good luck; let us know how you did. Consider starting an auto painting business if you succeed.

✔ Stare at the speed-limit signs on your daily commute and command them to raise the limit so you can speed your way along. By the way, don't start speeding until they actually change.

Unconfusing facts and feelings

Feelings serve many purposes. For example, feelings may give you joy and pleasure or they may warn you of impending danger. But when OCD kicks in, feelings lead you astray. That's because OCD causes the brain to turn on the burglar alarm when there's no actual sign of a break-in (see Chapter 4 for the biological explanation of this process).

People with OCD are flooded with feelings of dread and doom when no logical cause for alarm exists. However, the OCD mind tells them that there must be a real reason for these feelings. And if the feelings are true, whatever meaning you associate with those feelings must be true, too. For example:

✔ I feel ashamed, so I must be a sinner.

✔ I feel dirty, so I must be contaminated.

✔ I feel dizzy, so I must have a brain tumor.

✔ I feel guilty, so I must have done something wrong.

✔ I feel out of sorts, so I must be coming down with something.

✔ I feel scared, so there must be real danger.

Feelings like the ones listed above can be very powerful. Anxious, negative feelings are merely an indication that your brain's alarm system has been set off — but just like a home burglar alarm system, lots of false alarms can occur. Winds, a neighbor's cat, your teenage son sneaking in late at night, and an electrical short can also start the sirens blaring.

To get a grip on your feelings, start reminding yourself that feeling bad doesn't mean you *are* bad or that something bad is going on. When your brain's alarm system goes off, resist the urge to scream, run, or hide. Hold off on making a judgment, and carefully check for evidence. If you can't find clear signs based on what you can see, hear, smell, taste, or feel, consider assuming the alarm was false. With lots of practice, you can stop your brain from setting off so many false alarms.

Overcoming the need for perfection

Perfection permeates the OCD mind by telling you that mistakes are horrible and must be avoided at all costs. Perfectionism leads to procrastination and avoidance because perfection is impossible to obtain. For example, a student may write and rewrite a paper and never turn it in because she knows it must contain errors. Although many people without OCD struggle with perfectionism from time to time, OCD ups the ante. How can you ever be 100 percent sure that

- ✔ You will never say anything that could offend anyone, ever?
- ✔ The books are lined up precisely and perfectly?
- ✔ The kitchen counters have absolutely no microbes or germs of any kind?
- ✔ The tone of voice and words in your prayer are exactly what God demands of you?

If these kinds of concerns plague you, you may want to ask yourself these questions:

- ✔ Does my perfectionism benefit my life?
- ✔ Does my perfectionism hurt me in any way?
- ✔ If a friend of mine had such perfectionistic thoughts, what would I tell him?
- ✔ What would my life be like if I allowed for a little more leniency in the way I judge myself?

Most perfectionists have far more compassion and understanding for the flaws and foibles of others than they have for themselves. Learning to judge yourself by the same standards you set for your friends may help you let go of the excessively harsh standards you set for yourself.

Sidestepping obsessive thoughts

One of the hallmarks of OCD is that the thoughts, urges, and impulses known as obsessions become extremely upsetting and unwanted. Therefore, most people with OCD feel driven to rid themselves of their obsessions. The problem with that strategy is that it flat-out doesn't work. Not only that, trying to suppress thoughts actually intensifies them. And as the thoughts intensify, so does the distress.

In the story that follows, Marty is plagued by the obsession that any dirty thoughts could alter his brain and actually cause him to contract brain cancer. Marty believes that his thoughts have special powers (see the earlier section, "Rethinking the idea that thoughts have real power"), so this belief causes him to work very hard at ridding himself of any dirty thoughts. The story shows you what happens as he tries to suppress his thoughts.

> **Marty** works at an electronics store at the mall. He has obsessions about the possibility that he could lose control and fondle women inappropriately when they walk into his store — abhorrent, dirty thoughts. Whenever Marty has those thoughts, he believes his brain begins to become contaminated with carcinogens.
>
> From that premise, it's pretty easy to understand why Marty desperately tries to suppress all such thinking. However, the more he tries not to have the thoughts, the more they grow. He finds that day after day, he spends more time trying to "not think" about these things. He sings to himself, he tries to repeat phrases such as "Clean thoughts/clean mind," and he repeatedly counts the inventory even though that task is only required once each month. His co-workers start noticing that he seems distracted all the time.

Attempting to suppress thoughts causes them to increase for a pretty simple reason. When you try to avoid thinking about something, you have to constantly search your mind for any sign of the thoughts that you're trying to avoid. The act of being on the lookout for the unwanted thoughts actually causes them to pop up to the surface more easily.

If you find yourself trying to control your OCD obsessional thoughts, try this experiment. You will see how trying to suppress thoughts usually just adds to your difficulties:

1. **Pick one obsessional thought that you wish you didn't have.** Write that thought down in your OCD notebook.

2. **Spend one day trying as hard as you can not to have the thought at all.** At the end of the day, estimate how many times the thought managed to break through your defenses and pop into your mind and write it down. Also rate and record how disturbing the thought felt from 0 (not at all) to 10 (highly disturbing).

3. **Spend the next day allowing the obsessional thought to do whatever it wants** — pop into your mind or not. Again, write down your estimate of how many times the thought came into your mind and how disturbing it felt on a scale of 0 to 10.

4. **Continue alternating days for at least six days** (three suppressing days with three days of no attempt at suppressing).

5. **Write down your conclusions and reflections** about what attempting to suppress your thoughts does to you.

You're likely to discover that the harder you work to stop thinking about your obsessions, the more they increase and disturb you. If you find that thought control really works for you, go for it. We suspect that it won't. If it does seem to work, most likely the effect will be temporary and partial. We suggest you work with a therapist if you discover that you're continuing to struggle with attempts to control your thoughts.

Letting go of feeling excessively responsible

People with OCD often believe that their thoughts, urges, or images — as well as their actions — actually cause harm to others or to themselves. They spend lots of time worrying about whether they may have done, said, or thought something that may possibly hurt someone. They dwell on the slightest possibility of causing such harm. Whenever an event has a bad outcome, they feel totally, morally responsible, even though they had little or no influence on the event and did not want it to happen.

One way to challenge your beliefs about being excessively responsible is to develop a picture of how responsible you really are by using a pie chart. The pie chart is a graph that illustrates all the factors that generate a particular outcome. The process goes like this:

1. **Estimate the percentage of the bad outcome for which you believe you're personally responsible.**

2. **List any other factors that could conceivably have contributed to the event.** Assign percentages indicating the extent to which these other factors may also be responsible.

3. **Make a pie chart to graph the percentages from Steps 1 and 2 accordingly.**

4. **Examine the resulting chart to assess your relative responsibility for the outcome.**

5. **Develop a statement that affirms the fact that you are not solely responsible, and repeat it to yourself often.**

The following example of Raul illustrates this process.

Raul works as a physical therapist at an assisted living facility. He obsesses about hurting the residents. He imagines pushing frail, elderly people down the stairs, dumping them from their wheelchairs, or suffocating them. Of course he has never hurt any of his patients and finds the idea totally repugnant, but he has repeated urges, images, and thoughts. When any of the residents becomes ill or dies, Raul believes that he is fully responsible for the outcome. He thinks he surely could have done something to prevent the illness or death. He obsesses over whether he failed to wash his hands or maintain perfect care, or whether his thoughts alone caused the patient's condition. He is disgusted with himself and believes that someday he will be punished for his horrible obsessions.

Following the death of one of his elderly patients, Raul's distress is so great that he admits to his therapist how he believes he caused the death. His therapist, Dr. James, asks him to estimate exactly to what extent he owns personal responsibility for the patient's death. Raul responds, "100 percent." This is illustrated by the pie chart in Figure 8-1.

Dr. James draws a circle on the white board in his office. He labels it "Responsibility for Patient's Death" and writes Raul's name on it. He then turns to Raul and asks, "Are there *any* other possible factors that could have caused the death of this patient?"

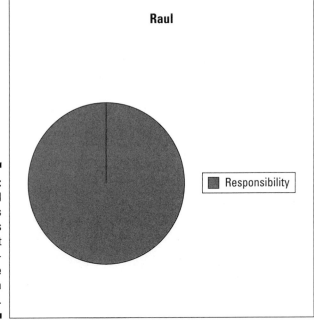

Figure 8-1:
Raul believes that he is 100 percent responsible for the death of a patient.

Raul responds, "Well she was in her late 90s and she started with a bad cold. Then she caught that flu that's been going around."

"So Raul," Dr. James expands, "her age may have been a factor, she had the flu, and she was already pretty frail. Let's add these to the pie chart. Were there any other things that may have contributed?"

Raul goes on to say, "Well, she did have advanced chronic obstructive pulmonary disease (COPD), which greatly increases the chances of dying from almost anything. And she'd had congestive heart failure for six years."

Their conversation ultimately produces a wide variety of potential contributors to the patient's death. At the end of the session, Raul and Dr. James conclude that he probably did not have much to do with the death of the 98-year-old woman. The pie chart they develop is shown in Figure 8-2.

Raul remains concerned about his obsessions. Dr. James doesn't really buy that Raul owns even 2 percent of the responsibility for the patient's death. However, Raul still clings to feelings of guilt and shame. He dwells on the slight possibility that his 2 percent contribution may have been the tipping point. Thus, Dr. James tells Raul that continued work on his excessive responsibility OCD is necessary.

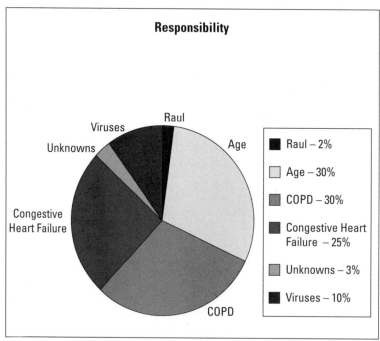

Figure 8-2:
Raul's pie chart indicates that Raul's responsibility for the patient's death is insignificant compared to the other contributing factors.

Is it a bird? A plane? No, it's COMET

A Dutch study published in the February 2008 journal *The Behavior Therapist* described the use of Competitive Memory Training (COMET) for a group of people with treatment-resistant OCD. The participants in the group had already averaged 30 weeks of Cognitive-Behavioral Therapy (CBT) before starting COMET. The premise behind COMET is that some people retain negative emotions in memory that seem extremely hard to change. CBT helps counter disordered *thinking,* but some people still *feel* dreadful after CBT. So COMET teaches clients a positive script to substitute for negative thoughts when they're feeling bad. In addition, they practice positive postures and facial expressions.

For example, a woman with an obsessive thought that she was going to harm a loved one would be taught to say, "I'm a good person who would never hurt anyone." At the same time, she would smile, sit up straight, and recall the times that she was helpful to others in the past. The training would progress so that whenever she had an obsession, she would automatically put on a "happy face."

Results of this small study were spectacular, given that they involved people who had failed to improve a great deal with standard effective therapies. Upon first glance at this article, to us it sounded a little like staring in the mirror and doing self-affirmations. However, we agree that the results appear to be promising and deserve more study.

However, this exercise helps Raul understand that his obsessive urges and impulses don't really have the power to hurt others. He still feels somewhat responsible, but using the pie chart technique helps him talk back to his OCD. He learns to say, "Just because I feel overly responsible, doesn't mean that I am. No one's care can be perfect, and even if it were, people would still die."

The pie chart technique helps people realize that many factors are involved in outcomes. Usually no one person or one reason can be held 100 percent responsible when something bad happens.

Pushing Out OCD Thinking with New Narratives

Mysteries, horror, and science fiction capture the minds and emotions of audiences all over the world. The audience is immersed in a story that may be highly unlikely or even illogical, but it appears possible because the audience suspends judgment and logic for a few hours. When the movie or book reaches a conclusion, the audience returns to reality.

OCD grabs your mind and emotions in much the same manner, but the story or movie never ends. Logic and reality remain suspended. Endless skewed narratives (obsessive thoughts) that misinterpret reality exhaustively plague the OCD mind.

It's as though those with OCD have a fiction writer living in their heads churning out compelling *narratives,* or stories, one after the other. The OCD mind sees just enough elements of *possibility,* to make the story *seem* totally believable. The best way to shut these OCD-fueled stories down is to rewrite your mind's narratives and give them a good dose of reality. This involves a three-step process:

1. **Making up OCD-like stories**

2. **Writing your own OCD narratives**

3. **Assessing and rewriting your OCD narratives**

But before you start writing fictitious OCD stories, it's a good idea to see what a typical OCD story looks like. Consider the story of Pam, whom we introduce in the earlier section, "Dismissing unrealistic doubts." Pam has doubts about the safety of food, the cleanliness of restaurants, and the possibility of contracting diseases from waiters. Her OCD story contains many OCD misinterpretations. Her therapist suggests that she write out her complete OCD narrative. Here's what she comes up with.

> Germs are everywhere. I keep thinking about filth. You never know who might be sick or have open sores. If a waiter with hepatitis has a cut and then touches my plate, I could easily get hepatitis. If I get hepatitis, I could pass it on to my family before I even know I'm sick. I saw a waiter smoking a cigarette outside in the parking lot. The parking lot is full of germs from rotting food and animal droppings. The waiters can pick up dirt and feces on their shoes, and then contaminate their hands when they tie their shoes. Then they touch everything on the table. I'm not certain that all the glasses, plates, and utensils are sterilized after each meal. I look at the plates and feel disgusted; if I feel disgusted, I'm pretty sure that means they must be contaminated. Walking into a restaurant feels like walking into a cesspool. I was lucky to just get food poisoning. If I eat in a restaurant again, I could get something much worse. So, it makes sense to carry my own food in sterilized plastic bags. If I have to go to a restaurant for work, I just don't eat. As soon as I'm out of there, I shower for at least 30 minutes, and then I sanitize my clothes.

Pam's OCD narrative has many elements that seem reasonable. Germs *are* everywhere, miniscule amounts of feces *are* found in food, parking lots *are* dirty, and hepatitis *is* occasionally transmitted by food handlers. What makes this an *OCD* story is that Pam has no direct evidence to confirm or disconfirm her concerns about all these contaminants making their way to her dinner plate. Her OCD story illustrates the following OCD misinterpretations:

- ✔ Confusing facts and feelings
- ✔ Doubting her own senses' ability to detect cleanliness and safety
- ✔ Inflating the importance of her thoughts
- ✔ Overestimating the risk of getting sick
- ✔ Seeking unobtainable perfectionism (perfect cleanliness)

Due to the type of OCD misinterpretations she uses, her story spins entirely out of her OCD mind. You see how to write out your personal OCD stories and assess them for misinterpretations in the later sections of this chapter. But first, we want you to indulge in a little fantasy.

Creating made-up, OCD-like stories

In order to prepare you for dealing with your personal OCD stories, you may find it helpful to create OCD-like stories about things that *you normally don't worry about at all*. Doing so allows you to see how similar these completely made-up stories are to those your OCD mind has already created. You can see that there is absolutely no end to such stories, and remind yourself that your personal OCD stories are merely fictitious creations of your OCD mind.

These fictitious stories are actually sort of fun to write. But the point of writing them is to remind yourself that these fanciful stories are exactly like the OCD stories that run through your mind and scare you all the time. Try viewing your OCD stories as creative, emotionally interesting, and even a little entertaining. Follow this process to author your own work of OCD fiction:

1. **Think about some mundane, everyday event that causes you no particular worry or distress.**

   Examples include walking along a sidewalk, searching for a book on the library's shelves, going to the mall, or sitting in your hot tub. Just be sure to choose something that you do with no trouble and that's unrelated to the actual OCD stories that currently run through your mind.

2. **Include details concerning everything that could conceivably go wrong in your story.** This can include contamination, death, illness, harm to others, imperfections, and so on.

3. **Read your made-up story, and notice how similar it is to the ones that really do scare you.** Compare it to the stories that run through the movie theater in your mind on a daily basis.

4. **Practice watching how creative the OCD mind can be.** Consider writing two or three of these stories each day for a while.

5. **Consider becoming a Hollywood horror-movie author.** (Just kidding.)

We think you'll discover that it isn't difficult to imagine many conceivable scenarios of danger. For example, how worried are you right now, *this very moment*, that your house may ignite into a ball of fire? Probably not very (at least until we brought up the possibility).

Now turn on the OCD fiction writer and watch how the story unfolds:

> Maybe the electrician who installed the wiring in your home office was smoking marijuana that day and crossed a few wires. It's also possible that moisture has accumulated behind the walls and some connections are about to short out. Maybe your neighbors haven't cleaned their fire-place chimney and an ember could spark, fly out, and land on your roof. And the U.S. Navy just shot a satellite out of the sky. You can imagine a big chunk falling onto your house, setting it ablaze. It's been awhile since you cleaned out the dryer vent. What if the cat tips over a lamp while you're out and it ignites the curtains? Are you absolutely, positively certain that you turned off the stove?

The point is that the above scenario is remotely possible. But the OCD story is not based on anything that is happening right now. Of course you should take reasonable precautions to keep your house safe. But, the OCD fiction writer keeps these thoughts churning despite the lack of any objective supporting evidence. And OCD doubt would not be assuaged by cleaning out the dryer vent — *there's always something else* that could be done to prevent fire. In actuality, the list is potentially endless. You could no doubt spend every waking moment of each and every day trying to eliminate risks of fire and still not succeed 100 percent.

There is a small chance that writing fictitious OCD stories could cause you to develop a few new worries. If you find that to be the case for you, please stop this process and seek professional consultation. If your OCD is fairly severe (that is, quite worrisome and disruptive to your life), you should seek such consultation before attempting any of the exercises in this book on your own at all.

Writing down your OCD narratives

In order to change the endings to the OCD stories that run continuously through your mind, you need to write them out. Take some time to start writing your personal stories — the ones that actually run through your mind and worry you from day to day. Be sure to tell the whole story (or as they say in New Mexico, "the whole enchilada"), including all your doubts, distorted interpretations, beliefs, reasoning, images, and worries — everything your mind tells you about your obsessions and compulsions. Here's how:

- ✓ **Write a complete narrative about every OCD fear or worry that bothers you.**

  You don't have to do all of these stories at once — you may need several writing sessions to complete the task. Write them down one at a time. Go back to your story a number of times and add details as they occur to you.

- ✓ **Be sure to include all thoughts, images, and urges that run through your head as they relate to the OCD story.**

- ✓ **Write down what makes you believe in your OCD story — your reasoning process (regardless of whether it seems logical).**

- ✓ **Don't forget to include your fears of what may happen if you fail to obey your OCD and take actions to avoid bad outcomes.**

- ✓ **Include any people or characters that may be involved in your story.** Often stories revolve around harm to others.

Review your story fairly often and embellish it further if additional details come to mind. Don't worry; we plan to help you change your story. In the next section, you find out how to write alternative, non-OCD stories to live by. But for now, you need to be aware of the existing stories and hear what they're telling you.

Assessing and rewriting OCD narratives

After you've written out your OCD story, you're ready to rewrite it with a different outcome. There are two steps to rewriting your OCD story:

1. **Assessing your story**

2. **Creating a balanced story**

Assessing your OCD narrative

In order to assess your OCD narrative, you need to determine what types of OCD misinterpretations (such as exaggerating risks, doubts, confusing facts and feelings, and so forth) your personal OCD story contains. Then you'll have the information you need to write an alternative, balanced story. Here are questions that can help you analyze the elements of your narratives:

- ✓ Does your OCD story involve doubt? If so, is your doubt based on direct evidence?

- ✓ Would other people agree with your story or find it illogical?

✔ How great is the risk of your OCD story happening? Are you exaggerating the risk?

✔ Are you viewing your thoughts as having special powers or as being real?

✔ Are you confusing your feelings with facts?

✔ Are you too worried about being perfect?

✔ Are you trying to control your thoughts?

✔ Are you being overly responsible and believing that you should be able to protect yourself and others from harm?

Write out the answers and take some time to reflect upon them. The answers alone will not greatly impact your OCD, but they will prepare you to write a new, more balanced story.

To give you a better idea of how this step works, take a look at Tracy's story. **Tracy** is a 45-year-old elementary school teacher with contamination fears. Her story provides an opportunity for you to practice analyzing OCD stories for OCD misinterpretations. Then you'll be ready to analyze your own OCD stories and, finally, rewrite them.

> The modern world is full of radiation and unknown dangers from cell-phone towers and other signals in the air. Whenever I spot a tower, I feel nervous and my entire body tingles. I am pretty sure it's due to the signals bombarding my body and disrupting nerve cells. The danger lurks everywhere. Thousands of satellites beam signals all over the planet. So I've lined my car roof with aluminum foil. I also had contractors place rolls of foil across my entire attic. But I still worry. I wear hats lined with foil everywhere for a little extra protection. I try to explain these problems to my family, but they think I'm crazy. I tell them the things they should do to protect themselves. I'd just die if they got cancer when I could have prevented it. Sometimes, I try hard not to think about these dangers because the thoughts just upset me. But the thoughts keep coming back. Maybe my brain has become contaminated, and that's preventing me from being able to control my thoughts.

Now let's take a look at Tracy's story and analyze it for OCD misinterpretations. Is her story based on faulty logic or thinking? By applying the eight questions noted earlier, we can detect any faulty thinking:

✔ **Does her OCD story involve doubt? If so, is her doubt based on direct evidence?**

As far as we can determine, Tracy's story is full of OCD doubt and not based on any clear evidence. Perhaps someday science will figure out whether the types of signals Tracy worries about pose any real risk — but until that day, no justification exists for her actions.

✔ **Would other people agree with her story or find it illogical?**

Everyone that Tracy has shared her story with finds it quite unlikely.

✔ **How great is the risk of Tracy's OCD story happening? Is she exaggerating the risk?**

As is typical with OCD, Tracy is profoundly exaggerating risks.

✔ **Is Tracy viewing her thoughts as having special powers or as being real?**

She believes that merely because she has these thoughts, they must be real.

✔ **Is Tracy confusing her feelings with facts?**

Yes. She feels tingling in her body, which is probably due to anxiety. She then assumes that the tingling represents proof of damage to her body.

✔ **Is Tracy too worried about being perfect?**

Tracy's story does not show evidence that she is too much of a perfectionist.

✔ **Is Tracy trying to control her thoughts?**

Yes, but like most people, she finds that attempts to control her thoughts just make the situation worse.

✔ **Is Tracy being overly responsible and believing that she should be able to protect herself and others from harm?**

Yes, Tracy is assuming that she can do things to prevent cancer from occurring in her family by getting them to take the same actions she has — that is, by creating barriers to block signals and radiation.

By answering the preceding questions, you can see the types of OCD misinterpretations Tracy has been making. You can assess your own OCD stories the same way.

Creating a balanced narrative

Now it's time to start writing an alternative, non-OCD story. This story will stand in sharp contrast to your OCD story. Your new story needs to take the opposite view. Consider how someone who doesn't have OCD might tell the story. You probably won't believe in this new story right away — that's expected. However, with time and practice, you will make slow but sure progress toward buying into your new story.

Writing and rewriting your OCD stories will likely be much easier to do with the collaborative help of a therapist. If your OCD is fairly severe, please realize that while these exercises are likely to help you, you'll also need to do many of the other strategies presented throughout this book. And we strongly suggest professional help.

Here's how to proceed:

- ✔ **Take your time.** Don't expect to write your new story in one sitting.

- ✔ **Include at least as many details in your non-OCD story as you have in your OCD story.** Add even more details over time.

- ✔ **Make sure your story is based only on evidence that you can see, touch, taste, feel, or hear.**

- ✔ **Act as if you believe your story.** Read it and imagine it to be true several times each day. Continue this process for a number of weeks.

- ✔ **Don't pull out your story to deal with distress that arises when your OCD story becomes active.** Instead, read your new story repeatedly when you're feeling okay.

- ✔ **As you practice your story, start rating how much you believe in your balanced, non-OCD story.** Also rate your belief in your OCD story and see whether it starts to slowly decline.

Following is Tracy's new, non-OCD story. (See "Assessing your OCD narrative" for the OCD version.) Because Tracy's OCD is pretty severe, she enlists the help of a therapist to complete this exercise.

> I realize that no one is on a mission to contaminate the world. Overall, most cancer rates have actually declined a little in the past decade. Telephone companies certainly don't want to kill their customers off. Real people work for those companies and those people care about their own families and probably other people as well. My house and my car are safe, nice places to be. I enjoy spending time driving as well as having friends over to my home. I like going to other people's homes. Their homes are as safe as they need to be. Cellphone towers help people stay in touch with each other. Satellites allow us to predict the weather, view movies on demand, and enjoy modern life.

Tracy reads and imagines scenes from her story regularly. She remembers not to pull it out in order to deal with her OCD story when it pops up. With lots of support and practice, she discovers that her OCD story feels less and less believable. Her new story slowly becomes more comfortable. She finds that living her life as if the new story were true feels much better.

Chapter 9

Managing the OCD Mind

*I*n this chapter, we tell you about a treatment for OCD that involves applying various techniques based on the ancient practice of mindfulness. Practicing mindfulness involves adopting a set of attitudes and is a good precursor to meditation. Research supports the use of meditation and mindfulness as adjuncts to Cognitive-Behavioral Therapy (CBT).

Mindfulness has been increasingly incorporated into CBT. Exciting research on mindfulness-based techniques has shown significant promise. In fact, CBT that includes a mindfulness component has demonstrated actual, positive changes in brain areas thought to be involved with OCD. We expect many more studies on mindfulness to be carried out in the upcoming years. However, to date, relatively fewer large controlled studies on this approach exist than on the effectiveness of exposure and response prevention (ERP) — the focus of Chapter 10.

Separating Your Thoughts from Who You Are

The concept of mindfulness means attending to the present moment with openness and without judgment. Achieving mindfulness can seem very challenging when your mind is busily bubbling with obsessions and compulsions. You may wonder how you can be accepting of the present moment when the present moment feels so distressful and uncomfortable.

To achieve mindfulness, you must be able to recognize that the thoughts you think and who you are as a person are not one and the same.

Building bridges from Buddhism to Western psychology

In the October 2006 issue of *American Psychologist,* Dr. B. Alan Wallace of the Santa Barbara Institute for Consciousness Studies and Dr. Shauna L. Shapiro of Santa Clara University discussed their views on and approach to integrating Buddhist philosophy and mental-health practices. In contrast to traditional psychology that often focuses on what is wrong with people, Buddhist philosophy is concerned with achieving states of balanced well-being. Wallace and Shapiro believe that good mental health consists of mental balance in four areas. Achieving this balance could help relieve OCD symptoms. The four areas are

✔ **Conative Balance:** Conative behavior means purposeful and goal-directed. A person must have willful intentions and carry them out. These intentions must be realistic, and consistent with the well-being of one's self and others. For example, with OCD, there must be an intention or willingness to face fear and some discomfort in order to benefit from treatment.

✔ **Attentional Balance:** Attentional balance refers to the ability to attend to and focus voluntarily. Lack of attentional control is a problem for those who suffer with OCD. They can be distracted by their obsessions and unable to concentrate on what is important. The development of voluntary and sustained attention allows a person with OCD to practice mindfulness instead of dwelling on obsessional thoughts.

✔ **Cognitive Balance:** Maintaining cognitive balance means having a clear mind that is open to experiences and not distorted by thoughts or emotions. A person with cognitive balance is grounded in reality. For OCD sufferers, this means identifying OCD distortions that cloud their thinking (see Chapter 8).

✔ **Affective Balance:** Affective refers to one's emotions. People with affective balance experience a full range of emotions and respond to reality with appropriate emotional expressions. They are empathic, compassionate, and joyful as appropriate, based on reality, as opposed to those with OCD who tend to become overly fearful and anxious because of their OCD beliefs.

People with all types of emotional disorders universally fall into a trap set by their minds. And in truth, people who do not suffer from clear-cut emotional maladies sometimes fall into this same trap. The nature of this trap is that the mind tells you to take the thoughts it generates very seriously. The mind further dictates that you should believe that you and your thoughts are synonymous — one and the same.

But you need to realize that these directives from your mind are erroneous illusions. And believing in these illusions can lead you down a very rocky path indeed. The only way to avoid this trap is to find a way to step back and observe your OCD mind at work.

Here's an exercise to help you see what we're getting at. We call it "Discovering the Observant You versus Your OCD Thoughts."

1. **Sit down and make yourself comfortable.**

2. **Close your eyes and wait for a thought to pop into your mind** — any thought at all. Your thought could be about

   - How you're feeling (relaxed, anxious, sad, whatever)

   - The temperature in the room

   - What this exercise has to do with OCD

   - What you want to cook for dinner

   - Wondering when a darn thought is finally going to pop into your mind — yes, that's a thought too!

   You may have to wait a few seconds or perhaps a few minutes, but we're pretty confident it won't take too long for some sort of thought to cross your mind. After all, the mind is a master at generating thoughts one right after another.

   Obsessions are thoughts too. If an obsession is the first thing to pop into your mind, consider it a thought.

3. **Now, ask yourself this question about your thought:** *Who noticed* **the thought?**

The answer to that question is that there is an observant part of you that can see your thoughts separately from the part of you that generates your thoughts. Thus, *you* are not your thoughts. With time and practice, you can separate yourself from your thoughts — especially your OCD-related thoughts. Start listening for those OCD thoughts. Typical examples include

- ✔ I can't stand not being certain that things will be okay.

- ✔ I could die from touching doorknobs.

- ✔ I could never use a public restroom.

- ✔ Public telephones are dangerous collectors of germs.

- ✔ Restaurants are full of contaminants that could kill me.

In Chapter 8, we tell you how to rethink the content of your thoughts — by examining the evidence, rewriting OCD stories, looking for OCD misinterpretations, and so on. Now we suggest that you try your hand at viewing your OCD thoughts as simply random, meaningless output from your OCD mind. These thoughts can be interesting to observe, but they shouldn't be taken too seriously.

Some simple mental exercises can help you put your thoughts into the proper perspective and let them go effortlessly. To that end, try the following:

- ✔ Close your eyes and imagine writing your OCD thought on a leaf. Then toss the leaf into a stream. Watch the leaf swirl in the eddies of the water as it slowly heads downstream.

✔ Close your eyes and imagine you have a magic laser that writes your thoughts onto a cloud high in the sky. Just watch the cloud slowly drift.

✔ Repeatedly remind yourself that "thoughts are merely thoughts, nothing more." Repeat this phrase over and over, but don't let it become a new compulsion for dealing with your obsessive thoughts!

The point of treating your thoughts this way is that slowly, but surely, you can relate to them differently. You can call upon the observant part of you to help you step back from your thoughts. Think of your thoughts as analogous to having your hand smashed up against your face, blocking your vision. The observant you can help you take the hand away, allowing you to see (think) more clearly.

Acquiring the Attitudes of Mindfulness

Mindfulness consists of a set of adoptable attitudes, which we describe in this section. Once you embrace these attitudes, you can start ever-so-slowly to form a new perspective on life that can help you manage your OCD mind instead of allowing it to manage you. These ways of thinking can also prepare you for mindful meditation. These attitudes are

✔ Making time

✔ Having patience

✔ Letting go

✔ Learning acceptance

✔ Suspending judgment

✔ Living in the now

Making time to be mindful

Adopting mindful attitudes and becoming skilled at mindfulness require you to open up some space and time in your life. Simply put, to change, you have to want to change, and you have to make time to change.

We can almost hear you saying, "Okay, but I'm awfully busy. Exactly how much time will I need to put in on this?" That question actually comes from the OCD part of your mind, which doesn't want you to spend time on things that will take you away from your OCD!

In actuality, you don't need to practice mindfulness for any absolute amount of time. If you're feeling really pressed, try giving mindfulness ten formal minutes a day. As you get used to it and it begins to feel more natural, you'll probably find it easier to devote an increasing amount of time to it. Try to work up to 30 to 45 minutes a day.

If you're thinking, "Gasp, I could never devote 45 minutes a day to something like this," don't forget that less time can be helpful too. You can always try being mindful for a couple of minutes ten times a day, or develop some similar strategy. The more time you spend on being mindful, the less time you will be devoting to your OCD. Most people find that if they can reduce their OCD by 50 percent or more, a big chunk of time is freed up that was unavailable to them before.

Pursuing patience

Humans tend to be a rather impatient lot. But impatience can derail the most determined efforts to change. For example, dieters give up on dieting because they don't see results quickly enough — even though studies indicate that the more slowly you lose weight, the better you'll do in the long run. In the same way, impatience causes people to stop physical training when they can't observe results after a few weeks.

You simply cannot rush the process of adopting mindful attitudes. An analogy we like is that of running a long distance race using the wrong motivation. Somewhere along the way, after running for what seems like an eternity, you realize you have not yet reached the finish line. To prod yourself to do better and run faster, you start smacking yourself on the head. We hope you can see the futility in this approach. It is only by accepting where you're at now that you can move forward.

OCD often devours hours of time and mental energy every day, so it's very understandable that you want quick relief. Be patient. Don't expect immediate balance and absolute well-being after a few days of practicing mindfulness.

Letting go of striving for striving's sake

In the Western world, and especially in the United States, people tend to emphasize hard work and striving for a purpose. The message is usually that if you aren't where you want to be in life, all you have to do is work harder, and you'll get there. Still not getting the results you want? Work even harder. Whew! We're tired just from thinking about it! What about working *smarter* with mindfulness?

Adapting a mindful attitude may feel very strange indeed if you, like most people, belong to the "work hard and then work some more" school of thinking. Mindfulness just doesn't happen that way. Rather, unlike almost everything else you do, mindfulness comes from letting go of working harder. In a sense, you want to strive to not strive. You *allow* mindfulness to come in while allowing yourself to let go of striving for striving's sake.

You could easily conclude that we are suggesting that hard work is a bad thing. But that's not the case at all. For example, the treatment of OCD usually involves hard, difficult work. Most people will need to participate in some type of psychotherapy in order to get better. That means going to sessions, talking about difficult topics, and even doing things that may be really hard (see Chapters 8 and 10 for more information). But our experience with people is that when they work too hard at therapy and become, well, obsessive, then progress can be slowed.

Discovering acceptance

Most of our clients start therapy wanting to change something about themselves or their world. They come for help because they're uncomfortable and feeling great distress. They want something different in their lives. They want to feel better. Although we can help them feel better, we cannot eliminate all the bad stuff they will encounter the rest of their lives. If we could do that, we'd do it for ourselves first, and then implement world peace!

Certainly, if you suffer from OCD, you want change — change from suffering and change from feeling overtaken and overwhelmed. What if we tell you that the only way out of suffering is to accept that you will suffer? But the pain of your suffering will impact you far less when you practice acceptance.

Life is difficult. If you live a long life, you will necessarily experience pain, loss, and sadness. We all do! But, you may wonder, why do some people fall apart when bad things happen while others march on or even benefit from hardship?

Lots of factors play a role in how people respond to life's bumps in the road. People are made stronger by having supportive family and friends, enjoying productive work, and being strong mentally and physically. But something else protects against misfortune. People who are shocked and surprised when the inevitable obstacle shows up have a harder time handling it than do people who acknowledge and anticipate distress. Knowing and *accepting* that some moments in life are going to be uncomfortable, and even expecting those moments, make those difficult moments less, well, difficult.

Acceptance means cultivating a willingness to experience life as it comes your way. Allow bad feelings in when they arrive, and embrace them. The more you fight, the bigger the battle. That is the paradox of acceptance. Thus, acceptance is neither pessimistic nor optimistic. Acceptance is *realistic*.

Okay, enough of the philosophical chatter. Here, in a nutshell, is what acceptance has to do with you and your OCD: When you struggle against your own thinking, your mind bubbles over with even more obsessive thoughts. This means the more you can't stand to have an obsessive thought, the more likely that obsessive thought is to materialize.

Here's an exercise to make the point clearer. Think of a pink elephant. Bright pink, big, and fat. Concentrate. Picture that big, fat, pink elephant in your mind. Now, stop. Stop thinking about that pink elephant. Think about paying your bills or something. Seriously, we mean it! Whatever you do, don't think about that elephant. Don't let any thought of pink elephants enter your mind for the rest of the day. Tell yourself that the absolute worst thing you can do is think about pink elephants.

Did it work? Did you succeed in having absolutely no thoughts about that pink elephant? Probably not. That's because it is pretty hard to stop yourself from thinking. Active attempts to suppress thoughts usually boomerang.

By contrast, when you accept your thoughts for what they are — just thoughts — they lose some of their stranglehold over your OCD mind and dissipate more quickly. See, you've probably already stopped thinking about that pink elephant. Oh, sorry.

Mind you, acquiring acceptance takes time. Most humans will never be fully and readily accepting of whatever happens to them 100 percent of the time. For example, if you suffer a serious loss, we aren't suggesting that you simply accept the loss and instantly move on. That's not fair. Rather, it's important to accept the grief into your life. Feel it, observe it, and don't try to push it away. This approach will gradually guide you toward a healthy resolution of the loss. If you try to simply squelch difficult thoughts and feelings (whether related to loss or OCD), they will hang around far longer. Acceptance acknowledges the loss, the grief, and the lessening of the pain over time.

Suspending judgment about emotions

The vast majority of OCD thoughts that produce difficult emotions, such as anxiety, distress, sadness, stress, and controllable urges, include making strong judgments about the thought or events. The powerful emotions brought on by these judgments frequently trigger troubling episodes of OCD. The process is cyclical and looks something like this:

1. A thought enters your awareness or an event occurs.

2. You make an OCD-biased judgment about the thought or event.

3. Your judgment of the thought or event triggers an emotion.

4. You make an OCD-biased judgment about the emotion.

5. Your judgment of the emotion triggers OCD behavior.

6. As it says on the shampoo bottle, lather, rinse, and repeat. . . .

With practice, you can learn to release judgments and harsh evaluations of yourself and the world. Here are a few common OCD-related judgments and evaluations of the self and the world that you may want to watch for so that you can defend yourself against them:

- ✔ I am a defective person who must always be on the lookout. Otherwise, I am bound to seriously harm or kill someone.

- ✔ I could never forgive myself if I failed to keep my kitchen 100 percent clean and someone in my family came down with food poisoning.

- ✔ If I mess up in any way at all, I am a truly horrible person.

- ✔ No sane person would ever have thoughts like mine. I'm a disaster!

So how do you defend yourself against these kinds of judgments and evaluations? As an alternative, try realizing that all humans are an incredibly mixed bag of actions that can be judged positively or negatively. We're not saying that people are not responsible for intentional, immoral, illegal, and unkind actions. However, devoting much of your time to negatively judging yourself or others only makes you miserable and provides further fuel for your OCD mind. As Forrest Gump said, "Stuff happens!" When it does, remember that emotions are neither right nor wrong — they just are.

Please realize that suspending judgment and acquiring self-acceptance is an ever-evolving process. As with all mindful attitudes, you'll never achieve perfection with it. But that's okay, because considerable research has shown that people who struggle for perfection wind up feeling much worse than those who can accept themselves as they are.

Try to avoid judging your attempts at becoming nonjudgmental! Of course you will make many slips along the way. Just remember that no one is keeping score — other than the OCD part of your mind.

Living in the now

Everyone tends to worry now and then about things that haven't happened, and in many cases never will. For those with OCD, this kind of worrying is persistent, with one thought leading to another. What if I lose my job? What if that table is contaminated? What if I can't control myself? Or, you may feel guilty or depressed about what has happened in the past. Why did I say or do that? I wish I could go back in my life and do something better with my relationships. If only my childhood had been better.

Even though we write lots of books on how to think better, we're not always masters of our thoughts. Much of the time when we're thinking, we're not focused on the here and now. Instead, we're somewhere else in time, often in the future. But we're always aware that we are *living* in the here and now, and that we're not time-traveling in our thoughts.

If you suffer with OCD, thinking about the future can feel like being in the future. This can lead to experiencing the emotion of dread toward the future, even though the event has not and may not occur. So, if today is sunny and warm, yet you are focused on tomorrow's forecast of cold and rain, you miss the joy of the good day that *is* and experience the dread of the rainy day that may or may not actually occur. After all, the TV weather people are not infallible!

The following example is taken from our own experience and illustrates what focusing on anticipated dread versus present moments does:

> Friday mornings we travel down the road to a small gym near our home. There, we are met by our personal torturer, uh, we mean personal *trainer*. All the way there in the car we gripe about how early it is and how we didn't have enough coffee. Our minds are spinning and spewing negative thoughts. We begin to conjecture. What if
>
> - She makes us go up on our weights this time?
> - She makes us stand on one leg and twist into a pretzel?
> - We fall over and everyone laughs?
> - We have to jump rope for three minutes and can only do two?
> - We stop breathing and die?
>
> Still, when we arrive at the gym, we drag ourselves out of the car, continuing to dread what is coming next.
>
> Our trainer greets us, smiling. "Hi, I've been taking some great continuing education classes. I've got some new routines that involve abs, core strength, triceps, and biceps. Oh yeah, and the gluteus too!"
>
> Oh goodie, we think.
>
> But, then something happens. As we give ourselves to the magic of rigorous, physical exercise, within just a couple of minutes, the dreadful thoughts disappear. Attention focuses purely on how to balance, coordinate, and sustain the muscles necessary to complete each set. The "now" we are experiencing is really not that bad, and its aim is to keep us healthy. The mind calms. After the workout, smiles and happy moods prevail. See you next week!

This example from our own lives shows you how absurdly self-defeating thoughts about the future are typically poor predictors of actual experience (like those faulty weather reporters). The OCD mind is particularly good at this kind of catastrophic thinking about the future.

However, the mind becomes still when you fully engage with the present moment and live in the now. When you pay attention — full attention — to what is in front of you rather than what is behind you or ahead of you, your mind fully engages in the now.

Minding Meditation

Acquiring mindful attitudes (see the preceding sections) greatly enhances your ability to engage in what's known as meditation. Both being mindful and practicing meditation can help relieve your OCD.

OCD involves intolerance of distress, discomfort, urges, and uncertainty. Meditation teaches you to tolerate these frustrations. Meditation also increases your concentration and helps OCD sufferers view intrusive thoughts as less important.

The really great thing about meditation is that it's not especially complicated or expensive — you don't even need formal lessons or classes, although many people find them helpful. You can get started just by setting aside a few minutes each day.

There are many types of meditation. You may be instructed to focus on a candle or pay attention to each breath. Some forms of meditation ask you to concentrate on your body as you walk. Yoga is considered by many to be a type of meditation.

Which form of meditation is the best one for OCD? No one knows, and we rather suspect almost any one of them will work as well as any other. Although large studies on meditation for OCD are lacking, we think future studies will ultimately demonstrate that meditation works for OCD. We show you the basics of two easy-to-learn forms in the next two sections.

One form of meditation uses mantras (a word, phrase, or meaningless sound that you repeat over and over in order to focus and block out thoughts). You can use this approach to meditation, but if you do, be sure *not* to use it in direct response to an obsession. If you do, you run some risk of the mantra becoming a type of compulsion — in other words, something you feel compelled to do in order to reduce the distress brought on by your obsession. Definitely not something we recommend for those with OCD.

Breathing meditation

Breathing meditation is a common type of meditation. We recommend you do this one while sitting down in the following manner:

- ✔ **Find someplace pleasant where you will be undisturbed.** This place can be inside or outside. Quiet is nice too, but less important than finding a place where you won't be interrupted.

- ✔ **Find something to sit on.** Many people choose to purchase formal mats and pillows called *zabutans* and *zafus* for their meditation. But you can also use a chair or couch.

- ✔ **Experiment with a sitting position.** You can assume any of quite a few different postures while meditating — nothing is especially magical about any of them. Try to maintain the posture you choose for a period of time. Practice remaining still. Not many people find this easy to do, but you'll get better with practice. Physical training and/or yoga are great for strengthening your body so that you can remain still for increasing amounts of time.

- ✔ **Invite all feelings in, including discomfort.** Yep, that's right. Notice little feelings of unease, discomfort, anxiety, obsessions, and urges. Sit with them a while. Stay connected with these feelings, and try not to judge them. You'll see over time that you can tolerate these feelings longer and longer if you don't evaluate them as "horrible" or "awful."

- ✔ **Allow whatever thoughts you have to go through your mind — including your obsessions.** Some people think meditation involves blocking thoughts out. But meditation actually teaches you to relate to your thoughts differently — dispassionately observing them rather than taking them so seriously. So if you hear an obsession or other negative thought calling, just notice the thought. Allow it to pass, as eventually it will.

- ✔ **Don't hold onto positive thoughts.** Everyone enjoys positive thoughts, but this instruction involves just noticing your positive thoughts. They too will pass, and that's okay.

- ✔ **Focus on your breathing.** Notice the air as it passes through your nose and down into your lungs. Take slow, deep breaths. Allow the tension in your muscles to release. Let go of any tightness you sense. Scan your entire body and allow it to relax. Let your eyes and face soften.

- ✔ **Be kind and accepting of yourself.** Realize that no one finds meditation immediately rewarding and beneficial. If you struggle with meditation, give it more time. You can take a class later if it continues to be difficult. Results come slowly. But studies show it has benefits well beyond OCD. Improvements may occur in blood pressure, chronic pain, anxiety, and general health.

Engaging in regular meditation enhances the mindful attitudes discussed in the previous sections. And mindful attitudes aid your efforts with meditation.

In a few cases, people find that meditation triggers especially troubling feelings, such as anxiety or panic. Although meditative practices call for allowing and noticing difficult feelings, don't let things get out of hand. If you find the approach too disturbing, stop immediately! You still may want to learn meditation, but in these cases, you should get assistance from a mental-health professional who is also trained in meditation. This distressing reaction is less common with walking meditation, described next.

Walking meditation

Consider observing people scurrying about on a busy sidewalk or in a shopping mall. Notice how they rush to and fro. Take a glance at their faces and bodies — furrowed brows, tense foreheads, and arms swinging wildly. Many folks rush through their days, never noticing their own keyed-up states.

Mindful walking meditation can help you let go and refocus. Walking meditation is probably one of the easiest meditation methods around, so it's often a good way to start. And the great thing is that you can do it almost anywhere. Here's how walking meditation works:

1. **Pause for a moment before you start, and take a deep breath.** Focus on the air as it flows through your nose and lungs.

2. **Start walking.** The pace doesn't matter much, but don't rush.

3. **Focus on the sensations in your body as you walk.** Pay attention to your leg muscles, feet, thighs, ankles, calves, and the rhythmic swinging of your arms.

   If thoughts, obsessions, or bad feelings intrude, allow some space for them. Notice those thoughts and feelings, but do not judge them. When you can, shift your focus back to the sensations in your body.

4. **Concentrate on your feet for a while.** Focus on how they strike the ground as your heel hits first, your foot rolls, and you use your toes and the ball of your foot to push off. Just notice these sensations.

   Again, thoughts, obsessions, and bad feelings are welcome. Do not judge them negatively.

5. **Focus again on the flow of air as you breathe.** Inhale slowly and exhale as you notice the rhythm of your breath.

6. **Focus on any sights, smells, or sounds that you encounter on your walk.** Do this without judgment or evaluation.

7. **Shift your focus back to the muscles in your body and the rhythm of your walking.**

   If any of your obsessions come in, allow and notice them, but resist acting on them. You can tell yourself that when the walking meditation is over, you can engage in a compulsion if you feel you must — but continue the walking for at least 15 minutes.

That's it. Consider practicing walking meditation every day for 15 or 20 minutes. The exercise from the walking can't hurt, and the meditation is likely to help you.

The "Four R's" approach

Jeffrey M. Schwartz, M.D., began working with OCD patients at the U.C.L.A. School of Medicine in the mid 1980s. In a book he coauthored with Sharon Bagley, *The Mind and the Brain: Neuroplasticity and the Power of Mental Force*, Schwartz expressed concerns about what he considered to be the highly distressing and objectionable nature of exposure and response prevention (ERP) therapy, "... with its visits to public toilets and patients wiping urine-impregnated paper over themselves." As an alternative to ERP, Schwartz and his team developed what they call the "Four R's" approach to OCD treatment. He considers his approach to be cognitive-behavioral, with an emphasis on mindfulness techniques. He describes this treatment in the previously mentioned book as well as in *Brain Lock* (both published by Harper Perennial). The Four R's approach consists of four steps, as follows:

1. **Relabel:** When you have a compulsion or an obsession, you want to label it as exactly that — an obsession or a compulsion at work. Thus, if you touch something and fear getting AIDS from it, you need to remind yourself that the thought is an obsession.

2. **Reattribute:** When you notice an obsession or a compulsion, you not only realize that it is an obsession or compulsion, but you also tell yourself that it is being generated by faulty wiring and chemicals in your brain.

3. **Refocus:** After you have relabeled and reattributed, make a decision to focus on something else, such as reading a book, taking a walk, or playing a game. The key in this part of the program is that you delay any compulsive act at least 15 minutes.

4. **Revalue:** This step slowly evolves from repeatedly going through Steps 1 through 3. Dr. Schwartz advises that you can become an impartial, nonjudgmental observer of your mind. Over time, you can come to realize that your obsessions and compulsions are not who you are, but merely stem from your OCD mind. You will come to see that your obsessions and compulsions have no actual value for you. They are the equivalent of brain junk and ought to be ignored.

Dr. Schwartz's program has generated a lot of excitement, and we also see it as quite interesting and promising. We do, however, have reservations about abandoning ERP totally and replacing it with the Four R's as some have suggested, for the following reasons:

- Large, randomized, controlled studies supporting the effectiveness of the Four R's treatment are lacking, unlike other approaches for OCD, such as ERP, medication, and cognitive therapy.

- The Four R's plan actually includes a few elements of exposure and, ultimately, response prevention.

- ERP as usually practiced only rarely requires some of the horrid, more extreme exposures Dr. Schwartz describes.

There is no absolute, correct way to do breathing or walking meditation. You can experiment with varying what you decide to focus on, but generally you want to concentrate on bodily sensations and your breath. Finally, with meditation, you do not want to block out thoughts, including obsessions. Rather, you want to relate to them differently, by allowing them to come in and pass through as they will.

Chapter 10

Tackling OCD Behavior with ERP

. . . .

In This Chapter

▶ Understanding exposure and response prevention (ERP)

▶ Executing ERP

▶ Troubleshooting ERP

. . . .

*O*ver the past 30 years or so, we've consulted with clients who previously had received many years of treatment for their OCD — including various medications, all types of psychotherapy, and even electroconvulsive shock therapy — to virtually no avail. Sometimes OCD had not been correctly assessed and diagnosed. Other times the diagnosis was on target, but the therapies and medications were ill-chosen. A few of these cases had even been described as hopeless, and family members had been told to expect a lifetime of serious disability, if not institutionalization. We're happy to report that we were able to provide significant relief for the vast majority of these cases.

Fortunately, in recent years the outlook for OCD clients has been improving. Many more mental-health professionals are aware of how to recognize OCD and accurately diagnose it, as well as which treatments work and which ones don't. Of the available treatments for OCD, the specific type of Cognitive-Behavioral Therapy (CBT) called exposure and response prevention (ERP) stands as the most widely researched and accepted treatment strategy.

In this chapter, we explain what ERP is, why it works, and how to implement this strategy. Unless your OCD is very mild, you will want to collaborate with a professional in using ERP. In fact, it may be best to consult with a therapist before using ERP alone in any case. This chapter lays out the essentials and can help you prepare to work with your therapist. See Chapter 7 for information about seeking the services of a professional with appropriate training in ERP.

Exposing the Basics and Benefits of ERP

Don't panic! The "exposure" part of ERP doesn't mean we're going to suggest that you take off your clothes and walk around in public nude — that's *not* what ERP is about! But exposure *is* involved. ERP is pretty straightforward, and can be broken out into two parts:

✔ **Exposure:** The exposure part of ERP involves putting yourself in contact with the situations, cues, events, and triggers that lead to your *obsessional fears* (frequently recurring thoughts, images, or urges that are unwanted and cause considerable distress). For example, if you fear touching numerous everyday objects like telephones, doorknobs, and kitchen counters, you're asked to gradually start touching these feared surfaces.

As you make contact with these triggers, you're asked to pay close attention to how you feel, which will likely involve some distress. However, that distress will diminish as you continue making contact. In fact, you will be expected to repeatedly come in contact with these triggers and cues until your distress *does* diminish. It may take a while for you to feel better, but you will.

✔ **Response prevention:** The response prevention part of ERP simply refers to resisting the urge to engage in or carry out your usual *compulsions* (behaviors or mental acts that you use to reduce the distress caused by an obsession) in response to the discomfort you feel from making contact with the triggers. In the preceding example, after touching objects, you're likely to want to wash your hands (a compulsion), but while practicing ERP, you're instructed to work very hard to avoid hand-washing.

The description of ERP initially may sound like we're simply saying, "Just stop having your obsessions and compulsions!" We understand that reaction. But we suspect if you could, you would have already stopped your OCD.

So how is ERP more than an instruction to "just stop"? Well, with ERP you are carefully guided to systematically — slowly but surely — make contact with your problematic triggers while gradually building up your ability to resist engaging in your compulsions.

It seems to us that psychologists are pretty much addicted to acronyms, but they don't particularly agree on which ones to use. Exposure and response prevention is sometimes referred to as ERP, but you may also see acronyms such as E&RP, EX/RP, and ERPT used to refer to the same thing. Occasionally, you may see the terms Behavior Therapy (BT) or Cognitive-Behavioral Therapy (CBT) used to refer to ERP, but those are actually much more general types of therapy that may or may not include ERP.

Understanding why and how ERP works

People learn best through repeated, direct experience and practice. The more times you do something, the more ingrained the learning becomes. Your OCD is well practiced and deeply ingrained. ERP helps you unlearn your

OCD behaviors by reconditioning your responses to an increasing hierarchy, or staircase, of stimuli (triggers). You start with the least problematic trigger and progress to the most challenging one.

Ringing in change with ERP

In the late 1890s, a Russian scientist by the name of Ivan Pavlov conducted experiments that demonstrated a learning principle that helps explain how ERP works. Pavlov noticed that dogs begin to salivate upon seeing the person who normally feeds them. He then decided to see if he could teach the dogs to associate the same response with the sound of a bell (something that dogs would normally never salivate in response to). He rang a bell and closely followed the sound with giving the dogs food. Soon the dogs began to drool merely in response to the bell — even without receiving food. Even more importantly, he discovered that this response could be *unlearned* (essentially, that the association could be broken) by repeatedly sounding the bell over and over again without following the sound with food.

Humans also have used dinner bells for centuries to announce that dinner is ready. The users of dinner bells find that they, like Pavlov's dogs, begin to salivate in response to the bell — and sometimes even bells other than dinner bells. But if someone continuously rang bells with no food to follow, humans would also unlearn the response.

The first principle of why ERP works is based on this same idea. The triggers, cues, situations, and events (what shrinks call *stimuli*) that set off your obsessions and compulsions have a powerful negative emotional charge — in other words, you associate them with great distress. So if touching a doorknob triggers an obsession about contamination, you feel freaked out. Just looking at a doorknob may even make you feel upset.

However, if you make repeated, prolonged contact with doorknobs, you can actually unlearn this association. The association is broken or unlearned because the anticipated horrible outcome doesn't occur. In other words, you hold onto the doorknob until your freaked-out feelings diminish — and they will with enough time and repetition.

It may take you a while to believe that nothing bad will happen during exposure to fearful, distressing stimuli — which is why many, if not most, people need some assistance in going through ERP.

Reconditioning behavior with ERP

For those people who have both obsessions and compulsions (the vast majority of those with OCD), an additional principle explains why ERP works. That principle is known as *reinforcement*. Reinforcement refers to the fact that people tend to do more of almost anything that makes them feel better (see Chapter 5 for a more detailed explanation of both positive and negative reinforcement). Thus, if what you do results in either pleasurable feelings or marked reductions in anxiety or distress, you have a strong incentive to keep doing more of what leads you to these feelings.

Compulsions are powerfully reinforced because they temporarily make you feel better. ERP therapy instructs you not to carry out your compulsions so that your brain won't remain stuck in the OCD loop of an obsession causing distress and a compulsion reducing that distress, which reinforces the cycle.

See Chapter 4 for a description of how the brains of those with OCD differ a little from the brains of those without OCD. In OCD, certain brain areas are enlarged and others show increased activity. Particularly exciting research shows that ERP (as well as medications) can restore these alterations to normal. Remind yourself repeatedly that with each ERP trial, you are literally rewiring and normalizing the way your brain works. That's actually the best incentive we can give you for undergoing ERP.

Seeing the upsides and downsides of ERP

ERP has been extensively studied as a treatment for OCD since the 1970s. These studies have consistently demonstrated that ERP is highly effective as a treatment for OCD, as long as the patient stays the course.

The major downside of ERP (and it's significant) is that it has a moderately high dropout and/or refusal rate. Some people just won't consider doing ERP, and others drop out after they start. Combining cognitive therapy or medication with ERP appears to reduce the rate of refusal, but it's unclear whether fewer people ultimately drop out of such combined treatments. More studies are needed on this issue.

However, the positives of ERP, when you follow through, are many. Here are the major findings at this time:

✔ ERP appears to be at least as effective as medication and may be even more so, although the literature on this issue is mixed. A combination of ERP and medication does not lead to dramatic improvements over either one alone, but is generally recommended for those with severe cases.

✔ The effectiveness of ERP appears to be similar to that of other CBT techniques for OCD (see Chapter 8 and 9), but those techniques have not been studied as extensively. Furthermore, most studies of CBT for OCD to date have included at least some component of ERP. And ERP usually has a few elements of CBT. Therefore, the jury is still out regarding the overall comparable effectiveness of CBT alone for OCD or, for that matter, ERP with no other elements of CBT.

✔ ERP can be done in a therapist's office or in a patient's home environment. There's no rule as to which works better, but our clinical impression is that home applications sometimes appear useful.

✔ ERP usually works better when guidance is provided by a trained professional. However, self-directed ERP seems to work fairly well for some people, especially those with mild cases.

✔ ERP works better than psychological treatments aimed only at anxiety reduction (like progressive muscle relaxation and deep-breathing techniques).

✔ ERP works over the long term, and those who practice it appear to resist relapse for a number of years (if not longer). By contrast, medication alone leads to rapid relapse if discontinued.

Exploring an alternative when ERP isn't appropriate

Real-life exposure generally works best whenever carrying it out is practical. However, a lot of people with OCD experience obsessive thoughts or images having to do with worries about engaging in violent, inappropriate, danger-ous, or immoral behaviors. For example, some people with OCD obsess about shouting obscenities out loud and compulsively chant to prevent them from losing control. ERP would not have those people shout obscenities at a reli-gious service.

Obviously, exposure is inappropriate when obsessions have to do with horri-ble or socially inappropriate things, such as murder, rape, or doing something indecent in public. However, another approach to exposure *can* be used for these kinds of problems. This alternative is called imaginal exposure.

A very small percentage of those with OCD report experiencing obsessive thoughts without any compulsive mental or behavioral actions. Some of these people may have horrible images of hurting someone else without any com-pulsive actions to keep them from doing so. Imaginal exposure also can work for this issue when regular exposure would be impractical.

Imaginal exposure strategies include:

✔ **Scripts:** With this approach, you write out a vivid story about your obses-sions. For example, you might write out a scene involving catching a terrible disease from eating contaminated food. Or, if your OCD theme is about harming other people, your script might include detailed descrip-tions of you losing control and doing what you fear, such as stabbing all your family members to death. The scripts are usually one to five minutes in length. Scripts should be listened to or read multiple times.

✔ **Video:** Sometimes you can find a scene closely related to your OCD theme from a horror movie that you can play repeatedly.

 ✔ **Imaginal hierarchies:** You can also arrange a set of specific scenes into a hierarchy, or staircase. You proceed with imagining each stair on your hierarchy again and again until your Ugh Factor Ratings drop substantially. Then you move onto the next stair on your hierarchy. (We discuss hierarchies, staircases, and Ugh Factor Ratings later in this chapter.)

If your obsessions are highly disturbing and include themes about harming yourself or others, engaging in violence, or doing illegal activities, we strongly recommend that you consult a therapist. Although those with OCD are at lower risk than most people for actually engaging in such behavior, you need a mental-health professional to assess your risks and provide an actual diagnosis.

Working through ERP Therapy

Setting up and working through ERP involves a series of five steps. Although you can read most of this book in any order you want, if you're ready to consider ERP, we recommend you start with Step 1 and proceed through Step 5. Most people find going through ERP is easier when working with a therapist.

1. **Find your OCD theme.**

2. **List your OCD triggers and their Ugh Factor Ratings.**

3. **Build an ERP staircase.**

4. **Warm up to ERP.**

5. **Work through your triggers by doing ERP.**

Determining your OCD theme

Although obsessions and compulsions vary widely from one person to another, in almost all cases, OCD consists of one or more unifying themes or subjects. These themes are often referred to as OCD types (see Chapter 2 for more specific information). The most frequent themes are fears and worries about:

 ✔ Collecting and hoarding

 ✔ Contamination

 ✔ Doing something inappropriate (usually sexual or aggressive)

 ✔ Doubts (or checking)

 ✔ Physical health

 ✔ Sinning

 ✔ Symmetry

The first step in ERP is to determine the main theme or type of *your* OCD. That isn't difficult to do. Simply review the list above and/or look through Chapter 2 and find the types of OCD concerns that give you the most trouble. You may identify more than one.

Because contamination is the most common OCD theme, we focus on it in this chapter as well as the previous two. However, you will see these same principles applied to other OCD themes in Chapters 13–19. So don't feel left out if your OCD theme is a little different — we're likely to have you covered.

Tallying up your OCD triggers and assigning Ugh Factor Ratings

Once you know the theme or themes surrounding your obsessional thoughts and worries, the next step is to look for all the triggers, actions, events, cues, and situations (also known as stimuli) that set your whole OCD cycle off. These triggers include a variety of situations that you probably avoid much of the time right now. For instance, if your obsessional theme is contamination, you may stay away from public bathrooms or avoid touching doorknobs, dirt, kitchen counters, or telephones. A trigger is something that sets off your desire to use a compulsion (like washing your hands) if you encounter it.

The nature of a given person's OCD may involve triggers that don't lend themselves to standard ERP in real-life situations. For example, someone who fears exposure to radioactive material would not be encouraged to actually take a field trip to the national labs at Los Alamos, New Mexico, and walk into a room labeled: "Warning! Highly Radioactive Material Inside!" If your OCD involves impractical triggers like this example, see the earlier section, "Exploring an alternative when ERP isn't appropriate."

After you've made your list of problematic OCD triggers, actions, cues, events, and situations, rate each one for the amount of difficulty it would cause you if you were to make contact with it. We like to whimsically call these *Ugh Factor Ratings*. We like to use Ugh Factor Ratings because the word "Ugh" captures the essence of distress and upset.

The technical term that most psychologists use is Subjective Units of Distress or SUDS. Only psychologists would come up with an acronym like SUDS. These ratings are personal and arbitrary — basically, good guesses. SUDS sounds important, but it just means a good guesstimate.

Here are the steps to follow for listing and rating your OCD triggers.

1. **Make a list of about 10 to 20 distressing situations — the events, cues, actions, and triggers for your OCD.**

   All items in your list should relate to your particular OCD theme, such as contamination. Make a separate list for each theme or type of OCD you struggle with. As you create your list, consider the following guidelines:

   - Include situations that you normally completely avoid, but that would upset you if you were to encounter them. Thus, if you never go into public restrooms (and you fear doing so), that would go on your list.

   - Try to include items on your list that vary in the difficulty they would cause you if you were to make contact with them. Have several relatively easy items, a few that would cause you moderate distress, and some that would be very difficult.

   - Don't include items that would require almost no effort at all (those with an Ugh Factor Rating below 20 or 25).

   - Unless you're working with a professional therapist, do not include items that someone without OCD would probably be unwilling to do. For example, most people would be pretty reluctant to touch the inside of a dumpster or the inside of a public toilet.

2. **Go through your list and give each item an Ugh Factor Rating on a 0 to 100 point scale of difficulty.**

   On this scale, a 0 indicates that you would anticipate no distress whatsoever, while a 100 indicates that nothing imaginable could cause more distress. Thus, a 25 would cause you mild distress, a 50 would start feeling intense, and a 75 would set off strong negative feelings.

Gil's story illustrates the process of making a list of OCD triggers related to contamination fears and assigning an Ugh Factor Rating to each item on the list.

Gil is a 19-year-old college student majoring in physics. Since he was about 10 years old, Gil has worried about germs and becoming ill, and he fears exposure to all kinds of possible environmental toxins. Through an ad in the school newspaper, he discovers that the student mental-health clinic on his campus happens to have a clinic for treating OCD. Gil recognizes himself in the ad's description of OCD, and makes an appointment at the clinic. A therapist interviews him carefully, gives him some questionnaires about OCD and concludes that Gil indeed has OCD.

The therapist then suggests that Gil list his problematic OCD triggers (events, situations, and cues). He recommends that Gil rate each item on his list in terms of the Ugh Factor. Table 10-1 shows Gil's list and associated Ugh Factor Ratings.

Table 10-1	Gil's OCD Trigger List and Ugh Factor Ratings
OCD Trigger	*Ugh Factor Rating (On a Scale of 0–100)*
Touching doorknobs	70
Walking on lawns (fear of exposure to toxins)	30
Touching classroom desks	50
Using public toilets	80
Eating at a public restaurant	65
Eating at the school cafeteria	75
Picking up the mail	25
Touching money	50
Touching the door to a health clinic	80
Touching motor oil	50
Touching handrails	55
Pressing elevator buttons	55
Using a public phone	60
Visiting a hospital room	90
Being close to someone who is sick or disabled	95
Driving by a homeless person	30

Gil's therapist is pleased with his list and Ugh Factor Ratings. However, the therapist notices that there are no items in the range between 30 and 50. Because that's quite a jump, they work together to come up with two items that are a little tougher than a 30 and easier than a 50 — specifically, shaking hands (40) and checking out at the grocery store (45).

Gil's list is typical of someone with the OCD theme of contamination. Now he's ready to turn his list and ratings into an ERP staircase.

Each person's list will differ both in content and Ugh Factor Ratings. For example, one person with contamination fears may not feel any distress at all in touching doorknobs while someone else may dread doing so. Compiling your list and rating each item is likely to take you a little time and creativity — don't rush the process.

Developing and rating your list can cause anxiety. In a way, that's good because the process actually represents the beginning of the exposure task — just writing down the items and rating them is a type of exposure. However, if you experience overwhelming anxiety, get professional assistance.

Placing your OCD triggers on an ERP staircase

Now it's time to take your OCD triggers and construct an OCD exposure staircase. Look for the item with the lowest Ugh Factor Rating and put it on the bottom stair, as illustrated in Figure 10-1. Continue to fill in the staircase with items, progressing from the least difficult on the bottom stair to the most difficult on the top stair. See Appendix B for a blank staircase form for your use, and feel free to make extra copies as the need arises.

Steps in your staircase should have reasonably even spacing between them in terms of their Ugh Factor Ratings. So if you have two steps that are more than 10 or 15 Ugh Rating points apart, try to come up with another one to place in between them. Try breaking a difficult item into two or three parts. For example, if the thought of touching the doorknob of a health clinic feels terrifying, consider starting with a glove on. Then work up to touching the knob with the back of your hand — anything that makes it easier, so long as you keep going after you master the easier item.

If you are trying ERP on your own, you definitely want to use a carefully constructed staircase, one step at a time. However, if you are working with an experienced professional with ERP, you may find that a formal staircase (also called a hierarchy) may not be utilized. If the therapist determines you can do it, a more fluid, rapid approach is sometimes employed.

In Figure 10-1, Gil's OCD triggers from the preceding section have been turned into an OCD exposure staircase.

Being close to someone who is sick or disabled (95 Ugh Factor Rating)
Visiting a hospital room (90 Ugh Factor Rating)
Using public toilets (80 Ugh Factor Rating)
Touching the door to a health clinic (80 Ugh Factor Rating)
Eating at the school cafeteria (75 Ugh Factor Rating)
Touching doorknobs (70 Ugh Factor Rating)
Eating at a public restaurant (65 Ugh Factor Rating)
Using a public phone (60 Ugh Factor Rating)
Touching handrails (55 Ugh Factor Rating)
Pressing elevator buttons (55 Ugh Factor Rating)
Touching classroom desks (50 Ugh Factor Rating)
Touching motor oil (50 Ugh Factor Rating)
Touching money (50 Ugh Factor Rating)
Checking out at the grocery store (45 Ugh Factor Rating)
Shaking hands (40 Ugh Factor Rating)
Walking on lawns (30 Ugh Factor Rating)
Driving by a homeless person (30 Ugh Factor Rating)
Picking up the mail (25 Ugh Factor Rating)

Figure 10-1: Gil's OCD exposure staircase.

Now that Gil has his staircase in hand, he's ready to start climbing his stairs. Well, almost ready. First, he has to look out for the responses (compulsions) he usually tries to use as a way to reduce his distress. (We address this later in the section "Preventing the response to compulsions.") But before we move on to compulsions, you should know that variability exists within each OCD contamination type or theme.

Seeing variations on the contamination theme

Some people with the contamination type of OCD worry about germs from dirty surfaces. Others have fears about environmental contaminants. The actual content of each person's hierarchy, or staircase, will vary somewhat, not only due to having slightly different themes, but also because each OCD mind is unique in what it chooses to fear. The following example illustrates a staircase for someone concerned about toxins.

> **Corwin** has always tended to be anxious. Some of her friends have teased her in the past about her obsessive concerns regarding toxic chemicals. Corwin stays away from pesticides, uses environmentally friendly cleaning products, and refuses to microwave her food. She has trouble keeping a job because of her excessive concern about toxins. She even carries her own paper products that have been produced organically without exposure to "unnatural chemicals."
>
> Corwin takes a new job at a busy call center. She enjoys talking to the customers, but the stress of her new position starts to get to her. She finds herself thinking more and more about what contaminants she might pick up at work. She has always cleaned her headset with her spray bottle of alcohol before putting it on — not to eliminate germs or viruses, but because she believes the alcohol removes toxic fumes from the plastic — at least for a little while. Now she is beginning to feel the need to spray the headset many times a day. She's also starting to worry about getting sick from using a phone all day. She imagines that the phone puts out some kind of toxic radio waves.
>
> One day she observes the cleaning crew using harsh chemicals to clean the employee bathroom. She begins to worry about the chemical contaminants pulsing through the air. Her ability to concentrate on the job is decreasing by the minute. On the day she wears a surgical mask to work (to avoid breathing in imagined toxins from cleaning supplies), her supervisor asks her to come to his office to discuss the problem.
>
> Rather than get fired again, Corwin decides to get help for her OCD. Figure 10-2 shows her staircase.

Eating a donut from the employee lounge (95 Ugh Factor Rating)
Using a headset without cleaning to remove toxins (90 Ugh Factor Rating)
Using the toilet paper from the employee restroom (75 Ugh Factor Rating)
Eating snack food from the machine in the break room (75 Ugh Factor Rating)
Touching my desk without wiping off toxins (70 Ugh Factor Rating)
Using paper towels from the employee restroom (65 Ugh Factor Rating)
Microwaving the water for my organic tea (65 Ugh Factor Rating)
Eating at a fast-food restaurant with co-workers (60 Ugh Factor Rating)
Carpooling with a co-worker in an old car that may emit fumes (55 Ugh Factor Rating)

Figure 10-2:
Corwin's
ERP
staircase.

As you can see, Corwin's staircase is quite different from Gil's. A couple of the items actually look rather similar to Gil's, but the underlying obsessional worry has to do with fear of toxins rather than viruses and germs, as is the case for Gil.

Preventing the response to compulsions

When you look at your staircase, your first reaction will likely be "Ugh." That's perfectly normal. Ask yourself what you want to do when you see those stairs. Most people feel compelled to engage in a compulsion when an obsessive worry is activated. Compulsions come in two forms:

- ✔ **Actions:** Examples include washing your hands, spraying disinfectants, touching or moving in a certain way, or arranging things in a certain order.

- ✔ **Mental acts:** Examples include counting, praying, chanting, or having certain good thoughts.

Are toxins OCD or real?

Global warming, greenhouse gases, pesticides, Escherichia coli (E. coli) in the food supply, air pollution — all represent legitimate concerns. People get sick and die from environmental contaminants. So when do normal concerns about toxins cross the line into OCD? You probably don't want to hear this, but there is *no absolute, definitive line.* Perhaps some people viewed Al Gore as a little OCD when he began to rail against the dangers of global warming. Others thought he was visionary, and today most of the scientific community sees him as the latter.

Al Gore's interest in the environment was passionate, welcomed, and under his deliberate control — all signs that he wasn't suffering from OCD. If your concerns are based on clear warning signs or a body of consistent, scientific evidence, they probably don't constitute OCD. On the other hand, if your concerns feel out of your control, highly disturbing, life disrupting, and intrusive, they are more likely to be indicative of OCD.

Compulsions may seem logically connected to the OCD triggers, as in the case of wanting to wash your hands after touching something you see as contaminated, or they may have no clear logical connection to the trigger at all — they may simply feel like the right thing to do in order to alleviate your discomfort. Thus, after touching a doorknob you may feel compelled to think certain "clean thoughts" over and over as a way of neutralizing your obsessional fears — that may not be logical, but somehow it makes you feel better.

In either case, compulsions bring a sense of temporary relief and are therefore very rewarding. Some people with OCD describe the compulsive act as somehow protecting them or their loved ones from danger. Others say that performing a compulsion neutralizes the obsession.

Very good reasons exist for preventing your compulsions. They include the following:

- ✔ In the long run, the feelings of relief are short-lived while compulsions usually take more and more of your time.
- ✔ Compulsions prevent you from discovering that obsessions are merely obsessive and rarely, if ever, come true.
- ✔ Compulsions can involve other people and make you feel foolish.
- ✔ Compulsions ultimately make OCD worse.
- ✔ Compulsions often hurt your self-esteem. They don't mean you are crazy, but they can sure make you feel that way.

Developing an awareness of the compulsions that your OCD mind urges you to do is essential. After making your staircase, list any and all actions (whether mental or physical) that you feel compelled to do when encountering any of those OCD triggers. This is your compulsion list — a list of the things you want to work very hard not to do.

In Gil's case (see the preceding sections), after going over his OCD exposure staircase, he realizes that he has a variety of compulsions, including

- ✔ Counting backwards from 100 to 0 slowly
- ✔ Disinfecting what he's touched
- ✔ Repeating the phrase "I'm clean" seven times
- ✔ Showering four or five times each day
- ✔ Washing his hands

Your list of compulsions may be quite short, such as only wanting to wash your hands, or you may have a lengthy list of compulsions that you turn to. Jot down any and all compulsions that you notice yourself tempted to do in order to feel better. Keep your list handy — you may find that you discover new compulsions popping up. If you do, add them to your list.

The "RP" in ERP stands for *response prevention*. That means not engaging in a compulsion.

Preparing to engage in ERP

For many people, starting ERP feels like standing at the end of the highest diving board before taking the plunge (of course, if you're an Olympic diving champion, this is not a good metaphor). Nevertheless, we have a couple of tips for boosting your courage before you make the dive. You can think of these as warm-up exercises. They're not as intense as the real thing that comes next, but they're a great start.

- ✔ **Take a few deep breaths and delay your compulsive act.** Put it off for 15 minutes, then, later, put it off for 30 minutes. Even later, go for an entire hour. Pay attention to how you feel during your delay time.

- ✔ **Do something different — alter your compulsions in some way.** If you usually have to count to 10 six times, count to 10 five times. Or perform your compulsion at top speed one time and at slow speed the next. Clean with a different hand if cleaning is your problem. Wash your hands in cold water or with just a trickle coming from the faucet. In other words, the more you change up your compulsion, the better. Again, pay attention to how you feel. These altered compulsions aren't likely to feel as satisfying to you, but they prepare you for living without compulsions altogether.

- ✔ **Remind yourself that you are not your OCD.** You will get better. You've started to reprogram and rewire the OCD part of your brain.

Stepping up through your triggers with ERP

Take a look at your OCD staircase as well as your list of usual compulsions. Set aside a couple of hours, because ERP takes some time to work. That doesn't mean you'll hold onto a doorknob for two hours straight. Rather, you will touch a doorknob while not using any compulsions. Then you'll keep touching the doorknob frequently, but not constantly.

Realize that ERP is hard work, and that you need to be prepared to feel some discomfort. However, you're quite likely to find that you can tolerate that discomfort.

Exposure is sort of like jumping into a cool swimming pool on a hot day — it feels freezing at first, but you get used to it. Acclimating to exposure takes a lot longer than getting used to the temperature of a pool, but you get the point.

You'll find that the discomfort involved with ERP is well worth the effort because your symptoms will decrease greatly — and in some cases, a nearly complete cure is possible.

Here's how you proceed with your staircase and list of usual compulsions:

1. **Pick the lowest stair on your OCD staircase.**

   Some therapists recommend starting on a stair that has an Ugh Factor Rating of at least 50. You can do that, but we like the idea of starting slow, especially if you're doing this on your own.

2. **Write the label for the stair you're working on in the "Checking Your ERP Progress" form.**

   Refer to Table 10-1 to see Gil's progress form for an example. See Appendix B for a blank progress form for your use.

3. **Step on the stair.**

   In other words, make contact with the OCD trigger. The nature of your contact very much depends upon the nature of the specific trigger. Thus, if your trigger involves touching doorknobs, you'll remain in close proximity to doorknobs and actually touch them repeatedly and often, but not for a single, extended period of time. If your trigger involves eating a certain food or shaking someone's hand, obvious time limits will be necessary. Frequent, repeated contact is what usually matters most. If you're uncertain how to proceed, consult a professional.

4. **Record your Ugh Factor Rating (refer to Table 10-1) when you first make contact with your stair. Stay in close contact with the trigger for about ten minutes or so.**

   Refrain from resorting to a compulsion.

5. **Re-rate your Ugh Factor Rating every ten minutes.**

   This rating may increase for a while, but stay in contact with your trigger anyway.

6. **Remain in close contact with your trigger until your Ugh Factor Rating decreases.**

   Ideally, you want it to come down by 50 percent before you move on to another step or conclude your ERP session. But don't be rigid about the amount of the drop — any truly significant improvement in your feelings can suffice if the ERP has gone on for over an hour.

As you go through the process of ERP, keep the following guidelines in mind:

✔ Be on the lookout for subtle compulsions that you find yourself tempted to do in order to decrease your distress. You want to avoid coming up with a new compulsion, such as wanting to count in your head or repeatedly say a poem or prayer.

✔ Don't try to suppress your obsessions. Go ahead and let yourself worry about contamination or whatever. Notice the thoughts, but don't try to suppress them. In fact, it's a good idea to actively imagine the most feared and dire outcomes you can think of actually occurring — such as being stricken with a horrible disease and dying a slow, torturous death.

✔ Sometimes you may be able to climb two, three, or more steps in a single exposure session. Other times, one step will feel like plenty. You may even need to stay with one step for several sessions. Use drops in your Ugh Factor Ratings as your guide — slow and steady works just fine.

✔ Conduct at least two or three exposure sessions each week — the more the better.

Gil's OCD exposure staircase began with three stairs that had Ugh Factor Ratings of 25, 30, and 30. He recorded each of these triggers in his "Checking Your ERP Progress" form. His first exposure session required about 2 hours, but he only needed to work on his next stair for about 30 minutes for his Ugh Factor Ratings to drop a great deal. His third step took him two separate sessions that each lasted close to two hours. You can see Gil's progress in Table 10-2.

Table 10-2	Gil's "Checking Your ERP Progress" Form
Exposure Step	*Ugh Factor Ratings*
Picking up the mail	45, 50, 55, 55, 45, 45, 50, 45, 40, 30, 25, 20
Driving by a homeless person	20, 20, 10
Walking on lawns	60, 65, 65, 70, 55, 65, 70, 75, 70, 60, 50, 40
Walking on lawns	65, 60, 60, 65, 55, 45, 40, 45, 50, 40, 40, 30

Gil's "Checking Your ERP Progress" form demonstrates several important issues:

✔ Sometimes your initial Ugh rating is inaccurate and you discover that your distress is considerably higher (or lower) than you thought it would be. That's no problem. If any step is utterly too intense for you, try to come up with another, easier step. If it's way too easy (such as Gil's stair involving driving by a homeless person), move on to another step quickly.

> ✔ Your Ugh Factor Ratings will likely go up and down during your exposure session, though they will generally diminish over time.
>
> ✔ Notice that Gil's third exposure session (involving walking on lawns) did not result in a 50 percent reduction in his Ugh Factor Rating. Therefore, he repeated the session on another day.
>
> ✔ Gil found that tracking his progress in this manner gave him incentive for continuing his exposure sessions.

Managing the ERP Process

Successfully carrying out ERP involves paying attention to a variety of important issues. It's easy to find yourself tempted to cheat, so you need to know what's cheating and what's not. You'll probably want to enlist support from a helper so you need to keep a few things in mind when you do (see Chapter 22 for more information about bringing family and friends into the picture). When things go wrong, we have some tips for dealing with the problems. And don't forget to pat yourself on the back when you pull all this off — ERP is hard work and you deserve some credit.

Did you wash your hands?

How many times did you hear that growing up? Parents are always telling their kids to wash their hands. If you work around food or in a healthcare setting, you're frequently reminded to wash your hands — in such cases, you should follow the rules that have been designed for those specific settings. Frequent hand-washing is one of the best ways to prevent getting sick and spreading germs to others. No wonder one of the most common compulsions of OCD is hand-washing. In ERP, the idea is to stop compulsive behavior. However, we don't want people to stop washing entirely. Therefore, if you have OCD involving fears of contamination, you probably need a few rules to know when and how washing your hands is okay.

✔ **How to wash your hands:** Wash your hands with clean water and soap. Rub your hands together for about 20 seconds (singing "Happy Birthday" to yourself takes about that long). If soap is not available, using hand sanitizer is okay. Rinse your hands well, but briefly. Dry your hands with a clean towel.

✔ **When to wash your hands:** After using the bathroom, before preparing food, after changing a diaper, after coughing or sneezing, before and after being around someone who shows obvious signs of illness, after picking up after or playing with an animal, after handling garbage, or after handling something that is *visually* dirty.

Knowing what's cheating and what's not

Your OCD mind will want to come up with clever ideas for helping you deal with the distress that ERP involves. Consuming alcohol, smoking pot, and taking other illegal drugs to numb you before engaging in ERP are definitely forms of cheating. But you need to be on the lookout for other interesting, but misguided, strategies. Ultimately, caving in and using any of these tactics will sabotage your efforts at ERP.

Staying above the fray with dissociation

You may attempt to neutralize or diffuse your distress by *dissociating,* or finding ways to remove yourself psychologically from what's going on. Some people try to numb their feelings. Others imagine that they're removed from their bodies and are viewing the ERP process from a distance. Both techniques may make you briefly feel a little better, but they block ERP's benefits.

Getting propped up with reassurance

You may want to seek reassurance from other people that everything will be okay. This strategy seems reasonable and helpful, but it's actually just like the other forms of cheating. Obtaining reassurance makes you feel better, but only briefly, and it ruins the effects of ERP. So, if you're using a friend or helper with your ERP (see Chapter 22 for much more information about how helpers can do and say the right things), ask them specifically not to reassure you by saying things like "It will be alright," "You're perfectly safe," and so on.

Dabbling in distraction

We generally recommend that clients not use distraction to keep themselves from engaging in mental compulsions. So you typically want to avoid watching television, talking on the phone with a friend, or surfing the net during exposure tasks. Distraction that almost completely takes you away from feeling any discomfort is not a good idea. You don't learn to break the associations between your OCD triggers and the discomfort if you aren't really "there."

However, if all else fails, distraction is better than using the compulsion. So if you have an uncontrollable mental obsession (such as constant images of germs invading your body), studies say that using simple distraction by focusing on everyday tasks is better than using your usual mental or behavioral compulsions, such as washing or repeating certain phrases. The key is that if you do use distraction, try to maintain at least some attention on the exposure task and your feelings of distress.

Finding fair relief

So is there anything you *can* do to reduce your distress during ERP if it feels really awful? In a limited way, yes. If you're already on prescribed medication for OCD, keep taking it. Also, you may consider using a brief relaxation strategy, such as the following:

1. **Inhale slowly and deeply.**

   Do so by pushing out your abdominal muscles in order to fill the bottom part of your lungs first.

2. **Hold your breath for a few seconds.**

3. **Slowly exhale as you pull your abdominal muscles in.**

   Exhale to a slow count of eight while making a very slight noise with the air in between your lips.

4. **Repeat up to ten times or so.**

This brief breathing/relaxation strategy should be considered a temporary stopgap. You can use it for your initial contacts with any given step on your OCD staircase. However, you want to stop using the breathing for subsequent contact. You should not use this breathing to eliminate your distress, but rather to merely help you cope with it for a little while.

Brief breathing/relaxation can be an effective strategy for dealing with many feelings of stress. Thus, you may want to use it while stuck in traffic and feeling frustrated. However, you want to be sure not to allow this strategy to turn into a compulsive response associated with your obsessions and/or your OCD triggers.

Troubleshooting ERP

We wish we could tell you that ERP works, that it works every single time, and that it works extremely well each time. Ah, but this is the real world, isn't it? It's true that ERP usually works and, for the most part, improvement is quite dramatic when it does. But, just like your car and everything else in life, sometimes things misfire. This section is about knowing what to do when problems arise in carrying out ERP.

Struggling with getting out of the starting blocks

It's not uncommon for people with OCD to hear about ERP and respond, "Thanks, but no thanks." That's because it can sound pretty scary. We would say, "Trust us; it's not that bad and you'll be able to do it," but we have a feeling you may not believe us.

So instead of just trusting us on this one, we suggest you do something else first. If you find yourself unable to get out of the starting blocks with ERP, read or reread Chapters 8 and 9 first. These approaches may work for you by themselves, or they may simply help you feel more ready to tackle ERP. If that doesn't work, seriously consider medication for your OCD (which is, of course, always an option and an especially good one for severe cases).

In addition, if you find ERP particularly scary, see if someone (such as a therapist or good friend assisting you) would be willing to model or demonstrate the ERP steps for you before you try them. If they do this, it's very important that you continue the work without their modeling at some point. However, a demo or two can provide a boost to get you started. The reason the demonstrations need to cease at some point is that you could easily start to rely on them for excessive reassurance (see the previous section, "Knowing what's cheating and what's not").

Finally, work on accepting the idea that nothing — not ERP, medication, or anything else — will ever totally remove all uncertainty for you. The OCD mind desperately wants to eliminate uncertainty, and ERP looks pretty dubious and uncertain to many people. Remind yourself often (but not obsessively) that one must accept a certain amount of uncertainty.

Constructing huge hierarchies and endless staircases

Many people with OCD construct huge exposure hierarchies with staircases that seem to rival the tallest buildings! They want to be certain that they don't miss *anything* that could be relevant. We've seen lists that run many pages in length. However, ERP hierarchies work best when the number of items runs in the range of about 10 to 20.

So what do you do if your hierarchy has gotten out of hand in length? Try condensing your list. Select items that have high priority. *You do not need to include everything in order to make excellent progress.* When people make progress on one item, like doorknobs, they usually find that similar things, like shaking hands or touching plates, get a little easier too. Finally, make sure that the items in your hierarchy all relate to a single OCD theme, such as contamination. If another theme appears to be involved, make a separate hierarchy for that theme.

Avoiding avoidance

Always be on the lookout for whether you're engaging in subtle forms of avoidance and/or reassurance seeking. Maybe you give your friend or therapist a "certain look" to solicit reassurance that things will be safe and okay. Or you may try to avoid ERP by putting it off and procrastinating for reasons that may seem good, but are really designed for avoidance.

When progress bogs down

If your progress stalls along the way (or even if your progress is slow from the get-go), there are a few things you can do. First, make sure your ERP sessions are long enough and frequent enough. Sessions lasting 90 to 120 minutes usually work pretty well. We've found on occasion that prolonging the exposure even more can help — anywhere from half a day to several days straight in a few cases. With prolonged exposure sessions, you obviously won't remain in constant contact with your triggers, but you will hit many triggers repeatedly without engaging in your compulsions.

Another possibility to improve progress is to take a short step backwards. In other words, go back to earlier steps and redo them until your Ugh Factor Ratings diminish even further. Then proceed ahead once more. If you find that one of the steps involves much more distress than you anticipated, you can always design a new step to fit in between.

Sometimes progress slows because compulsions crop up despite your best efforts to refrain from them. Probably the most difficult compulsions to keep from enacting are the mental ones — such as counting inside your head, repeating comforting phrases, or mentally trying to either burn or blow up a disturbing obsessive image. In this case, your best strategy is to actively refocus on the disturbing obsessive image or thought.

Mental compulsions are not the same as obsessions. Obsessions are unwanted, feel out of your control, and are highly disturbing. Mental compulsions, on the other hand, are the things you do inside your mind to reduce your distress and discomfort. The goal is to prevent mental compulsions, while remaining in contact with your mental obsessions.

If you get stuck and can't get going again, that's the time to get some help. Most people with OCD can use help — sometimes from family and friends and quite often from professionals. See Chapter 7 for more info on getting help.

Wavering motivation

If you find that your motivation for engaging in ERP wavers, we suggest that you jot out a cost/benefit analysis for doing ERP. Make a list of all the advantages and disadvantages of continuing with ERP. Appendix B gives you a cost/benefit analysis form that's designed for dealing with problematic OCD beliefs. Your lack of motivation qualifies as a problematic belief. You may also want to read or reread Chapter 6 on overcoming obstacles to change.

Coping when bad stuff really happens

People do get robbed; illness happens; houses catch on fire; cars do run over people; people die — that's life, and such events cannot be avoided with or without OCD. However, if bad luck strikes during your exposure treatment, it can set you back. You may conclude that your OCD thinking was right on target after all. In such cases, a therapist can help you cope.

Rewarding yourself

Fighting OCD with ERP can be hard work. Appreciate yourself and your efforts. When you have completed a particularly hard exposure or successfully resisted engaging in a compelling compulsion, do more than give yourself a pat on the back. Reward yourself with a treat.

Deliberately decide on a reward. Set a goal to complete two (or more) sessions of ERP, and then pay yourself. Think of some activities that are special, such as getting a massage, going out to dinner, watching a performance, or taking some time to relax — whatever gives you pleasure. Congratulations on your hard work — you deserve it!

Limiting ERP

The idea of ERP is to push yourself pretty hard and do some things you find quite difficult to do. You're expected to keep at it until you feel substantial improvement in your OCD, and then do a little more. However, we do not recommend that you include items on your OCD staircase that most people would find extremely difficult or dangerous. For example, we don't think it's a good idea for you to lick toilet seats or share needles with someone who has HIV. If you're unsure whether a given exposure item is "over the top," ask your therapist or a healthcare provider.

Chapter 11

Considering Medications for OCD

· ·

In This Chapter

▶ Figuring out what makes sense for you

▶ Weighing the pros and cons of taking medication

▶ Taking a closer look at medications that may help

· ·

Some people are good candidates for medication and others are not. For those who are, certain antidepressant medications have been found to be effective in treating OCD. Fortunately, for those who either fail to benefit from medication or cannot take it, good alternative treatments are out there (see Chapters 8, 9, and 10). In this chapter, we guide you through the information you need in order to make an informed decision about taking medication.

Many people are helped by psychotherapies that are useful in the treatment of OCD — treatments like exposure and response prevention (ERP), Cognitive Therapy, and mindfulness, as well as various combinations of these strategies. Rest assured that the purpose of this chapter is not to pit medication against these treatment options. The use of medication doesn't preclude other treatments; on the contrary, many people combine the use of medication with psychological treatment.

Deciding whether Medication Is Right for Your OCD

The decision to take medication for your OCD needs to be a cooperative effort between you and your healthcare provider. In order to play an active role in the decision-making process, you should be well-informed of the pros and cons involved. Your doctor will need access to your health history, and will do a complete physical exam to assess your current health status.

Getting a thorough check-up

In order to help you determine whether taking medication is right for you, a thorough physical exam is in order. Your primary healthcare provider should coordinate a comprehensive evaluation of your current health and health history. Appropriate laboratory and diagnostic tests should be conducted to rule out physical causes of or contributors to your OCD symptoms. Your primary care doctor can also be someone to turn to for advice and recommendations for specialists in treating OCD.

 Some primary care providers do not feel comfortable prescribing medications for OCD because they have limited experience in dealing with the problem. Be sure to ask your primary care provider whether a referral to a psychiatrist who specializes in OCD would be a good idea.

Coming clean with your doctor about your health and medications

Medications that affect your mind and your mood are powerful agents. If you and your healthcare provider decide to use them as a tool to help alleviate symptoms of OCD, you must work in close collaboration. If you are honest and open, you can expect your doctor to be respectful and nonjudgmental.

Before you begin taking any new medication, talk with your doctor about the following:

- Inform your doctor of any other health problems you have, including allergies, a history of heart problems, head injuries, seizures, problems with blood pressure, diabetes, glaucoma, or substance addiction.

- Be open about other problems you may be having such as insomnia, poor appetite, or fatigue. Be sure to let your provider know if you have ever been diagnosed with a mood disorder.

- Discuss concerns you have about taking medication.

- Provide a list of all other medications, either prescribed or over-the-counter, that you take. Include any herbs or supplements you are taking in this list.

- Tell your doctor if you are pregnant, considering getting pregnant, or breastfeeding.

- Be honest about habits such as drinking, smoking, or using other drugs.

If you decide to give medication a try, keep the following tips in mind:

- ✔ Take your medication as prescribed. If you decide to discontinue your medication, talk to your healthcare provider before you actually stop taking it. You may experience significant side effects from abrupt discontinuation.

- ✔ Discuss any side effects you may be feeling. Let your doctor know if you are feeling more depressed, suicidal, agitated, or uneasy, or if you're experiencing any sexual side effects.

- ✔ Be patient. Positive treatment effects may not be noticeable for a while — up to twelve weeks in some cases. Furthermore, your dosage may need to be adjusted, or you may need to try different medications before you find what works best for you.

Looking at reasons for medicating your OCD

Most experts in OCD agree that psychological treatment is the preferred choice for most cases of OCD, especially for OCD in children. However, in some cases, psychological treatment may not have the desired effect, or it may not be enough in and of itself. Medication may be a good choice when

- ✔ **Your OCD is severe.** If your symptoms are ruining your life and you cannot work, function at home, or be independent, medication may decrease your symptoms enough so that you can start psychological treatment. You're still likely to benefit from ERP treatment (see Chapter 10).

- ✔ **Your OCD is combined with depression.** Most people with OCD have at least some symptoms of depression, and about $2/3$ of sufferers have had a major depressive disorder at some point in their lives. Depression alone can be treated by psychological treatment and/or medication. However, when you add OCD to the mix, both forms of treatment may prove to be necessary.

- ✔ **Your OCD is accompanied by suicidal thoughts.** If you feel hopeless and have thoughts of suicide, you must get help immediately. If you're unable to reach a mental-health professional, go to the emergency room of a hospital or call 911. Don't wait. Help is available.

- ✔ **You have bipolar disorder.** Most people with bipolar disorder need medication management. Your best bet is to consult with a psychiatrist who has expertise in both OCD and bipolar disorder.

✔ **You see or hear things that others do not see or hear.** These symptoms are quite serious and almost certainly require medication. You will likely need a psychiatrist to evaluate your condition and prescribe treatment.

✔ **Your thinking is very confused.** If you can't seem to concentrate or think rationally, medication may be appropriate. We still recommend a mental-health therapist to support you with psychotherapy.

✔ **You refuse to try ERP.** A significant number of people with OCD can't stand the thought of ERP. For those people, medication may help take the edge off so that later they can try exposure. Or, in a few cases, they may discover that medication works so well that they feel little need for ERP.

✔ **You've tried therapy and it hasn't worked.** Some people don't benefit from the various OCD-specific psychotherapies (see Chapters 6, 8, 9, and 10). Medication can sometimes decrease symptoms sufficiently so that therapy can work.

✔ **You can't find a therapist nearby or one that you can afford.** Unfortunately, some areas do not have sufficient numbers of trained therapists who can do ERP or cognitive therapy. Some insurance plans do not pay for mental-health services.

If money is a factor in your treatment, you may be able to find a university, community mental-health clinic, or a few private practitioners who provide services on a sliding fee scale — you just have to ask.

✔ **You can't find the time in your schedule for psychotherapy.** We hope this isn't the case. But we realize that some people don't have the time. Frankly, if you can't find a couple of hours a week for therapy, that may be part of the problem. Stress can certainly make OCD worse. Furthermore, OCD steals considerable amounts of time from your day. Think of how much more time you will have without obsessions and compulsions. That said, medication, if it works, takes less time.

The story of Max illustrates a positive use of medication. Max's thinking was too confused for him to benefit from psychological treatment. For Max, taking medication was necessary to get him on the path to recovery.

> **Max** believes that food purchased at restaurants and grocery stores is contaminated by fecal matter in the groundwater. Max used to think shopping at an organic grocery store was safe, until a couple of years ago, when he read about organic spinach being contaminated by fecal matter. Max's OCD has caused him to lose his job and his friends, and to isolate himself from his family.
>
> One day, his brother shows up at his apartment and is appalled to see Max, emaciated, with several pots of boiling water on his stove. Max has restricted his food intake to boiled potatoes and boiled ground beef. He boils each for 45 minutes. Max seems to be out of touch with reality, so his brother takes him to the emergency room.

There, Max is given a prescription for an antidepressant and an appointment with a psychiatrist. Family members make sure that he keeps his appointments. After two months, Max no longer believes that the food supply is contaminated. However, he still has many OCD symptoms. The psychiatrist keeps him on the medication and refers him to a psychologist for ERP.

Understanding the side effects and risks of medications

If popping a pill once or twice a day can help rid you of OCD, why not? There are downsides to taking medications, which can vary from person to person. Here are some issues for you to ponder before starting medication:

- ✔ **Side effects:** Antidepressants can have very distressing side effects. Dry mouth, weight gain, constipation, tremors, diarrhea, insomnia, nausea, headaches, and dizziness are all commonly reported. For most people, these effects decrease over time. And your doctor can sometimes recommend other medications to decrease your discomfort. Unfortunately, the side effects cause many people to stop taking medication before it has a chance to work.

- ✔ **Sexual problems:** This one can be pretty bothersome. Some people report loss of sex drive and others have trouble achieving an orgasm. These symptoms usually go away or can be treated with other medications.

- ✔ **Discontinuation Syndrome:** People on antidepressants sometimes have a difficult time stopping their medication. Some report feeling out of sorts or anxious; others feel like they have the flu. These symptoms can usually be avoided by slowly tapering the dosage of the medication under the guidance of your healthcare provider.

- ✔ **Pregnancy and breastfeeding:** No long-term, well-controlled studies have been done on the effects of many medications during pregnancy or breastfeeding. We urge caution. Psychotherapeutic alternatives should be considered first.

- ✔ **Concern about relapse:** When medications work for treating OCD, they generally work very well, though rarely do they accomplish a complete remission of OCD symptoms. And if a person decides to stop medication, the symptoms usually return. Psychological treatments, on the other hand, provide greater protection against relapse.

- ✔ **Suicide risk:** The FDA warns that there may be a slight increase in the risk of suicidal thoughts in children, adolescents, and young adults who start antidepressant medication. Because of this risk, people who start on antidepressant medication should be seen regularly and encouraged to call their healthcare provider if they experience any of the following:

- Thoughts about dying

- Thoughts about suicide

- Worsening depression

- Agitation

- Irritability

- Aggression

- Unusual behaviors

- Inability to sleep

Looking at Your OCD Medication Options

Medications that are used to treat OCD are all antidepressants that increase the availability of serotonin and, sometimes, other chemical messengers, or *neurotransmitters,* in the brain. Serotonin supports communication between neurons in the brain. It affects your mood, your level of anxiety, your perception of pain, your memory, and your ability to control impulses. See Chapter 4 for more information about the brain's role in OCD.

Yikes I feel a yawn coming on

Decreased libido and inability to have an orgasm are quite common side effects of many medications for OCD. However, extremely rare, unexpected, spontaneous orgasms have also been linked to certain antidepressant medications. Some researchers suspect that many of these cases aren't being reported to the prescribing doctor. No kidding.

Case studies reported in the *Canadian Journal of Psychiatry* and the *Journal of Biological Psychiatry* have documented these unusual side effects. One woman reported a three-hour orgasm while shopping! Wow. She found the experience pleasurable, but a tad socially awkward. Incredibly, there have been numerous reports of yawning spells with simultaneous orgasm while taking antidepressants. Yawning can occur at any time and the orgasm appears to be uncontrollable. This can be particularly uncomfortable for men when accompanied by ejaculation. On the other hand, obviously this reaction can also be quite pleasant. So, if you are being treated with antidepressants, and you want to feel good, try watching reruns of *Green Acres*. Yawn.

People with OCD usually require higher doses of these drugs than the amounts typically prescribed for treating depression. Prescriptions are often started at a low dose and gradually increased. Furthermore, medications for OCD frequently require six to twelve weeks to significantly improve OCD symptoms, whereas these same medications sometimes work a little faster when used for depression.

Generally, medication treatment continues for about a year — after which a gradual discontinuance is sometimes attempted. However, many people find that they need to go back on medication, frequently for a lifetime, for successful OCD treatment. The odds of long-term success with medication withdrawal are improved greatly if ERP has been provided at some point.

Seeking serotonin with SSRIs

The first choice of medication for most people with OCD is one of the selective serotonin reuptake inhibitors (SSRIs). SSRIs appear to work by increasing the level of serotonin that's available to the nerve cells. Exactly how that increased availability impacts OCD specifically is an unresolved issue.

These drugs have been extensively studied and found to be effective in decreasing symptoms of OCD. Currently the SSRIs that have been found to be effective for OCD and officially sanctioned by the Food and Drug Administration (FDA) include:

- **Luvox (Fluvoxamine):** This antidepressant was the first SSRI to receive FDA approval for the treatment of OCD. Luvox is somewhat sedating. Therefore, it often provides immediate relief from the anxiety part of OCD. However, you may have more gastrointestinal side effects.

- **Paxil (Paroxetine):** This medication works for anxiety and depression. It tends to be sedating and is associated with weight gain. Some find discontinuing this medication very uncomfortable.

- **Prozac (Fluoxetine):** This antidepressant boosts energy for many people. When beginning treatment, you may experience an increase in anxiety and have difficulty sleeping. Withdrawal symptoms tend to be milder with Prozac than for the other SSRIs.

- **Zoloft (Sertraline):** Like Prozac, this antidepressant is associated with increased energy. It is often considered the best choice for people with heart disease.

Other antidepressant medications that affect not only serotonin but also a few other brain neurotransmitters (see Chapter 4 for more information about neurotransmitters) appear to work for OCD as well. However, they haven't received as much study as the ones listed above. A few of these options include:

- ✔ **Celexa (Citalopram):** This SSRI medication may have fewer negative interactions with other medications.

- ✔ **Lexapro (Escitalopram):** Similar to Celexa, this SSRI may work faster than some of the others.

- ✔ **Effexor (Venlafaxine):** Effexor boosts both serotonin and norepinephrine. It sometimes appears to work for OCD when other SSRIs don't. This drug can boost energy. Effexor sometimes increases blood pressure. It is not suggested for those with heart problems.

Trying tricyclics

An older antidepressant, Anafranil (Clomipramine), was the first antidepressant medication found to be effective for OCD. Clomipramine is still used, especially when other SSRIs have not worked. The primary reason that Clomipramine is sometimes avoided is that an overdose can be fatal. It is at least as effective as the SSRIs, but it has more unpleasant side effects. Clomimpramine also carries some risk of inducing seizures, increased heart rate, and problems with withdrawal.

Clomimpramine belongs to the class of antidepressants known as tricyclics. *Tricyclic* refers to the chemical structure of the drugs in this class rather than the effects they have on neurotransmitters, as is the case with SSRIs. Clomimpramine appears to affect various neurotransmitters, including serotonin and norepinephrine.

Other than Clomimpramine, tricyclic antidepressants (such as Imipramine or Amitriptyline) do not appear to be helpful in the treatment of OCD, nor does the class of antidepressants known as MAO inhibitors.

Adding other medications

Prescribing medicine is part science and part art. At this point, the understanding of exactly how antidepressants work and which one is best for a particular person is pretty primitive. Patients frequently have to try multiple antidepressant medications in order to find the one that works for them. For unknown reasons, one SSRI may do nothing for a particular individual, yet another one will prove to be quite helpful.

Biological Alternatives to Medication

A few people with OCD are not able to benefit from standard treatments. These people are severely impaired and not able to function because of their disorder. In these cases, there have been multiple trials of antidepressant medications, as well as other types of medications. For some of these people, ERP as well as cognitive techniques have been tried without success. This type of OCD is called *treatment refractory*, meaning it is resistant to ordinary means of treatment.

When *all else* fails, brain surgery is a controversial option. These surgeries are very rare and involve destroying a small amount of the brain. This destruction interrupts the circuit of the brain that has been implicated in ODC (see Chapter 4). For obvious reasons, there are no "controlled" studies where people with OCD are randomly assigned to brain surgery or other treatment. Therefore, the success of these surgeries is based on case reports. Unfortunately, over half of those treated with brain surgery continue to have OCD.

A less extreme option, but still a last resort, is deep brain stimulation. A few case reports have found this technique to reduce OCD symptoms. These results are promising and this technique does not require destruction of brain tissue. As knowledge of the brain increases, treatments that are less invasive and more specifics will likely be discovered.

Sometimes, other medications are added to the first to augment the effects of the first medication. Furthermore, many people with OCD have other problems such as depression, attention problems, or another anxiety disorder (see Chapter 3). In those cases, other drugs may be used to treat the co-occurring disorder. Be willing to work with your doctor in order to find the best regimen for you. Some of those drugs include:

- ✔ **Buspar (buspirone):** This medication helps reduce anxiety symptoms. It does not cause dependence or problems with withdrawal. It is considered relatively safe and does not cause severe sedation. However, effects may not be noticeable until you've taken the drug for a week or more.

- ✔ **Clonazepan (Klonopin):** Like Buspar, this drug decreases anxiety. The effects can be felt immediately, but unlike Buspar, this medication can cause dependence.

- ✔ **Lithium carbonate (Eskalith):** Lithium and other mood stabilizers (Depakote, Tegretol, Neurontin, Topamax, Lamictal) are used when OCD occurs with bipolar disorder. They are also used to enhance the effectiveness of antidepressant medications.

✔ **Other medications:** There are numerous other drugs that your doctor may try to help reduce your symptoms. Stimulant medications can be used to improve attention. However, stimulants can increase anxiety, which many of those with OCD already have in abundance. Atypical antipsychotics are sometimes given when there is severe depression or disordered thinking.

Many of the drugs listed above have not been studied specifically for use with people suffering from OCD. However, specialists have used different combinations successfully to treat their patients with OCD and other disorders.

Chapter 12

Responding to and Recovering from Relapse

*R*elapse is part of the treatment process. Most OCD sufferers experience a recurrence of OCD symptoms at some point during or after their treatment. But take heart: Relapses are normal, and with patience and persistence, you can continue on your road to recovery.

By the conclusion of treatment, many people have successfully reduced their OCD symptoms by 50 to 75 percent. Occasionally, people succeed in completely eliminating their symptoms. Even moderate reductions in symptoms usually result in more time for pleasurable pursuits, enhanced relationships, and a substantially higher overall quality of life. These benefits are obtainable for most folks with OCD — even for many whose symptoms are severe.

Regardless of where you are in treatment, the information in this chapter can be useful. Maybe you want to know about relapse risks before you even begin treatment for your OCD. Or maybe you know someone who is recovering from the disorder. After all, forewarned is forearmed!

In this chapter, we give you the straight dope on relapse and OCD, like which treatments have a higher rate of relapse, what to do if relapse comes knocking at your door, and how you can reduce the risk of relapse.

Knowing the Risks of Relapse

Relapse occurs with varying frequency after successful treatment of most emotional disorders, and OCD is no exception. Relapse from OCD treatment can be very high, but the risk greatly depends on the type of treatment you receive as well as how you handle your relapse. The sections that follow give you an idea of what you may encounter as far as OCD relapse challenges.

Medication relapse rates

As discussed in Chapter 11, various medications have a good track record for demonstrating the ability to greatly reduce OCD symptoms. But for a host of reasons, many people with OCD choose to discontinue their medications. Sometimes they want to become pregnant and worry about possible effects on the developing fetus. Other times, they experience distressing side effects, such as weight gain, dizziness, nausea, loss of sexual desire and/or inability to experience orgasms. And for some, discontinuing medication simply reflects a personal philosophical preference.

If you have experienced success with medications and decide to discontinue them, you should do so only under a doctor's supervision. That's because abruptly stopping certain medications can cause discontinuation syndromes that involve various distressing physiological reactions, depending on the type of medication involved and the individual person.

Be prepared to experience an increase in your OCD symptoms — especially if medications were the only thing you used to treat your OCD. Relapse rates following medication discontinuation are disturbingly high — estimates vary widely, but can run from 75 to 90 percent or so *if you had no other type of treatment for your OCD.*

If you choose to go off your medication, you can reduce the risk of relapse by heeding the following advice:

- ✔ Continue medication for at least a year or two before considering discontinuance. Taper off your medication slowly and under your doctor's supervision. If symptoms return, consider going back on medication, perhaps even for a lifetime.

- ✔ Seriously consider exposure and response prevention (ERP) therapy, either while you're on medication or when you start to taper off of it. Studies suggest that if you combine medication with ERP, your risk of relapse plummets.

ERP relapse rates

We have some pretty good news about ERP and the risk of relapse. If you successfully treat your OCD with ERP therapy, your odds of relapse are fairly low. A number of large studies have shown that if you respond well to ERP, you have a very good chance (perhaps as much as 70 to 80 percent) of maintaining your gains after treatment is completed — possibly for several years. Your improvement may even last much longer — we simply don't have a lot of studies that have followed participants for more than a few years.

If you took medication in combination with ERP, no problem. Most studies suggest that medication does not increase your risk of relapse following successful combined treatment. However, adding medication to ERP doesn't substantially improve the relapse rates once medication is discontinued. It's possible that your odds of maintaining gains may improve somewhat if you remain on medication for a lifetime.

CBT and mindfulness relapse rates

Cognitive-Behavioral Therapy (CBT) and mindfulness techniques (see Chapters 8 and 9) are two approaches that have similar strategies and goals. Unfortunately, the data on relapse risk with these approaches is rather thin — we need more studies before we can make definitive statements about the relapse risks associated with these two forms of OCD treatment. Given that early studies have shown that CBT and mindfulness appear to work pretty well for OCD, at least in the short term, we suspect future research is likely to show that they help reduce relapse risks as well.

This is particularly true if the track records of these treatments' success in treating depression are any indication. When used to treat depression, CBT has been shown to substantially reduce the risk of relapse as compared to medication. Similar evidence suggests that mindfulness may also reduce the risk of depression relapse.

Responding Well to Relapse

Only a few people who are treated for OCD are truly, 100 percent cured. Just because relapse happens doesn't mean your treatment is not successful. The vast majority of people continue to have some mild symptoms that are occasionally irritating or annoying. Others have a few lapses here and there, especially when under stress. Another group of people (we don't have the long-term studies to say exactly how many) suffer a full-blown return of their OCD. (See the later section, "Knowing the difference between a lapse and a relapse," for a more detailed explanation.) So what should you do if your OCD symptoms return? Here are three approaches for dealing with relapse:

- ✔ **Do what worked for you before.** If you used ERP, do that again. You can try ERP on your own or go back to a therapist. Treatment is usually more efficient the second time around because you already know what to expect. If you took antidepressant medication, try going back on it.

- ✔ **Try something new.** If you go back and find that what worked before is no longer effective, other treatment alternatives are available. From what we know, ERP is probably the best bet for long-term management of OCD. So, certainly, if you were only taking medication and you experience a relapse, we strongly suggest trying ERP (see Chapter 10). If you've previously done ERP, consider reviewing Chapters 8 and 9 for additional ideas. If you've tried ERP and/or CBT but not medication, by all means, review Chapter 11 for medication options.

- ✔ **Accept a little OCD in your life.** Is OCD always bad? Not necessarily. Millions of talented people — artists, writers, scientists, and other good people all over the world — have OCD. (Oh, and did we mention book editors?) A little OCD can encourage creativity, hard work, and carefulness.

OCD can be an enemy of well-being. But a little OCD once in a while can be okay. The more you can embrace OCD as a friend, maybe as a pesky friend, but nevertheless a friend — the less OCD will overtake you.

Strategies for Reducing Relapse

The best defense against relapse is getting the right treatment (or combination of treatments) for your OCD to begin with. Although medication alone works well (see Chapter 11), you can reduce your relapse risk substantially by either remaining on your medication for a very long time (perhaps for life) or by combining medication with ERP. Also, combining ERP with CBT and/or mindfulness can help.

Nevertheless, relapse happens no matter what the problem is or what therapy is being used. In the following sections, we discuss steps you can take, or at least be aware of, to help you guard against OCD relapse.

Knowing the difference between a lapse and a relapse

Chapter 8 tells you that the way you interpret events makes a huge difference in the way you end up feeling. That principle holds for an occasional return of obsessions and compulsions. A lapse can be defined as a mild slip involving a mild increase in symptoms. By contrast, a relapse is considered to be a major regression toward pre-treatment functioning. We give you examples of each of these in the following sections.

Looking at a lapse

A lapse is usually mild and transient. In the following example, Jeremy gets treatment for his OCD and then experiences an occasional obsession, which indicates a lapse.

> **Jeremy** suffers from OCD that centers on the theme of contamination. He avoids public restrooms and restaurants. He is first referred for help when his primary care provider notices that his hands are raw and bleeding. Jeremy confesses that he often spends an hour in his shower and washes his hands hundreds of times during the day.
>
> After 12 sessions of ERP, Jeremy's symptoms are under control. Jeremy continues to have moments when obsessive thoughts return. He reminds himself that the obsessions are normal and to be expected. He purposely waits until the thoughts pass and does not engage in compulsive washing. Most days Jeremy feels that he is leaving OCD behind him.

Jeremy had been told by his therapist that thoughts that seem like obsessions occur in everyone from time to time (see Chapter 2 for information about how people without OCD frequently have thoughts that look much like obsessions — but they just don't take them all that seriously). And Jeremy had been informed that such thoughts would no doubt pop back into his mind from time to time. Armed with that information, Jeremy understands that his obsessions are normal, expected, and something that he can handle. He knows if they happen to worsen, he now has skills and tools for dealing with them. Such brief visits from his old obsessional thoughts are merely mild, temporary lapses — not a full-blown return of his OCD.

Revealing a relapse

A relapse can begin with a lapse and then spiral downward from there, resulting in a full-blown return of obsessions and compulsions.

In the following example, Todd initially makes a good decision to seek help for his compulsive hand-washing. However, when he encounters a normal uncomfortable situation — the flu — his obsessions return.

Todd has OCD focused on contamination concerns. He is a compulsive washer and avoids public places as much as he can. His washing takes up hours of his day. Todd talks about this with his primary care doctor, who tells Todd about different kinds of treatment. Todd and his doctor choose to try an antidepressant to see whether that will help. Todd's doctor reminds him that the medication can take a while to have an effect. Todd is relieved to know that he may get better. After about eight weeks, his symptoms seem to lessen. He doesn't always think about contamination, and his compulsions to wash have lessened.

An early flu season hits, and Todd comes down with the flu. He finds himself obsessing about what may have made him sick. The more he thinks about it, the more he begins to avoid public places and engage in compulsive washing. Todd calls his doctor to complain that the medication is no longer working. The doctor encourages Todd to stay on the medication and consider seeing a psychotherapist for ERP therapy. Todd throws the pills away and hangs up the phone. Within a few weeks, Todd is back where he started with OCD controlling his life.

Todd's story illustrates how a lapse can turn into a relapse. The lapse began when Todd started to obsess a little about how he got the flu. The relapse came when he became discouraged and threw away his pills — resulting in a return of his symptoms with a vengeance. Todd would probably have benefited from psychological treatment in the form of CBT, mindfulness, or ERP in order to help him understand and deal with his setback.

An OCD lapse need not turn into a full-blown relapse. It all depends on what you do with it.

Prolonging treatment

Realtors have a saying that success all comes down to three words — location, location, location. When it comes to OCD treatment, we like to say success boils down to persistence, persistence, persistence — no matter where you are in your treatment process. As we explain in the section "Medication relapse rates," if you choose medication to treat your OCD, you should be willing to continue taking it for at least a year or two, and perhaps a lifetime.

If you treat your OCD with ERP, CBT, mindfulness, and/or medication, with luck and considerable effort you will see a great deal of improvement within a few months. Many people see significant, sustained improvement within four or five months. On the other hand, sometimes severe cases and/or OCD that's combined with other problems can require prolonged treatment. Some people benefit from working on their problem over several years. In almost all of those cases, we suggest multi-pronged treatments involving most of the strategies we discuss in this book.

Phasing out your sessions gradually

The relationship between you and a therapist is unique. Therapy is a time when you can be open about your weaknesses, fears, and secrets. Within this relationship there is trust, confidentiality, and safety. You have the undivided attention of someone who wants to help. That can feel pretty good.

However, usually a point is reached when therapy can and should be terminated. Most of the time, this happens when the client and therapist agree that the goals of treatment have been met. Nevertheless, when you realize that progress has been made, you may worry that you won't be able to maintain it on your own. When that time is approaching, the following suggestions can ease the process.

- ✔ **Taper off the frequency of your sessions slowly.** When you're close to reaching your goals, try seeing your therapist every other week and then monthly.

- ✔ **Have your therapist help you develop a relapse plan.** How will you handle upsetting times or increased symptoms?

- ✔ **Be sure to talk about how you can be your own therapist.** You can engage in ERP on your own. You can also return to using other CBT strategies, such as Cognitive Therapy and mindfulness described in Chapters 8 and 9.

- ✔ **See whether your therapist can offer you limited contact.** We sometimes set up occasional e-mail contact or a brief follow-up phone call. These can cut off trouble before it gets out of hand.

You should also know that you usually can return to therapy for a tune-up. The nice thing about a brief return to your previous therapist is that you don't have to start from square one.

Staging a fire drill

If you work in a school or hospital, you probably run through fire drills from time to time. That way, if a real fire ever breaks out, everyone knows what to do. We recommend you do the same for your OCD.

Fire drills for OCD start with making a list of high-risk situations — anything that may trigger a return visit from your OCD obsessions and compulsions. Depending upon the focus or theme of your OCD concerns, the following may trigger your OCD:

- ✔ A burglary occurs in your neighborhood, causing obsessions about checking your locks.

> ✔ A fire breaks out somewhere and triggers obsessions about your home's fire-safe worthiness.
>
> ✔ You have a thought about harming someone and fear you may act on it.
>
> ✔ You run over an unexpected bump in the road that you didn't see and fear that you may have run someone over.
>
> ✔ You shake hands with someone you later learn has cancer, and fear you may have caught it (even though cancer isn't transmitted this way, those with OCD sometimes have this fear).
>
> ✔ You step in a pile of dog poop and worry about becoming contaminated.

As you can see, we could list dozens, hundreds, maybe thousands of such items. Gosh, that would make filling up the rest of the pages of this book really easy. Hmm, we're guessing our editors wouldn't particularly like that idea though.

The point of making such a list is to be prepared. Expect to encounter such situations. When you expect the inevitable, you won't be shocked or surprised when it happens, and you can have a plan ready. Perhaps you'll want to try some mindfulness or a brief regimen of ERP (see Chapters 9 and 10).

Finally, it's not a bad idea to read about all the various types of OCD themes discussed in Chapters 13 through 19. You're not very likely to develop a new type of OCD, but it can happen. If it does, you'll already have some ideas about how to handle it.

Remaining vigilant

Very few people will eliminate their OCD virtually 100 percent and not experience an occasional setback. You can nip these setbacks in the bud if you catch them early. Therefore, we suggest that following successful treatment, you actually create a log and track your obsessions and compulsions. You don't have to keep this log all the time — start by tracking once a month for a few days at a time.

If your symptoms remain low, that's great. You may then reduce your monitoring to a day or two every few months. If your obsessions and compulsions even start to creep up, take them seriously. Check out the earlier section "Responding Well to Relapse" for ideas.

Zeroing in on especially problematic beliefs

We have found that two specific beliefs frequently seem to creep into the mind following successful OCD treatment, and these beliefs can pave the way for relapse. We discuss both of these beliefs so you can be on the lookout for them. (See Chapter 8 for more info on beliefs that provide fuel for OCD.)

Feeling as if something is true when you know it isn't

After your symptoms have been substantially reduced, you very well may find yourself thinking things like:

- ✔ "I don't believe that using a public telephone is a threat to my health, but it still *feels* like it could be."

- ✔ "I understand that walking into an Alzheimer's ward isn't going to make me demented, but it *feels* like it might."

- ✔ "Well, sure I now know that I can't really get toxic contaminants into my body by touching drywall, but I *feel* like I can."

Obsessions and compulsions love to try sneaking in the back door. And it's easy to have thoughts like, "Big deal, so what if I cave into a few of my obsessions?" On the one hand, it isn't a huge problem if you slip a little. On the other hand, if you start having strong feelings that run counter to what your observant, rational mind tells you (see Chapter 9), this contradiction can serve as an important warning sign that your OCD mind is attempting a comeback. We recommend you conduct a cost/benefit analysis of buying into the OCD part of your mind rather than the observant, rational mind. See Chapter 9 for information about how to conduct such an analysis.

You may also find it useful to ask yourself whether these feelings are based on clear evidence that most people would agree is valid. Generally speaking, such evidence should be based on things that you can clearly see, touch, hear, smell, or taste.

Feeling as if you must avoid all negative feelings

Please realize that negative feelings absolutely cannot be avoided in life. If you try to avoid all such feelings, relapse may be waiting around the next corner, ready to pounce. We find that physical training provides an excellent analogy for helping you think about this issue.

Most people, including us, find that intense physical exercise causes a few discomforts — shortness of breath for a while, soreness, stiffness, sweating, and so on. However, the more you exercise, the more you feel the benefits — including less negative feelings. These benefits include:

- ✔ Enhanced sense of well-being
- ✔ Increased endurance
- ✔ Increased flexibility
- ✔ Increased mobility
- ✔ Increased strength
- ✔ Reduced pain

Tolerating the discomfort associated with obsessions works exactly the same way. In the short run, you feel distress, anxiety, and frustration. Sometimes those feelings can be quite intense. But the more you resist caving into the discomfort with your usual compulsions, the more your tolerance increases and the less discomfort you feel.

Recognizing events that trigger relapse

There are no guarantees in life. Roadblocks, setbacks, detours, and crashes inevitably occur. When these events happen, OCD symptoms may return. Increased stress decreases your ability to stay mentally healthy. Watch out for times of high stress that could trigger relapse, such as:

- ✔ Getting sick or injured
- ✔ Losing a friend
- ✔ Losing a job or failing to get an expected promotion
- ✔ Sleeping poorly
- ✔ Suffering a loss
- ✔ Watching the stock market tank and your 401K evaporate
- ✔ Working too hard

What some people don't realize is that even positive life events and changes can also trigger relapse. Whenever the status quo changes — even for the better — don't be shocked if some of your symptoms return. Most people with OCD struggle with the unpredictability and uncertainty that come with almost any type of change. The following events can trigger stress, and therefore, OCD:

- ✔ Getting married
- ✔ Graduating
- ✔ Having a baby
- ✔ Getting a new job
- ✔ Retiring

If a major life transition occurs shortly before a return of your OCD symptoms, you may find that it's very important to deal with the implications of that event prior to working on your OCD again.

Just because a negative or positive event occurs doesn't mean you are compelled to respond compulsively.

Part IV
Targeting Specific Symptoms of OCD

The 5th Wave   By Rich Tennant

"Oh no! I just stepped on a crack.
I need to call Mom and make sure
she's okay!"

In this part . . .

OCD expresses itself in a surprisingly wide range of themes and concerns. The chapters in this part detail the many faces of OCD and how each one can be treated. We provide strategies for dealing with Superstitious OCD, "Just So" OCD, Doubting and Checking OCD, Hoarding OCD, and Shaming OCD. The final chapter of this part covers a strategy called Habit Reversal Training (HRT) for some of the cousins of OCD.

Chapter 13

Dealing with Doubting and Checking OCD

*W*orry wears you out. People with the doubting and checking type of OCD feel uneasy and worried much of the time. Many of their concerns have a remote chance of happening, but a few are extremely bizarre and unrealistic. More than a few people focus on worries about illness and disease. Normal body fluctuations, such as muscle soreness after exercise, turn into an esoteric, degenerative neurological disease in their minds. For some people, these fears and behaviors occur hundreds of times each day.

Doubting comes in the form of an *obsession:* an unwanted image, urge, or thought. The doubt is intense, realistic, and vivid. These obsessions center on things such as damage being done to your house or harming someone, all through some imagined negligence on your part.

Checking is the compulsive part. There is a compelling need to see whether the lights are on, the door is open, or someone got hurt. See Chapter 2 for more information about the differences between obsessions and compulsions.

In this chapter, we provide more detail about the doubting and checking types of OCD. We give you specific strategies for dealing with doubt and resisting checking.

Defining Categories of Doubting

Doubt means uncertainty. Doubt leads to questions, hesitation, and, in the case of OCD, checking. Doubt is associated with many of the other types of OCD, but in the doubting and checking type, doubt towers over reason and logic. The individual, specific doubts of Doubting and Checking OCD vary endlessly but seem to cluster together into several areas of concern:

- ✔ Obsessions about the home
- ✔ Worry about harming others
- ✔ Obsessions having to do with unintentionally running someone over
- ✔ Personal health concerns

The next sections give examples of each area of concern.

Harming your home through negligence

One area of doubting involves concerns with harm befalling where you live. People with this concern worry about something terrible happening to their homes because of their own carelessness. The feelings of doubt are so intense that they lead to nearly endless loops of compulsive checking.

Those who are obsessed with such matters worry about fires breaking out, roofs falling in, and termites consuming their walls until they collapse. They worry about explosions from gas leaks and asphyxiation from carbon monoxide. They obsess about faucets that may have been left turned on resulting in flood damage. This type of OCD is difficult to overcome because you can never absolutely rule out the possibility of damage or harm occurring to your home — no matter how many times you check.

The following example illustrates the vicious cycle of Doubting and Checking OCD as it relates to household safety.

> **Carl** turns the oven knob to the off position. Actually, he turns it on, then off, then on, and then off. He looks to make sure it is still off. He leaves the house. But he fears the knob may have slipped back on. He goes back inside and checks. It's off. He leaves the house and gets in the car. But as he pulls out of the driveway, he wonders whether there's a chance that the oven could still be on. Maybe, just maybe, he thinks, it is. He pulls back in, gets out of the car, and goes back in the house. Checks the knob. It's off. Whew! He opens the oven door to see whether the oven is warm.

He thinks it is. He checks the knob. He closes the door. He checks the knob. He leaves the house. Gets into the car. Starts the car. Looks back. Was that smoke? Is the oven on? He stops the car. Goes back to the house. And checks everything all over again.

Just reading about Carl's doubting is exhausting! The pattern is difficult to stop. Doubt, check, doubt, check. . . .

Harming others through negligence

Another concern of people with Doubting and Checking OCD is fear that their behavior or negligence will somehow harm someone else. The specific content of the fear ranges infinitely. But the belief is one of hyper-responsibility for other people's welfare and safety. The afflicted person must constantly be on guard to make sure that something really bad doesn't happen.

This type of OCD worry escalates, with sufferers taking more and more drastic steps to keep others safe. Their attempts to protect others consume more of their time as the concerns go on. The following example illustrates how someone with this type of OCD concern attempts to protect people, but actually accomplishes little or nothing for her efforts.

> **Naomi** believes that she is responsible for warning her friends and family about bad weather. This problem gets worse after she hears about a child dying in a tornado that briefly touched down in her town. Her obsession causes her to constantly monitor the weather station. When there are reports of storms in the area, she calls each person on her list of 45 people. At first, she only calls when the storms are serious and imminent, but after a while she calls when there are mere threats of rain.

> Friends and family no longer answer their phones when they see her number on the caller ID. She leaves messages when they fail to answer, but worries that the voice mail won't get picked up in time. And if it isn't, and someone gets hurt, she feels she will be personally responsible. She begins driving to the house of each person on her list who doesn't answer the phone. Upon arriving, if no one answers the door, she leaves a note warning of the impending doom.

Naomi's story shows how the sense of responsibility inflates to incredible proportions. There is virtually no end to the efforts people with this type of OCD will make in order to protect the safety and well-being of those they love. Sometimes they expend this energy on protecting perfect strangers. But these efforts require huge amounts of time and fail to add significant safety to the lives of those they worry about.

Harming others with your car through negligence

The hit-and-run focus is actually a variant of the "harming others through negligence" concern discussed above. However, hit-and-run is such a common form of doubting and checking that it deserves some special attention. Those who dwell on hit-and-run issues greatly fear hitting someone with their car. Therefore, they interpret every bump in the road, unexpected honk, or random movement detected in their peripheral vision as evidence that they have run someone over.

Once they make that interpretation, they feel driven to go back and check on the victims or, more hopefully, find evidence that they did not actually cause a horrible accident. Sometimes they go back to the scene dozens of times — even causing them to be late. Additional ways these folks check on what they may have done include:

- ✔ Asking for reassurance from passengers in their car
- ✔ Calling hospital emergency rooms to inquire about recent arrivals
- ✔ Carefully rubbing the surface of their cars for signs of dents from an impact
- ✔ Listening to police scanners for calls on accidents
- ✔ Reading obituaries in the newspaper
- ✔ Scrutinizing the exterior of their cars for any signs of blood

No one really knows why this concern appears so often. Some have speculated that it stems from the importance of cars in modern society as well as the fact that automobiles cause many thousands of deaths and injuries each year.

Another contributor to the cause of Hit-and-Run OCD may be the fact that every so often a news story about someone backing out of the driveway and running over a child pops up in the newspaper or on TV. Almost always the person driving was unaware of the child's presence and the act was a tragic accident.

The following exercise asks you to put yourself in the shoes of someone who has actually experienced such a tragedy. Doing so gives you an idea of what this type of OCD feels like to those who have it.

> Imagine you are backing out of your driveway, maybe thinking about a grocery list or a dinner date. You feel a slight bump of the wheels. Then you hear the screams of neighbors. People are running toward your

car, pointing. The realization that something is horribly wrong floods your mind. You desperately wish that you could go back in time, but you can't. You stop the car, open the door, and there, on the driveway, lies a lifeless child.

People with Hit-and-Run OCD repeatedly have such images — with feelings to match — most days of their lives. The horror seems real and the urge to check irresistible. Paradoxically, a few people with Hit-and-Run OCD have been hurt or caused real accidents because of their compulsive need to stop and turn around in traffic to check.

Harming your health through negligence

People with Doubting and Checking OCD frequently have excessive concerns about their own health or sometimes the health of loved ones. Usually the health fear is specific to one condition or disease and often makes little sense to others. The following example shows you how someone with this OCD concern thinks.

> **Jack** believes that fibers from synthetic clothing contain carcinogenic material. He avoids wearing anything except cotton or wool. He calls stores and clothing manufacturers around the country asking about what types of thread they use for sewing on buttons. He inquires about the machines used to cut and sew the material to see if they are also used on the dreaded synthetic fabrics. If he is not fully assured that the machines are used only to manufacture natural materials into clothes, he won't buy the brand in question.
>
> He checks all fabric tags repeatedly before he puts on his clothes. He gets very upset when someone walks by too closely, fearing that synthetic fibers from clothes can jump from person to person. He monitors his body constantly for what he believes are possible signs of cancer, such as bloating, blemishes, swollen sinuses, and headaches.

Jack's story may seem pretty wacky to you. But that's how OCD works sometimes. OCD stories don't always make a whole lot of logical sense. Other examples of people with OCD health concerns include:

- ✔ A mother frequently fears she may poison her children by undercooking their meat, so she routinely burns their dinner.

- ✔ A father worries about his kids' health so much that he home-schools them to avoid exposure to contagions.

✔ A teenage boy obsesses about being killed by natural disasters. He convinces his parents to buy enough supplies to last for two months in case of an emergency. That's not such a bad idea, but his OCD is revealed by the fact that the boy does an inventory of the supplies each day. He also pressures his parents to move to Nevada because it has a lower incidence of natural disasters than California, which is where they live.

Categorizing Approaches to Checking

The compulsion to check momentarily decreases doubt, and that feels like a relief. But the doubt quickly returns. That's the nature of OCD. Checking is a very temporary solution because absolute certainty *never* replaces doubt. To the OCD mind, there is always a chance that something bad might happen. Over the long haul, continued checking produces increased uneasiness, frustration, and doubt.

Checking usually happens when the person with OCD is alone and further increases when the person feels stressed or unhappy. Checking falls into one of three forms: obvious or overt, mental, or assisted. The following sections describe each form in more detail.

Obvious or overt checking

These compulsions are active and can be seen — like clicking the car key fob again and again to make sure the car doors are locked or checking to see that the dryer is turned off. Obvious checking is also apparent when a driver turns around and goes back to the area where a bump in the road seemed suspicious. Another example of this type of checking is when a person scans the news for accident victims or repeatedly calls friends to make sure that they are okay.

Mental checking

Mental checking refers to thinking about or reviewing something over and over. Someone may think about all the details of driving to work repeatedly to check for the possibility of harming someone. Or, one may mentally review each step taken to make sure that the windows at home are closed. Still others may repeatedly review each conversation from the day in order to be sure that they said nothing offensive to anyone.

Getting others to check

One way to get others to help check is simply to ask. A man might call his roommate and ask him to check and see that the stove is off. A woman might ask a passenger in the car if he felt that bump. Another way of getting others involved is through *reassurance seeking* (see Chapter 5). A woman might ask her spouse whether he thinks she looks sick. A child might repeatedly ask his parents whether they think the house will be safe from intruders.

Taking Steps to Defeat Doubting and Control Checking

Treating Doubting and Checking OCD is relatively straightforward. However, it takes effort, a willingness to do a few uncomfortable things, and perseverance. In addition, you need to be very self-observant in order to pick up on all the important nuances that your OCD may involve. The following five sections take you through a typical treatment game plan, step by step.

If you don't feel ready to tackle your Doubting and Checking OCD, seriously consider reading Chapter 6 on overcoming resistance first. If the material in that chapter doesn't make you feel fully prepared, consult a mental-health professional for assistance. You should also make an appointment with a professional if your own efforts begin to stall at any point.

Note: You need a notebook or something to write on as you work through the following steps.

1. Searching for signals, triggers, and avoidance

The first step in treating Doubting and Checking OCD involves a little detective work. You must monitor your environment, actions, and behaviors carefully in order to determine what *triggers* (problematic situations and events) set off your doubting and checking cycle. Assessing and listing anything and everything that you find yourself avoiding is a good way to discover these triggers. But try not to be too obsessional in your search.

For example, if you have trouble leaving your home due to fear of burglaries, the need or desire to go out into the world may trigger a cascade of obsessions about the security of your doors and windows. Similarly, if you avoid watching television out of fear that you'll fail to hear someone breaking in, then turning on the television and perhaps other noisy appliances may trigger your OCD. Additional common triggers for Doubting and Checking OCD include driving, traffic, being in crowds, sneezing, feeling nauseous, and listening to news stories. Actually, the list of possible triggers goes on and on and on, but for now, choose ten or so items from your list so you won't feel overwhelmed. Write these items in your notebook.

Occasionally, your problematic triggers may seem to strike from out of the blue. However, usually when you look hard enough, you find something that likely triggered your OCD cycle. Typically, the trigger is a fairly clear-cut event or happening. Other times, it may be something a little more vague such as increased stress at work or having had a poor night's sleep.

2. Identifying obsessional doubts

The second step in treating your Doubting and Checking OCD is to figure out what you fear will happen if you stop avoiding your OCD triggers. These fears constitute your obsessions or doubts. Usually, whatever consequence you fear is rather horrible. That's why it's so hard to give up on checking.

For example, if you went ahead and drove in congested areas and over speed bumps, what do you think the consequence would be? If you have hit-and-run worries, the consequence is likely to be pretty clear — you fear that you will cause someone's death or serious injury. Write down the obsessions or feared consequences of encountering your triggers in your notebook.

3. Compiling compulsions

A critical component of your Doubting and Checking OCD treatment is making a list of your compulsions. These compulsions include checking and safety behaviors. Checking compulsions involve all the things you do to see whether your worst fears have actually occurred or not, such as:

- ✔ Checking your locks
- ✔ Returning to the scene of a feared accident
- ✔ Going to the doctor to check out your latest physical symptom
- ✔ Reviewing the newspaper for stories about car accidents you may have caused

Safety behaviors are another type of compulsion and encompass things you do to prevent your fears from occurring. These include rituals such as checking your stove exactly 14 times while counting out loud from 1 to 14. Other safety compulsions include repeating certain words or phrases to prevent bad things from happening and carrying lucky charms to accomplish the same goal. Safety behaviors often have a superstitious or magical flavor to them (see Chapter 17 for OCD that actually focuses on superstitions and other magical thinking).Write down your list of compulsions and safety behaviors in your notebook.

Robyn's story illustrates how someone with severe Doubting and Checking OCD goes about finding the triggers, obsessions (feared consequences), and checking compulsions for her OCD cycle.

> **Robyn** has Doubting and Checking OCD that focuses on worries about harming others with her car (see the section "Harming others with your car through negligence"). Her OCD has progressively worsened over the past few years. Today, she can rarely manage to drive anywhere at all. Robyn identifies the actual events, situations, and triggers for her hit-and-run concerns. She comes up with this list of triggers:
>
> • Driving in congested areas
>
> • Driving near bike lanes
>
> • Driving near crosswalks
>
> • Driving near sidewalks
>
> • Driving on bumpy roads
>
> • Driving with passengers in the car due to the distraction
>
> • Going over speed bumps
>
> Robyn ponders the obsessional fears that she believes will occur if she stops avoiding her OCD triggers. The answer is pretty obvious — she assumes that the likelihood of her harming or killing someone with her car will skyrocket.

She reflects on the following obsessions or feared consequences of encountering her OCD triggers:

1. She runs someone over.

2. The police pull her over and arrest her.

3. She is driven to jail in handcuffs.

4. She appears in court.

5. She is found guilty of negligent manslaughter, and is sentenced to ten years in jail.

These obsessions cause Robyn to engage in an array of compulsive checking. She does this by:

- Returning to the place of the perceived accident over and over again until she feels she can go on
- Examining the exterior of her car for an hour twice each week
- Having her car washed twice a week to facilitate her examination

Her compulsions also include safety behaviors:

- She drives only on certain uncongested roadways.
- She repeats the words "break a leg" as she drives.
- She drives five miles an hour below the speed limit.

With these lists of triggers, obsessions, and compulsions in hand, Robyn is prepared to take on the next step in her OCD treatment — disputing doubts.

4. Disputing obsessional doubts

If you suffer from the doubting and checking type of OCD, it is distressing for you. This type of OCD centers on obsessional worries about caring for others, keeping the home safe, and staying healthy. Checking feels like a logical response because the imagined consequences of harming others, watching a home burn down, or becoming seriously ill are harsh. The fact that you and others with this type of OCD may resist direct challenges to these worries is understandable. Resistance is a common response to exposure and response prevention (ERP) therapy (see the next section).

However, if you start by learning to rethink the way you view doubt, you may feel better prepared to undergo ERP (which is the next step). OCD doubts are not based on evidence. In contrast, realistic doubts stem from logical information. To help you figure out whether your doubts are realistic or based on your OCD, ask yourself the following questions (see Chapter 8 for more on this and other strategies for rethinking doubts):

- **Are your doubts based on direct information from your senses (sight, sound, smell, taste, or touch)?** Most OCD doubts are not based on one's senses.

✔ **Does your doubt seem to have a life of its own and keep coming back, even without new evidence to support it?** OCD doubts typically do continually return over and over without fresh evidence.

✔ **Is there anything about your doubt that other people would see as illogical?** If your doubt is OCD, people likely see it as very illogical.

✔ **Is there anything that would convince you that your doubt is likely false?** If you have OCD, you likely can't be convinced that your doubt is false, no matter what the evidence says.

Obsessional doubts come from your OCD mind. They are not grounded by rational thinking. If your doubts persist in spite of contradictory evidence, then OCD is at work.

For example, in the preceding section we discussed Robyn, whose obsessional doubts center on the fear of running someone over with her car, being arrested, and going to jail. Following are her answers to these questions:

✔ **Are your doubts based on direct information from your senses (sight, sound, smell, taste, or touch)?**

I've never experienced hitting someone with my car, so I guess I don't have any direct information about these doubts.

✔ **Does your doubt seem to have a life of its own and keep coming back, even without new evidence to support it?**

Yes, my worry continues even when I avoid lots of dangerous intersections and congested traffic. I've had no accidents and nothing has happened that logically would suggest that I might be at special risk for running someone over.

✔ **Is there anything about your doubt that other people would see as illogical?**

I don't talk about this with most people. But my close friends think it's pretty crazy. I guess I don't talk about it with more people because I know they would think it's crazy.

✔ **Is there anything that would convince you that your doubt is likely false?**

I've never thought about this question before. I guess I can't think of anything that would make me stop believing in my worries.

Robyn reviews her answers and concludes that it's pretty obvious that her doubts are coming from her OCD mind. She still feels wary, but is now more willing to consider that these doubts are groundless. And she feels more prepared to engage in ERP, as discussed in the next section.

5. Applying ERP to doubting and checking

In Chapter 10, we discuss ERP in depth. Please read that chapter prior to attempting to use ERP for your Doubting and Checking OCD. It contains step-by-step ERP instructions and guides for troubleshooting problems.

Here we provide you with three sample exposure hierarchies or staircases relevant to Doubting and Checking OCD. See Chapter 10 for more about constructing hierarchies and staircases and assigning Ugh Factor Ratings to obsessions for virtually any OCD concerns.

Hit-and-Run OCD exposure staircase

As discussed earlier in this chapter, the fear of hitting someone with your car is a relatively common form of Doubting and Checking OCD. Robyn's example in the preceding two sections typifies this concern.

She and her psychologist work out an exposure staircase together, as shown in Figure 13-1. Notice that they include a couple of imaginary steps. Obviously someone with this OCD concern cannot use exposure steps of actually running over a pedestrian! After she completes her hierarchy, she carries out ERP as discussed in Chapter 10.

Figure 13-1:
Robyn's
OCD
exposure
staircase.

Imagining the worst case – hitting someone and going to jail (90 Ugh Factor Rating)
Driving in congested areas (85 Ugh Factor Rating)
Driving near bike lanes (80 Ugh Factor Rating)
Going over speed bumps (70 Ugh Factor Rating)
Driving near crosswalks (65 Ugh Factor Rating)
Driving on bumpy roads (65 Ugh Factor Rating)
Driving near sidewalks (60 Ugh Factor Rating)
Driving with passengers in the car due to the distraction (50 Ugh Factor Rating)
Imagining going for a drive on a crowded street (40 Ugh Factor Rating)
Driving to the grocery store near home (30 Ugh Factor Rating)

Burning down the house

Fears about home safety dominate the thoughts of some people with Doubting and Checking OCD. If this reflects your concerns, here's a sample hierarchy for developing a staircase. Please realize that your own specific hierarchy or staircase could contain a very different list of specific items with different Ugh Factor Ratings.

✔ Imagining the house burning down (95 Ugh Factor Rating)

✔ Leaving the coffeepot unattended and turned on (with coffee in it) for one hour (90 Ugh Factor Rating)

✔ Imagining a small kitchen fire (85 Ugh Factor Rating)

✔ Imagining someone actually breaking into the house (80 Ugh Factor Rating)

✔ Locking the doors and leaving the house without checking the locks (75 Ugh Factor Rating)

✔ Checking the door locks only once when leaving the house (60 Ugh Factor Rating)

✔ Checking the door locks only twice when leaving the house (50 Ugh Factor Rating)

✔ Leaving the toaster oven plugged in (40 Ugh Factor Rating)

✔ Leaving the coffeepot plugged in at night (35 Ugh Factor Rating)

✔ Leaving the television plugged in (25 Ugh Factor Rating)

Healthy or not

Fears about the state of one's health plague the minds of some of those with Doubting and Checking OCD. Here's a sample exposure hierarchy for this concern. Your particular list could contain very different items and ratings.

✔ Imagining dying a slow, painful death from cancer (90 Ugh Factor Rating)

✔ Exercising intensely with an elevated heart rate (85 Ugh Factor Rating)

✔ Volunteering at a hospice (85 Ugh Factor Rating)

✔ Exercising moderately with a slightly elevated heart rate (80 Ugh Factor Rating)

✔ Being around old people (75 Ugh Factor Rating)

✔ Imagining coming down with a serious, chronic illness (70 Ugh Factor Rating)

✔ Failing to check yourself for injuries after handling sharp knives (65 Ugh Factor Rating)

✔ Going for a week without asking anyone for reassurance about your health (60 Ugh Factor Rating)

✔ Going for a day without asking anyone for reassurance about your health (50 Ugh Factor Rating)

✔ Not taking your blood pressure for a day (40 Ugh Factor Rating)

✔ Not listening to your heart with a stethoscope for a week (25 Ugh Factor Rating)

Check with your healthcare provider once for clearance on any items that call for changing your exercise or monitoring your health status. Don't keep going back to the doctor for reassurance about these issues.

Chapter 14

Subduing OCD-Driven Shame

In This Chapter

▶ Reviewing the types of shame

▶ Changing shameful thinking

▶ Exposing and experimenting with shame

Generally speaking, those with OCD are unusually caring, moral, kind, and decent folks. Unfortunately, those with a type of OCD called Shaming OCD *believe* quite the opposite of themselves. Their minds fill up with obsessional images involving blatantly immoral, shameful, inappropriate, and humiliating actions. They believe that because those images enter their minds, they will actually put those thoughts into actions.

People with Shaming OCD feel so ashamed of their thoughts that they often keep them secret. Therefore, many people with this problem suffer for years and fail to seek help. That's a shame, because treatment works.

In this chapter, we describe the major themes of Shaming OCD, and we tell you how to go about treating this problem. We discuss ways to think differently about your worries. Then we show you how to behave in ways that help tackle your Shaming OCD.

This chapter includes examples involving gruesome and horrific scenes. We are not trying to be sensational or to shock you. The reason we include this material is because people with OCD often have these terrible thoughts and worry that this means they may be dangerous or crazy. If you are plagued by gruesome obsessions, realize that you are not insane or a terrible person — you have Shaming OCD.

Surveying Shaming OCD

Shaming OCD draws on a deep well of self-distrust. People afflicted with this problem vary greatly in terms of the specific themes upon which they base their concerns. However, they all share a profound fear that they may act in ways that will bring them great shame. Thus, one person may believe that she is likely to kill all her loved ones, another may think he will sexually abuse children, and someone else may imagine that she is an immoral sinner who offends God.

In the sections that follow, we review the three most common areas of concern for those who suffer from Shaming OCD. Those concerns are

✔ Fearing loss of control

✔ Questioning sexual identity

✔ Adhering to extreme religious rules (scrupulosity)

Being afraid of losing control

Many of those with Shaming OCD fear that their thoughts will ultimately turn into actions. They envision themselves acting out uncontrollably. Three areas stand out as concerns for those with the losing-control issue — aggression, sexually acting out, and losing control of bodily functions in public.

When horrible thoughts come into their minds, people with this type of OCD become very judgmental and self-critical. They often say to themselves, "If I have these bad thoughts, then I must be a bad person."

Shame versus guilt

Feelings of shame and guilt are reminders that some action or behavior is not acceptable — either morally, legally, or ethically. Although both emotions are negative, they help people know when they have done something wrong. Most people use the words shame and guilt pretty much interchangeably. However, social scientists usually make a distinction between the unpleasant emotions of shame and guilt.

Shame is a personal feeling about one's self and is usually all-encompassing: "I am ashamed of myself" thus means, "I am a bad person." People who are ashamed tend to avoid others, get angry, or become depressed. They appear to be less likely to do something positive to make up for their deeds. On the other hand, guilt is more specific and adaptive: "I feel guilty that I ran that red light. Next time I'll try to pay more attention," or "I feel guilty about getting angry with my brother." Those who feel guilty are more likely to try to fix the problem or do something to make amends.

The bottom line is that a little guilt isn't all that bad as long as it motivates you to do better in the future. If you feel guilty here and there, you probably have a good, well-functioning conscience. By contrast, shame is rarely helpful because it doesn't point the way to improved behavior.

Struggling with thoughts of aggression

Thinking you may be a mass murderer is a whole lot better than actually *being* a mass murderer. But, even the contemplation that you may lose control and harm someone else can be quite disturbing.

People with this concern worry that they will snap and do something terrible to someone else. The target of the aggressive impulse could be a stranger or a loved one. Some common worries include

✔ What if I am swimming and I hold my child's head under water?

✔ What if I kill my pet?

✔ What if I push down someone who is handicapped?

✔ What if I slap my boss?

✔ What if I walk near a knife, pick it up, and stab someone?

Baby obsessions

The birth of a baby is a time of great joy for most families. It is also a time when many new parents experience obsessive thoughts. A study at the Mayo Clinic reported that more than a third of new mothers and more than half of new fathers experience these temporary obsessions. The obsessions are repugnant and contradict the parents' love and concern for their child. Thoughts can be accompanied by vivid images. Thoughts usually center around health, safety issues, intentional harm, sexual thoughts, and worries about contamination.

✔ Am I sexually attracted to this baby?

✔ What if I abuse the baby?

✔ What if I am walking by a sharp object and stab the baby?

✔ What if I drop the baby?

✔ What if I fall down the stairs and kill the baby?

✔ What if my baby catches a disease because I didn't clean properly after changing?

✔ What if the baby slides down into the water and drowns?

The increased responsibility of caring for a newborn child and the stress involved (not to mention sleepless nights) are believed to make this a prime time for the mind to generate these weird thoughts. Obsessions about harming a baby usually don't last long. They do not become diagnosable OCD unless the thoughts become increasingly frequent, lead to significant distress, and involve considerable amounts of time.

Obsessional thoughts about harming a baby are almost never carried out. People are generally frightened and disgusted by obsessions. Having these thoughts means nothing about the person. However, there are extremely rare cases that involve loss of touch with reality and irrational thinking in which violence can occur. Anytime obsessional thoughts feel out of control or very disturbing, please seek help from a mental-health professional.

Wrestling thoughts of acting out sexually

One common concern of those with Shaming OCD is the fear that they may act out sexually deviant behavior at some point. We aren't just talking about acceptable, though perhaps unusual, sexual practices between consenting adults. When OCD is involved, the feared sexual acts are typically considered highly immoral by the sufferer and even dangerously illegal. Some of the top worries of those with Shaming OCD involving sexual concerns include

- ✔ **Thoughts about pedophilia:** This issue involves worrying that one may sexually abuse a child. Mind you, these people do not *want* to abuse a child and actually find the idea utterly abhorrent. However, they have obsessional thoughts about the possibility and constantly check on themselves to determine whether this could really happen. They interpret minor, meaningless bodily sensations in the genital region as proof positive that they actually are aroused by children. These concerns often cause them to avoid being around playgrounds, schools, and other places where children congregate.

- ✔ **Thoughts about rape:** Those with this concern fear that they may lose control and rape someone. Although occasional rape fantasies are not uncommon, most people don't worry that they'll actually act them out. Those with Shaming OCD who have this problem have a different perspective. They believe that even a brief image of a rape scene floating through their minds means they are at real risk of acting it out. Therefore, these folks often avoid being around anyone they can imagine raping.

- ✔ **Thoughts about bestiality:** People who worry about this issue believe that they may actually engage in sex with an animal. They respond to any thought or image about sex with animals as though it means they are actually sexually attracted to animals. Like those with concerns about rape and pedophilia, these people find their thoughts about sex with animals disgusting. They typically avoid being around animals in order to control their imagined urges.

Worrying over losing control of bodily functions

Another interesting theme among those with Shaming OCD is the fear of losing control of bodily functions. Those with this affliction fear doing one of the following two distressing things:

- ✔ **Losing bladder or bowel control in public.** People suffering with this OCD issue constantly fret that they may wet or mess themselves in a public place. This feeling of uncertainty plagues people with elimination obsessions. The thoughts and accompanying feelings become so pressing that going out is avoided as much as possible. They monitor their bodies for slight changes and believe that they won't be able to control themselves.

When forced to leave the house, their first step is to find the nearest bathroom. They end up going to the bathroom at every opportunity — even when it's completely unnecessary — just to avoid having a humiliating accident.

✔ **Vomiting spontaneously in public.** Others with Shaming OCD obsess about the possibility of vomiting in public. Images come into their minds of uncontrollable projectile vomiting in crowded restaurants, at work, or in class.

To avoid such horrific happenings, those plagued with this concern often stop eating out. They also avoid other possible triggers for their concerns, such as opening their mouths to speak in public. These avoidance behaviors can make them seem strange. Finally, they commonly resort to safety behaviors such as taking antacids and anti-nausea drugs prior to going out.

Questioning established sexual identity

The sexual identity theme in Shaming OCD calls the very essence of a person's sexuality into question. Unlike the fear of sexually acting out, this worry does not involve aggressive or illegal acts. However, those with this torment feel considerable shame and distress, because the obsessional fears raise questions about their established sexual identity. These fears and thoughts are irrational and come out of the blue.

The example that follows describes someone with this issue.

> **Estabelle,** a happily married woman, begins to wonder whether she's gay. The woman enjoys a healthy sexual relationship with her husband but worries that she is attracted to other women. She starts to study herself for signs that she is aroused by women. She begins looking at lesbian pornography to see if she finds it arousing — and interprets almost any thought or bodily change as evidence of her newfound orientation. She constantly asks her husband for reassurance that he finds her attractive. She is so self-conscious about her sexuality that she finds herself distracted during sex. For the first time, she is unable to have an orgasm. This problem gives her OCD more fuel to question her sexual orientation.

Estabelle's example portrays someone who feels ashamed and extremely confused by the possibility that she may be gay. She is not aroused by thoughts of sexual encounters with women. These thoughts seem to have come out of the blue. Her obsessions are unwanted, frequent, and uncontrolled. And she's not gay.

Being homosexual is not a sign of an emotional problem. However, having obsessions about being gay — when you're not — is considered a form of OCD. People with this problem usually have some strategies to deal with their obsessions. Some repeatedly ask for reassurance from others about being gay or looking gay. Some challenge themselves by looking at pornography or going to gay bars. Many avoid situations in which they think they may be tempted to act on their thoughts. These coping strategies can be considered compulsive.

Taking religious or moral beliefs to the extreme

The category of Shaming OCD that deals with religion involves adhering to an overly demanding religious or moral code. Those with this form of "religious" Shaming OCD, which is also known as *scrupulosity*, obsess over perceived sins, fear losing control of their behavior in religiously inappropriate ways, or endlessly fret over failing to please God. They attempt to relieve the obsessions through compulsive acts such as praying, chanting, asking for reassurance, or confessing. Scrupulosity takes many forms; the following are a few examples:

- A woman repeats Bible verses over and over because she doubts that she says them correctly.

- A man at church sees a statue of the Virgin Mary and imagines having sex with her. Now he finds that every time he goes to church he has similar thoughts and images. He believes that merely having these thoughts is blasphemous. He frequently goes to confession for reassurance, which helps for only a short time.

- During Yom Kippur, a woman discovers that she has mindlessly chewed on the end of her pencil. Because her religion calls for fasting during this time, she believes that she has sinned. She views many such "transgressions" similarly.

- A teenager sits through church service believing that he will suddenly shout out obscenities against God. He resists going to church because of this fear, but then feels he has committed a horrible sin by not going to church.

Scrupulosity can also involve slavish adherence to moral codes that are not based on religion. These codes of conduct go far beyond what most people consider necessary. Thus, those with this concern may review all their actions for the slightest hint of a possible indiscretion or wrongdoing. Some rebuke themselves for giving a compliment that is not 100 percent true.

Others think they've committed an *unforgiveable* act if they fail to count their change from a cashier and later realize that they walked away with a nickel too much change.

Treating Shaming OCD

Shaming OCD involves thoughts, feelings, and behavior. The thoughts are usually distorted and highly judgmental. The feelings include self-disgust, shame, humiliation, anxiety, and guilt. Rarely, if ever, does anyone actually act out the behaviors they fear they will. Instead, they avoid situations they think could lead them into trouble. They engage in various safety behaviors and compulsive attempts to neutralize their obsessive thoughts.

Treatment targets both thoughts and behaviors — with the result being an improvement in the way the person feels. The following two sections discuss specific strategies designed to treat Shaming OCD thinking and behaving, respectively.

Changing OCD thinking by challenging the evidence

The primary approach to changing your Shaming OCD thoughts is what's known as "checking the evidence." This strategy has also been successfully applied to other emotional problems, such as depression and anxiety. It is particularly useful for Shaming OCD because the thinking component of this type of OCD is especially prominent.

Checking the evidence involves carefully reviewing and responding to a variety of questions that help you to challenge your OCD-related thoughts. These questions include the following:

- Do people I like and respect sometimes have bad thoughts too? (**Hint:** If you don't know, consider asking a few very trusted friends.)

- Have any of my obsessions gone up and down in frequency and intensity over time? If so, what happened in terms of my actual behavior, and why do I think my obsessions varied over time?

- How many times have my thoughts actually caused me to engage in unacceptable behavior?

- What would happen if I used the same standards for myself that I have for other people?

> ✔ What would I tell a good friend of mine who told me about having thoughts just like mine?
>
> ✔ When I am excessively critical of myself, do I end up feeling better or worse?

We encourage you to take some time considering these questions and writing out your answers. Keep a copy of your answers handy. When you have an obsessive thought, take a look at your responses. Read them out loud. Don't expect an immediate change; continue to work by completing the behavioral exercises in the section that follows on ERP. Here's an example that represents how someone with Shaming OCD may respond to the questions:

> **Tamara**, the mother of a 10-month-old boy, had been treated for Contamination OCD as a teenager and had recovered. She began having strange thoughts shortly after the birth of her baby. She changes a diaper and notices a rash. The thought that the rash is caused by her sexually abusing him flashes in her mind. After that first thought, she feels disgusted and repulsed. But why would that thought come to her mind? Maybe she wants to abuse him, or maybe she is sexually aroused by him. She starts to avoid looking at his genitals when she changes him, but this leads to her not getting him clean and his rash gets worse. He gets more and more fussy. Tamara can barely make herself hold him because she fears that she will act on her obsessions. Tamara's mind floods with horrible images and thoughts.
>
> Her family members notice how disturbed she is becoming and suggest she check in with her former therapist. Her therapist explains that she has had a relapse of her OCD. He tells her that because she responded to treatment before, she will likely get better fast. Together, they collect evidence regarding her new obsession. Here are her answers:

> ✔ **Do people I like and respect sometimes have bad thoughts too?**
>
> *I know a lot of people have OCD. And I read in* OCD For Dummies *that most people sometimes have thoughts that are just like the thoughts that those of us with OCD have. So probably most of my friends have similar thoughts here and there. They just don't take them as seriously as my OCD mind does.*

> ✔ **Have any of my obsessions gone up and down in frequency and intensity over time? If so, what happened in terms of my actual behavior, and why do I think my obsessions varied over time?**
>
> *Oh, yes. At one time I was afraid of contamination from all kinds of things — dirt, oil, food, you name it. I think stress had something to do with it. In any case, I guess I can see it's "all just OCD."*

> ✔ **How many times have my thoughts actually caused me to engage in unacceptable behavior?**
>
> *Well, in truth, it's never actually happened. I don't absolutely know that it won't, but it hasn't yet.*

✔ **What would happen if I used the same standards for myself that I have for other people?**

I never thought of that. I suppose it would make me less self-critical. Maybe my OCD would drop a little too.

✔ **What would I tell a good friend of mine who told me about having thoughts just like mine?**

I would tell a friend that she was just having OCD. My OCD from the past tells me that much. I'd tell her to repeat "There goes my OCD again" each time she had those thoughts.

✔ **When I am excessively critical of myself, do I end up feeling better or worse?**

Definitely worse. My OCD jumps up and I just spiral down. I guess trying to be more self-forgiving might help.

After completing the "checking the evidence" questions, Tamara feels significant relief. She still has work to do in therapy, but feels more emboldened to take on her OCD. She and her therapist work on some of the techniques described in the next sections.

Using ERP to change shaming OCD behavior

Changing your OCD-related behavior is probably the most powerful way to combat your Shaming OCD. The primary tool in your OCD toolkit is seen throughout this book and is called exposure and response prevention (ERP).

We cover ERP in considerable detail in Chapter 10. Please read that chapter thoroughly before you proceed further. There you will see exactly how to carry out ERP and what to do if and when you encounter trouble.

The purpose of this section is to present you with several ERP hierarchies (or staircases) for use with ERP. ERP *hierarchies* are lists. ERP *staircases* are pictorial representations of the hierarchies. Each places the item with the lowest Ugh Factor Rating at the bottom and moves progressively up the hierarchy or staircase, so the item with the highest Ugh Factor is at the top.

You won't know what to do with these hierarchies unless you read about ERP in Chapter 10 first. If you were to attempt something without that information, you could easily make things worse for yourself. And please see a professional trained in ERP if you encounter any snags or difficulty. Finally, consult a professional if you have scrupulosity OCD or any Shaming OCD issues that concern illegal or highly immoral acts. You need a proper diagnosis as well as careful guidance — but you can be helped! For religious issues, your therapist may want to collaborate with a spiritual advisor.

Losing bladder or bowel control in public

If worries about urinating and/or defecating in public pervade your mind, here's an ERP hierarchy involving this theme. Please realize that your personal concerns will vary somewhat (or even greatly) from these items. However, reviewing this sample should help you devise your own hierarchy.

Some people struggle with various medical conditions that may cause actual embarrassing moments. If that's the case for you, various medical treatment options may be available. Unfortunately, for some, the only solution is the use of adult diapers. These do manage to control the embarrassment, but we recommend checking into medical treatments first.

Some people with this form of OCD wear adult diapers not because of any medical condition, but to protect themselves from their worries about accidents — which they typically have never experienced. That's why we include going without adult diapers in our hierarchy — this is *not* advice for someone with a true medical condition to follow.

- ✔ Imagine peeing in my pants in a crowded mall — everyone stares (90 Ugh Factor Rating)

- ✔ Go to a public restroom without checking myself for possible "drips" (80 Ugh Factor Rating)

- ✔ Get on an airplane without going to the bathroom within 20 minutes of takeoff (75 Ugh Factor Rating)

- ✔ Go without adult diapers for an entire day (60 Ugh Factor Rating)

- ✔ Go out in public after drinking two full glasses of water (55 Ugh Factor Rating)

- ✔ Avoid going to the bathroom when out in the world for at least 30 minutes (45 Ugh Factor Rating)

- ✔ Go to a new mall without looking on the map for the restrooms (45 Ugh Factor Rating)

- ✔ Go to a restaurant without asking where the restroom is (35 Ugh Factor Rating)

- ✔ Avoid going to the bathroom for an hour while out in public (30 Ugh Factor Rating)

- ✔ Go without adult diapers for one hour (25 Ugh Factor Rating)

Don't get so compulsive with your ERP that you actually cause yourself severe pain and distress from avoiding voiding.

Notice that a hierarchy can contain items that occur only in the mind as well as some that you actually carry out. That's because carrying some of these situations out with real actions would indeed be pretty darned embarrassing! Fortunately, you don't have to venture out into the world and truly pee in your pants.

Vomiting in public

Now it's time to review a nauseating hierarchy. Just for the record, we're pretty sure that most people don't especially enjoy vomiting. However, those with this kind of Shaming OCD worry about vomiting every day. They avoid eating out and anything else that could possibly make them feel nauseous and vomit.

It is *possible* that carrying out this exposure hierarchy could result in you becoming somewhat nauseous and even vomiting. If a given staircase item starts to make you quite nauseous, you may want to back away from that stair and try an easier one. However, it's okay if you get nauseous or vomit. People do vomit, and the consequences of doing so are not nearly as horrific as your OCD mind tells you. If you find the tasks too scary, enlist the help of a professional.

- ✔ Put "vomit soup" in your mouth and spit it out — see sidebar for special recipe and instructions! (100 Ugh Factor Rating)

- ✔ Imagine walking into an alley behind a bar late at night and inhaling the smells (90 Ugh Factor Rating)

- ✔ Imagine vomiting on a subway train and causing everyone else to start vomiting (90 Ugh Factor Rating)

- ✔ Actually imitate vomiting/gagging sounds (85 Ugh Factor Rating)

- ✔ Actually listen to tapes of gagging sounds (80 Ugh Factor Rating)

- ✔ Actually go on an amusement park ride that spins (75 Ugh Factor Rating)

- ✔ Actually look at pictures of vomit on the Internet (60 Ugh Factor Rating)

- ✔ Actually let your mouth fill with saliva (55 Ugh Factor Rating)

- ✔ Actually go out to eat at a restaurant and eat the entire meal (55 Ugh Factor Rating)

- ✔ Actually spin in an office chair (55 Ugh Factor Rating)

- ✔ Imagine vomiting in your own bathroom (45 Ugh Factor Rating)

- ✔ Actually pull your stomach muscles in and out rapidly (35 Ugh Factor Rating)

Eeew, gross: Vomit soup

If you can carry out this instruction, you're very likely to make great strides with your vomiting-in-public worries. Note that this item lies at the very top of the vomit exposure hierarchy. Some therapists with considerable expertise in treating this issue concoct a brew that has much the same look and feel of vomit. Here's our own recipe.

The base of any good vomit recipe is soup. You can choose your own brand. We recommend a vegetable soup such as green pea, minestrone, or plain old vegetable. Make sure the soup has some color and good chunks in it. Next, you need a little more texture. Soft curd cottage cheese is always good. Exact portions are not important, but a little more than a quarter cup is enough. Add a little carbonated beverage of your choice to give the mix a few bubbles (we don't recommend champagne for this one unless you're also trying to give that up).

Mix some of this lovely potion up. Then fill your mouth with it while in a bathroom. Roll it around, make a good gagging sound and spit it out into a toilet. If you spill a bit on the toilet seat, that's great. This is true exposure. Repeat as needed until your anxiety drops significantly or until you can't stop laughing. Yum.

Complementary Treatments for OCD Shaming

The preceding strategies are your primary tools for use against Shaming OCD. However, we've found a few techniques to be useful add-ons. You can think of these techniques as experiments. Try them out and see what data comes in.

Revealing to others

Those with Shaming OCD usually hide their OCD thoughts from others. They work hard to conceal what they label as their hidden shame. That's because they're convinced that others would be repulsed and/or would reject them outright.

However, hiding your Shaming OCD prevents you from hearing a more reasonable perspective. Therefore, we suggest that you start by marshaling your courage and finding a therapist. Therapists are highly trained in being nonjudgmental.

Once you reveal your hidden thoughts to a therapist, the two of you can work out a plan to open up with a few highly trusted people in your life as well. Doing so enables you to see whether they interpret your OCD thoughts in a more benign, less judgmental way. If you open up with three or four close, trusted friends, the odds are you'll see that they attach less significance to your thoughts than you do. Hopefully, this information will help you see that your thoughts are not as meaningful as actions and that they stem from the OCD part of your mind.

Of course, it's always possible that you may pick a judgmental, rejecting person to reveal your thoughts to. But accepting a degree of uncertainty is part of treating OCD. If you do encounter a bad reaction, a therapist can help you through the incident. And one final word of advice: Don't *continually* seek the counsel of others because doing so can morph into reassurance seeking — something we frequently warn against.

Experimenting with being "off duty"

Most people with Shaming OCD vigilantly monitor their thoughts and behaviors in order to prevent themselves from actually carrying out their feared, shameful actions. They mistakenly believe that it is only this monitoring that stands in the way of them engaging in one of these acts, such as shouting out obscenities in church, acting out sexually, or vomiting in public.

We owe a debt of gratitude to Dr. Stanley Rachman for the following idea. He suggests experimenting with periods of "off duty" for this type of OCD. "Off duty" is a time span during which you consciously cease vigilant monitoring of yourself for the possibility that you might engage in some shameful act. You can start with an hour in which you decide not to monitor yourself at all. Then try extending that time period to three hours, a full day, and so on.

After each "off duty" period of time, jot down whether anything catastrophic occurred or whether you actually lost control. Then try experimenting with times of "ultra vigilance." During those times, try to control and actively monitor every single thought and action. After the "ultra vigilance" period, jot down whether you felt safer and whether you felt more in control or out of control.

Most of the time, this experiment leads people to conclude that their excessive vigilance does nothing to protect them. It doesn't make them feel safer or better. In fact, most people feel much worse during their periods of "ultra vigilance." The paradoxical lesson from this exercise is that *you will feel more in control as you let go of your need to be in control.*

Experimenting with self-critical versus self-accepting views

Those afflicted with Shaming OCD almost always believe that they suffer from severe deficiencies in control and morality. They seem to believe they are inherently defective as human beings. They manage to "prove" their inherent defectiveness by examining everything they do from a highly critical, judgmental perspective.

But what would happen if you experimented with turning this cycle on its head? That's what we ask you to do here. First, designate a full day to engaging in harsh, critical scrutiny of each and every thing you do. For example, right now, we could beat up on ourselves for not typing fast enough or failing to word each sentence in the best possible way. Similarly, you could berate yourself for failing to read fast enough or understand the full meaning of each word and sentence.

Jot down notes here and there during your "critical" day. Notice how you feel and whether your Shaming OCD concerns increase or decrease. We're betting that your concerns will rise.

Then choose a full day in which you decide to view yourself in a neutral, benign way. When you have OCD thoughts, merely say to yourself, "There goes my OCD mind again, how interesting." If a disturbing image floats through your mind, do the same. If you make a mistake, say, "I guess that makes me human." View all your OCD thoughts as though they are as meaningless as particles of dust.

Again, jot down notes on how you feel during your neutral, self-accepting day. See if you feel better or worse when you drop your self-critical stance. If you feel better, and we think you will, consider extending these periods to a week, then a month, and, ultimately, for the rest of your life.

Chapter 15

Messing with "Just So" OCD

. . . .

In This Chapter

▶ Working to make things just right

▶ Getting stuck with symmetry

▶ Thinking differently about order

▶ Messing things up

. . . .

Symmetry refers to pleasing balance and proportionality. Symmetry is found in classical art and architecture. Faces, leaves, and butterfly wings are generally balanced and symmetrical. People normally feel comfortable when surrounded by order and symmetry. Having a place for everything and seeing everything in its place can be reasonably satisfying. But, life has a way with messing with our neatly ordered garages, kitchens, and office desks. Most people are okay with this.

Some people with OCD crave order and symmetry all the time in everything. They are not satisfied or comfortable until certain things are done or ordered correctly, precisely, or "just so." Their concerns vary; some arrange books or cupboards; others rewrite letters or numbers. However, they share the same feeling of discomfort when things don't feel right, "just so," or complete.

In this chapter, we describe the common concerns of those with what we call "Just So" OCD. Then we tell you how to change your thinking surrounding this type of OCD. Changing your *thinking* helps you prepare for changing your *behaviors*. After you've changed your thoughts and behaviors, you're likely to start feeling better, even when things are out of place.

Being Driven to Make Things "Just So" All the Time

"Just So" OCD frequently begins in childhood. You can see elements of this issue in many normal childhood activities. Lots of children arrange their toys in special ways, enjoy reading the same book over and over again, and have bedtime rituals. Usually, these patterns, which help provide a needed sense of security and comfort, slowly fade over the years. As children grow and mature, they recognize that the comfort and security they experienced was not created by the patterns, but rather by parents and caregivers. But in some children, either because of biology or learning (see Chapters 4 and 5), OCD takes over.

For children with "Just So" OCD, the urge to find symmetry, order, and feelings of "just so" increases over time instead of fading. Their lives begin to fill with distress and rituals designed to make them feel better. This pattern can continue for a lifetime.

"Just So" OCD often exists along with other forms of OCD. For example, someone may believe that arranging the closet "just so" is necessary to please God. This driven, excessive need to please God stems from Shaming OCD that focuses on religious issues (see Chapter 14). Another person may arrange the closet just so in the belief that it's necessary in order to keep the family safe. In this case, the person has Doubting and Checking OCD along with the "just so" type. Finally, people with *just* the "Just So" OCD may arrange their closets because they feel driven to have their clothes "just so."

Unfortunately, research is currently lacking for the treatment of "Just So" OCD. In part, this neglect in literature appears to be due to the fact that many of those with this type of OCD don't seem as interested in changing as those afflicted with other OCD types. They view their need for symmetry and order as the right way to be. This belief may be held in spite of family and friends complaining, teasing, or even getting angry with the "just so" behaviors.

Yet, some folks with this problem do want to do something about their OCD. They may want to change because they realize how much time "just so" takes or because they are responding to others' complaints. If the desire to change describes you or someone you care about, read on. On the other hand, if you have this type of OCD and don't want to do anything about it, maybe you'll find what comes next in this chapter interesting.

Most obsessions and compulsions are not welcome by the person who has them. The technical term for this offensiveness is *ego-dystonic*. On the other hand, *ego-syntonic* refers to the feeling that one's obsessions and compulsions are appropriate and merely reflect one's values. Symmetry, or "Just So" OCD, is often ego-*syn*tonic.

In the rest of this section, we look at the two primary expressions of "Just So" OCD:

- ✔ **Arranging:** Seeking order
- ✔ **Repeating:** Seeking perfection

Shifting gears and symmetry

The symptoms of OCD are quite varied. Some people with OCD have obsessions and compulsions about harming others; others collect useless junk, while others have obsessions and compulsions requiring order and symmetry. These different forms of OCD may involve different areas of the brain.

A study reported in the 2006 journal *Neuropsychology* looked at the way people with and without OCD were able to shift their attention from one thing to another. They also looked at how types of OCD differently affected the performance of tasks that required this ability. Shifting attention or set shifting involves

responding to information from the environment by changing your focus. Set shifting is involved when you learn from your mistakes or solve problems through trial and error.

What they found was that people with the need for order and symmetry, what we call "Just So" OCD, had more trouble than others shifting attention. So how might this play out in real life? People with trouble shifting attention may have difficulty changing from one activity to another, multi-tasking, using feedback, or solving problems. And perhaps some of them have trouble shifting away from the need for order, symmetry, and "just so."

Enforcing order and symmetry on life

If you suffer with the *arranging expression* of "Just So" OCD, you are focused on arranging the environment in certain ways. You want particular things around you to be perfectly symmetrical, smooth, clean, or orderly. This need for order can take on any number of areas. Here are a few examples:

- ✔ **Books:** Some people spend hours each day ordering their books by size and shape. Others consume time by precisely measuring the distance between the edge of the shelf and each book. Some order books alphabetically by author or, oddly enough, the first word that appears in the book. Still others dust each book every day or arrange them by color. There's no end to the permutations of these arrangements, but everyone with this concern feels driven to arrange books in some special, personally meaningful way.

- ✔ **Carpet fibers and fringe:** This concern is surprisingly common. More than a few folks straighten the fringe on their rugs many times each day. You can imagine how easily a few pieces of fringe can be disturbed by a cat, the wind, or people walking around. Others repeatedly vacuum and pick at any stray fibers. They want each and every strand of carpet to stand up straight and in the same way. Yikes.

✔ **Food:** People with this focus arrange food in their refrigerators, cupboards, and pantries in various and sundry ways. The arrangement may be alphabetical or by size, shape, color, nutritional content, or weight. Another food-related compulsion is the need to arrange food on the plate or table in very specific ways — we aren't talking about a "nice presentation" here, but a precise, rigid pattern based on unusual rules. And after sitting down to eat, some people feel driven to eat in a fixed pattern — again, based on arbitrary ideas about what constitutes the right order.

✔ **Money:** Of course, many people like to arrange their wallets with the ones, fives, tens, and twenties in consecutive order. However, people with this OCD concern repeatedly arrange, smooth, and check their bills. Sometimes they even iron them each day. Others keep their change on their dressers in peculiar, precise, patterns.

✔ **Other stuff:** As we note earlier, the particular items that must be arranged, straightened, ordered, or made "just so" varies greatly. Pictures on the wall must be perfectly level and aligned. The hangers in the closet must be evenly spaced (see the picture on this book cover). Clothes, whether on hangers or in drawers, may have to be arranged in special orders by color, function, or texture. Items on a desk may need to be arranged in idiosyncratic ways. Shoes must shine without the slightest scuff.

Speaking of symmetry, we just bought new blinds that come down from the top or up from the bottom. Have you ever tried to make blinds perfectly even with each other? Across one room, we have eight blinds to line up. Enough to drive you crazy even if you don't have diagnosed OCD!

In order for concerns about symmetry and keeping things "just so" to be considered OCD, they must consume a lot of time and interfere with your life significantly. Many people have a dollop of fussiness without having OCD.

Trying to get it right by repeating and redoing

If you suffer with the *repeating expression* of "Just So" OCD, you focus on the need to repeat and redo actions until they feel just right. There are no objective criteria for what constitutes "just so" because it's based on a purely subjective feeling. If you ask people with this type of OCD how they know when something is "just so," they're likely to answer, "I just know; I can feel it." Sometimes the repeating and redoing goes on for hours. Examples of the repeating and redoing expression include:

✔ **Dressing:** This routine involves dressing and arranging one's clothes over and over again, until it all feels and looks just right. Picking just the right clothes can be part of this pattern, but the person may not know what's going to feel just right until everything is on.

✔ **Evening up:** This issue has to do with a need for achieving a feeling of evenness. Someone with this concern may feel a need to open doors with the left hand as often as the right hand. Some people feel driven to chew their food as much on the right side of their mouth as the left side. Still others work hard to make sure that their socks come up to exactly the same height on each ankle. A few folks try to keep conversations evened up by tracking how long each person speaks and trying to match them in duration. All of these actions require lots of repeating and redoing before that perfect feeling of evenness is achieved. And, of course, the feeling doesn't last.

✔ **Reading and writing:** Reading redoing entails the need to read, reread, and reread until the person feels that the material has been completely and fully absorbed and understood. Mind you, the person probably understands the material well enough on the first read; it's just based on a "feeling." Worry about the slightest ambiguity or imperfection in one's written work can cause someone to redo his or her writing many times over. It's a darn good thing we don't suffer from this problem!

✔ **Showering or washing routines:** You may think that long cleaning rituals sound like contamination OCD (see Chapter 2). But in this case, the worry isn't so much about contamination as it is in getting things to feel right. Therefore, the person scrubs and washes different body parts in certain sequences and ways until the feeling of "just right" occurs. This process can take hours.

The list for repeating and redoing potentially goes on and on and on. We could include more items, but this feels just right.

Taking Steps to Change "Just So" OCD

Earlier in this chapter, we note that many people with the "Just So" type of OCD waffle on whether or not they want to do something about the problem — or whether they view it as a problem at all. If that description fits you, we urge you to read Chapter 6 first on the topic of overcoming OCD obstacles. That's where you find ways of exploring and possibly enhancing your motivations for change if you indeed want to consider changing. If loved ones or others around you are indicating that you may have an issue, then working with a therapist to determine your need for change may be helpful.

Assuming you do find the motivation for change, you should know that there are two primary approaches to treating "Just So" OCD:

✔ By addressing ways to change your OCD thinking

✔ By tackling your OCD behavior

We generally recommend employing both strategies for this and other types of OCD. Medication is also an option (see Chapter 11), though medications may not be quite as effective for this specific type of OCD.

Rearranging your thinking

Chapter 8 reviews many of the ways that the thinking of those with OCD becomes distorted. That distorted thinking usually worsens OCD symptoms. Interestingly, many of these thought distortions do not seem to play a large role in those plagued with the "Just So" type of OCD. Thus, those with "Just So" OCD do not tend to exaggerate risk, struggle with uncertainty, feel excessive responsibilities, or confuse their thoughts with what's real.

However, those with "Just So" OCD do have some beliefs that get them in trouble and keep them bogged down. These beliefs are about

✔ Self-image

✔ Handling difficult emotions

We discuss each one in the sections that follow.

Rethinking self-image

At some level, most of those with "Just So" OCD feel that the directives from their OCD minds are the way things and they should be. You may feel like you wouldn't be you without your OCD. Papers should be orderly, books in their place, and everything smooth, perfect, and even. And within limits, a little order does feel good.

However, if you think that just maybe your "just so" issues have gone too far, try answering the following questions:

✔ Does the time I spend making everything "just so" take away important time for other, more meaningful activities?

✔ Would I tell someone I care about that this (ensuring that everything is "just so") is a good way to spend lots of time? Would I tell them that the OCD is about who they are as a person?

Heather's example shows how pondering these questions helps motivate her to work on this problem because she begins to see her OCD as OCD and not as herself.

> **Heather** keeps a clean house. Each day, she cleans every room from top to bottom. Each dish, food item, decoration, picture, and book has its own place. All the closets in her house are organized by type of clothing and hangers are $1/2$-inch apart. Heather spends hours keeping her house clean; she rarely goes out. Her teenage children are never home because they prefer to spend time at homes where the parents are less uptight.
>
> Heather is shocked to learn that her oldest son has been arrested for shoplifting. She is required to attend family counseling. Here are the answers she comes up with concerning her belief that she just wouldn't be herself without her "Just So" OCD.

> ✔ **Does the time I spend on making everything "just so" take away important time for other, more meaningful activities?**
>
> _I'd estimate that my "Just So" OCD takes me at least a couple hours each day. If I spent just a few of those hours each week on quality time with my family, everyone would be happier. The feelings are powerful, but so is the value in trying to overcome this problem._

> ✔ **Would I tell people I care about that this (ensuring that everything is "just so") is a good way to spend lots of time? Would I tell them that the OCD is about who they are as a person?**
>
> _No way. I'd tell my friends, my husband, or my kids to do anything and everything they could to stop spending time this way. I know doing the things I do is pointless and silly. I'd tell them that spending time this way will detract from their lives, as I can see it has from mine. This OCD stuff isn't about who they are or who I am as a person; it just feels that way sometimes to me._

These questions help Heather step back a little from the directives coming out of her OCD mind. She can now see that the time she spends on her OCD costs her a lot and that she would never recommend that anyone else do what she does. She can also see that the OCD is not about who she is as a person; it's just her OCD mind talking when she thinks otherwise. She starts making progress with her "just so" behavior.

Rethinking emotional responses

You may believe that you just can't tolerate having things unfinished, incomplete, or out of order. It no doubt does _feel_ like you can't stand the feelings you have when things seem this way. If you have this problem, you likely feel unbalanced, tense, anxious, and out of it, along with a sense of urgency to bring your feelings back to "normal." Once things are back in order, you feel significant relief for a while, but the out of sorts feelings soon return. Try answering these questions about not being able to stand these feelings.

✔ Have you ever had prolonged pain from an injury, dental work, or illness? If so, were you able to stand it, and was it as difficult as your OCD urges?

✔ Do you think the urges would continue at the same intense level forever if you kept yourself from caving into them?

✔ Were there ever things in the past that you detested doing, yet found ways to tolerate? Is it possible that your "Just So" OCD urges would be similar?

Jackson's story involves a slightly different form of "Just So" OCD, and he uses these questions to help him see that he probably can stand having some uncomfortable feelings for a while.

> **Jackson** has "Just So" OCD and focuses on a variety of ordering issues as well as redoing concerns. He has very specific ways that everything on his nightstand must be lined up or he feels he cannot go to sleep. He also reads notes about his job assignment for the next day each night. However, he feels he must read and reread until he has completely understood each and every part of the assignment. He knows this reading should require about five or ten minutes, but he usually can't stop until he's read the material at least ten times — a process that takes him an hour and a half most nights. He believes that stopping his driven OCD behaviors would drive him crazy and that he simply couldn't stand going through each day any other way.

> ✔ **Have you ever had prolonged pain from an injury, dental work, or illness? If so, were you able to stand it, and was it as difficult as your OCD urges?**

> *I remember playing on my college football team. I got injured often, but once I broke my ankle in two places. It hurt for weeks while I hobbled around. I'd have to say that the pain from that injury actually felt worse than the feelings of incompleteness I have when I resist my OCD for a while.*

> ✔ **Do you think the urges would continue at the same intense level forever if you kept yourself from caving into them?**

> *It does sort of feel like they would continue forever. But now that I think about it, I can recall a few times when I resisted the urges for a few hours and the feelings actually started to come down a little. Maybe if I continued that work, the feelings would come down even more.*

> ✔ **Were there ever things in the past that you detested doing, yet found ways to tolerate? Is it possible that your "Just So" OCD urges would be similar?**
>
> *I remember that for years I absolutely hated paying bills and balancing my checkbook. I almost couldn't get myself to do it at all. It's funny, but now I don't mind those tasks. Sometimes I even look at balancing the checkbook as a challenge when it seems a little off at first. I get the point; maybe if I work really hard at it, my "Just So" OCD could be a little like my hating to pay bills and balance my checkbook. Over time, it just might get better.*

Jackson's work on these questions helps him to see that feelings can change over time. And he now realizes that he can stand all sorts of uncomfortable feelings for a while. He feels more confident that if he tolerates the discomfort, his urges will slowly but surely fade. He happens to be right.

Redoing your responses to repeating

Exposure and response prevention (ERP), described in Chapter 10, is widely considered the most effective treatment for OCD. Refer to that chapter for detailed instructions on carrying out ERP. Here we give you some sample exposure staircases for "Just So" OCD.

The example ERP staircases and hierarchies are just that — examples. The actual content for your particular staircases will vary considerably. However, these staircases can give you ideas for how to construct your own.

Many people with "Just So" OCD may need some extra support in their attempts at ERP. We suggest getting help from a mental-health professional trained in ERP.

In the sections that follow, we give you examples of ways to use ERP to address the two primary expressions of "Just So" OCD: arranging and repeating.

Applying ERP to ordering and symmetry

Sometimes, being organized and having a place for everything is pretty nice. But when this type of OCD gets out of hand, life can become pretty miserable for the person with this arranging expression and any family members who are involved. Figure 15-1 presents an example of an ERP staircase for someone with order and symmetry concerns. In simple terms, you start on the bottom stair and move up as each "step" is successfully overcome.

Leaving the house without making the bed (90 Ugh Factor Rating)
Leaving the dishes in the sink for a night (85 Ugh Factor Rating)
Stacking some of the books on the shelf vertically (80 Ugh Factor Rating)
Putting the dishes in the dishwasher in the wrong order (75 Ugh Factor Rating)
Having the food in the cupboard placed out of alphabetical order (65 Ugh Factor Rating)
Shoving some hangers in the closet together and leaving them (65 Ugh Factor Rating)
Messing up the fringe on the rug (60 Ugh Factor Rating)
Tossing the pillows on the couch and leaving them messed up (55 Ugh Factor Rating)
Leaving the newspaper out on the counter (40 Ugh Factor Rating)
Stacking the mail on the table in the hall instead of filing it immediately (35 Ugh Factor Rating)

Figure 15-1:
A staircase
for ordering
and
symmetry.

Applying ERP to repeating and redoing

Repeating and redoing can become time consuming and interfere greatly with functioning. This can be especially problematic if you are required to read or produce written products at school or work. Having to do things over and over again slows you down. Here is a sample exposure hierarchy for this type of concern. (Hierarchies are the same as staircases; the only difference is that a hierarchy is a list, whereas a staircase is the list represented in a graphic.)

✔ Writing an e-mail to a colleague without editing it (90 Ugh Factor Rating)

✔ Limiting shower to 10 minutes with washing body only once (85 Ugh Factor Rating)

✔ Brushing hair on one side three times and the other side twice (80 Ugh Factor Rating)

✔ Using only my left hand to open doors all day long (80 Ugh Factor Rating)

✔ Writing an e-mail without using spell checker (75 Ugh Factor Rating)

✔ Reading work-related material only once (70 Ugh Factor Rating)

✔ Limiting shower to 20 minutes with repeating as little as possible (60 Ugh Factor Rating)

✔ Waiting to pick my clothes until morning and giving myself only 10 minutes to make a choice and get dressed (50 Ugh Factor Rating)

✔ Reading work-related material only twice (40 Ugh Factor Rating)

✔ Writing an e-mail to a friend with only one quick edit (35 Ugh Factor Rating)

Chapter 16

Throwing Out OCD: Hoarding

In This Chapter

▶ Revealing hoarding

▶ Examining the costs of hoarding

▶ Uncluttering the hoarding mind

▶ Cleaning up hoarding behavior

*M*ost people have some sort of collection in their homes, whether it is coins, stamps, or souvenirs. But those with Hoarding OCD acquire, accumulate, and purchase in staggering proportions — while rarely throwing anything out. Their homes eventually bulge at the seams.

In this chapter, we describe the mysterious nature of Hoarding OCD. A surprising number of people with this problem are found dead, seriously ill, or injured — victims of the consequences of their hoarding, which include the creation of unsafe or unsanitary conditions. Hoarders typically hide their problem from others and, rather than seek treatment, they are discovered by family members, police, social workers, and landlords. In fact, if hoarders do seek treatment, they usually wait until about the age of 50.

Hoarding seemed almost untreatable at one time, but that has changed. Today, hoarding presents a more hopeful picture, which we share in this chapter.

Defining Hoarding OCD

Professionals are increasingly considering Hoarding OCD to be a unique type of OCD. In fact, someday hoarding may have its own special category in the manual that professionals consult for determining official diagnoses of those who have various types of emotional disorders.

Hoarding OCD differs from other types of OCD in that sufferers frequently have low motivation for change. They also seem to think differently than those with other types of OCD (see the section "Uncovering problems in thinking," later in this chapter). But for the time being, hoarding is most frequently considered a type of OCD. Besides that, it's really interesting, so we'd hate not to include it in this book!

Like other types of OCD, Hoarding OCD has an inheritable component. But whereas non-hoarding OCD, like brown eyes, is a dominant trait, Hoarding OCD, like blue eyes, appears to involve a recessive gene. Hoarding also involves slightly different areas of the brain than other types of OCD (see Chapter 4). Thus, hoarding may be a biologically distinct type of OCD.

Describing characteristics of hoarding

So just exactly what is Hoarding OCD? Drs. Gail Steketee and Randy Frost have studied this problem for years and suggest that it has three defining characteristics:

- ✔ People accumulate huge quantities of possessions that have trivial value. At the same time, they may mix items into their piles of junk that do have value — jewelry, legal papers, and so forth. But it is the piles of items without real value that define this characteristic.

- ✔ Homes become so cluttered that the living areas can no longer be used for their original purposes (such as dining, watching television, bathing, or cooking).

- ✔ Those who acquire these possessions either feel very distressed by the effects of their hoarding or they show signs of impaired ability to work or carry out their lives in a normal manner.

Note that the third characteristic involves either distress *or* impairment — thus, one can have Hoarding OCD without actually feeling distressed about it. And not feeling concerned about the problem is quite common. The lack of distress is surprising, though, because Hoarding OCD causes substantial disability.

Hoarders usually begin acquiring things in adolescence. The accumulation of junk gradually increases over time. Mind you, lots of people collect things — sometimes far more than they need. But we're not talking about coin and stamp collections here. And we're not talking about an overstuffed garage, stacks of paper on your desk, or overflowing closets. If that were the case, far too many people would qualify as hoarders.

The tragic hoarding of the Collyer brothers

One of the strangest and saddest stories of hoarding involves the reclusive brothers Langley and Homer Collyer. Their story was covered by newspapers throughout the world. Sons of a doctor and an opera singer, the Collyer brothers inherited a 12-room townhouse in New York City. They had both graduated from Columbia University. While Homer worked for a time as a lawyer, Langley became increasingly reclusive. At some point, Homer became blind, apparently from various health issues. He was unable to work, and was totally dependent on Langley for his care. They filled their home with newspapers, magazines, broken furniture, thousands of books, 14 pianos, and junk. They kept their doors locked. Eventually utilities were turned off because of unpaid bills.

The brothers became increasingly paranoid and set booby traps so that anyone breaking in would be crushed by the rubble. Someone called the police in 1947 because of a horrible smell. A single officer was unable to get in — he faced a solid wall of broken furniture and newspapers. It took a squad of seven men to finally get through and then discover Homer dead from cardiac arrest, likely caused by malnutrition and dehydration. It took several weeks to find Langley. Police speculated that he'd been attempting to deliver food and water to his invalid brother when he was crushed by one of his own booby traps. More than 100 tons of hoarded stuff were cleared from the four-story building, which had to be demolished.

We're talking about useless junk piled in mounds so high that space is no longer useable or livable. See Figure 16-1 for a picture of a typical hoarder's living area. And that picture is not as bad as it gets. To understand how bad conditions can become, read on.

Seeing the consequences of hoarding

The consequences of having Hoarding OCD can be quite harsh and severe. As noted earlier in this chapter, some hoarders are found dead or injured as a result of malnutrition or poor home safety conditions. The clutter and resulting unsanitary conditions can result in high risk for:

- ✔ Chronic breathing problems
- ✔ Fire
- ✔ Gas or water leaks
- ✔ Insect and rodent infestations
- ✔ Tripping and falling

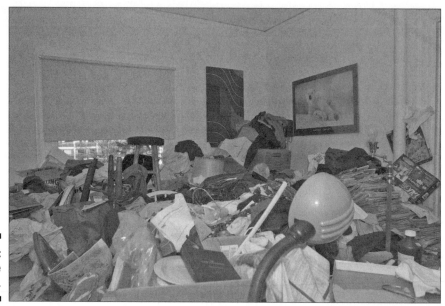

Figure 16-1:
An example
of hoarding.

Hoarders eventually stop inviting people to their homes. The stove may stop working, but they fear calling an appliance repairman because someone entering their house might alert health or welfare officials. Even a pizza delivery could result in a report to the police.

Sometimes homes suffer structural damage because of leaky water faucets. Insects or rodents feed on rotting food. Feces or urine often accumulate from rodents, large numbers of animals, or the unusual act of hoarding one's own excrement. If someone turns a hoarder in, officials may hospitalize or evict him. Cleanup when hoarders are discovered can be extremely costly — and is usually covered by tax dollars.

Perhaps not surprisingly, hoarders tend to be single. They develop an attachment to "stuff" rather than people. Those who do marry have a high divorce rate.

Those afflicted with Hoarding OCD often show profound signs of various other disabilities. They have an increased occurrence of depression, anxiety, and most other emotional problems. They miss more work than most people, and they often have many other health problems.

If you or someone you care about has Hoarding OCD, there's a good chance that another emotional problem such as depression or anxiety is also present. If you think that may be the case for you, please consult a mental-health professional. We also recommend reading two other books authored by us and published by Wiley: *Overcoming Anxiety For Dummies* and *Depression For Dummies*.

Piling up pets

Animal hoarding is a strange but relatively common type of Hoarding OCD. Over a thousand new cases are discovered each year. Yet, most animal hoarders go undetected, so we really don't know how many exist. Animal hoarders accumulate large numbers of animals, fail to provide adequate care, seem unaware of the poor health of their animals, and are oblivious to the horrible state of their environment. Many animal hoarders keep dead animals in their homes, don't attempt to clean up their waste, and avoid contact with other people. Animal hoarders usually live alone, lack basic sanitation, and are very resistant to treatment. After being caught, most animal hoarders immediately return to collecting. Here are four examples:

✔ A New Jersey couple living in a multimillion-dollar, 12,000-square-foot house was charged with hundreds of counts of animal cruelty. A delivery man contacted police after smelling an intense odor through an open window. The home was filled with boxes and bags of dead cats. Sixty-two sick cats were confiscated as well as six dogs. More cats were living between the walls of the home.

✔ A New Mexico woman was found dead of natural causes in her home. Some of the 33 cats and 4 dogs were feeding off of her body. There was at least a foot of filth and feces in every room.

✔ In Tucson, Arizona, authorities discovered 800 dogs (the majority Chihuahuas) in a triple-wide mobile home. In addition, 80 parrots inhabited the premises. Not surprisingly, the animals were in poor health.

✔ A psychiatrist was arrested when police discovered that not only was she hoarding cats and dogs at her home, but she rented a hotel room for 21 cats. Tragically, most of the animals found in these environments are euthanized.

Uncovering problems in thinking

Hoarders show some unusual types of thinking and a heightened, intense attachment to objects and possessions. Other types of OCD thinking tend to focus on doubts and uncertainty (see Chapter 5). The minds of hoarders are relatively less dominated by doubts and uncertainty. They work hard to maintain control over their collections and feel quite upset if anyone threatens to clean things up or throw anything away.

The kinds of things hoarders collect usually appear extremely illogical to others. But hoarders feel strongly that their collections are necessary, reasonable, and important. For example, a female hoarder may save an 8-year-old Christmas catalog from a department store because she likes one of the dresses, but wants to wait until she loses 50 pounds before she buys it. If someone points out that the store probably doesn't carry that dress any longer, she replies that they're likely to carry other items she'd like since they had that dress before. And she doesn't want to forget about the store. Never mind that that Christmas catalog probably lies under 4 feet of other papers, mail, bills, and miscellaneous junk.

Hoarders usually demonstrate deficits in the way their brains think and process information. Several of these cognitive problems have been identified through psychological testing and research. They include:

- ✔ **Attention:** Hoarders tend to be distracted easily by inconsequential sights, sounds, and events. For example, they'll zero in on the color or shininess of a piece of paper and save it because of how it looks rather than what it contains. They struggle to focus on what's truly important.

- ✔ **Categorizing:** Those with Hoarding OCD have profound trouble figuring out how to file things in a logical manner. They struggle to determine reasonable categories. Organizational strategies as simple as creating piles for unpaid bills versus paid bills or important legal papers versus interesting newspaper articles are not easy concepts for them to grasp.

- ✔ **Decision-making:** Hoarders have great trouble making even trivial decisions. They may ponder whether to drink out of the red glass or the blue glass. They can't decide what to eat. And they certainly can't decide what's truly important to keep or throw away.

- ✔ **Memory:** Hoarders can remember things, but they lack confidence in their memories. They tend to rely on the visual mode of remembering. For example, a man may be able to tell you that a given paper lies about "two feet down in a pile next to his sofa." He feels that he needs visual cues in order to remember. Putting things out of sight in a filing cabinet would feel like putting them out of mind.

Assembling uncommon collections

Hoarders hoard lots of different things. Their collections have personal meaning to them as individuals. Some hoarders save objects that may have small, possible — but dubious — future utility. Others report wanting to save things because they have sentimental value. They fear losing the slightest bit of conceivably useful information. In addition, they can't stand the idea of wasting anything, so they hold onto everything. Other objects are saved because they look interesting, beautiful, or unusual. Hoarders buy, find, or steal their collectibles in dumpsters, the mail, on the Internet, stores, or on the street — pretty much anywhere. Each hoarder's collection is unique, but some of the most common collections include:

- ✔ Books and articles
- ✔ Bottles, cans, bottle caps
- ✔ Cats, dogs, or other animals
- ✔ Cleaning supplies

- Clothes, shoes, jewelry
- Coins, money (not rare collectibles)
- Food items
- Mail — junk, bills, or catalogs
- Matches, lint, aluminum foil, gum wrappers
- Newspapers, magazines, or comic books
- Paper bags, plastic bags, or cardboard boxes
- Photographs, mementos, souvenirs
- Screws, nails, tacks, hooks
- Staples, paper clips, rubber bands, pens, pencils
- Tissue paper, wrapping paper, greeting cards
- Tools, batteries, parts of appliances and cars
- Toys
- Urine, feces, saliva, blood
- Yarn, string, cloth

Hoarders find comfort in these virtually useless collections. They even derive their identity from their collections. But at the same time, they realize that their possessions may be excessive and are embarrassed when others discover their piles of stuff.

People who collect items of significance in terms of either monetary or sentimental value, such as rare coins, license plates, wine bottle corks, rare or interesting stamps, matchbook covers, and so on, are not necessarily suffering from Hoarding OCD — even when their family members see their collections as silly or annoying. True collectors do not allow their collections to overtake their lives. They tend to maintain their collections in well-organized containers. They enjoy talking about and showing off their collections with other like-minded folks. They're not embarrassed about their collections, but feel pride instead. Although their collections may take up some space, they do not overflow halls, block doorways, or envelop appliances.

Treating Hoarding OCD

Until recently, treatments for Hoarding OCD had a dismal track record. Psychotherapies such as exposure and response prevention (ERP) did not seem to be as effective for this type of OCD as they had been for other types of OCD. And medications, at best, have demonstrated a minimal impact on the problem (see Chapter 11 for more information about medications and OCD).

Fortunately, the picture is improving. It now appears that treatments encompassing strategies for improving both thinking and behavior as they relate to Hoarding OCD appear to work pretty well, although they require more time (often close to a year of fairly intense work) than treatments for other types of OCD. So you may need to be a little patient, but if you have Hoarding OCD, you can probably improve your living situation significantly.

If you have severe Hoarding OCD and have lost major portions of your living space to your various collections, you should seek professional help. We also strongly recommend that you check out the *Compulsive Hoarding and Acquiring Workbook* by Drs. Gail Steketee and Randy Frost (Oxford University Press) to use in collaboration with your therapist. The book presents a comprehensive treatment approach for Hoarding OCD.

The information in this chapter may prove helpful to you if you suffer from mild to modest hoarding problems, and may even help you get started if you have more serious difficulty. Interested family and friends may also find this material informative. Additionally, millions of people suffer not from true Hoarding OCD (see "Defining Hoarding OCD," earlier in this chapter), but from definite issues with over-accumulation of junk. Thus, even we have learned how to toss out many unworn clothes from our closets by using some of the rules discussed in this section.

Tackling your OCD behavior involves four areas, which we discuss in the following sections:

- ✔ Weighing costs and benefits
- ✔ Challenging hoarding beliefs
- ✔ Recognizing what is essential
- ✔ Learning how to organize

If you are a friend or family member of someone with Hoarding OCD, please realize that pressure typically only makes things worse. You can suggest that someone with this problem consider conducting a cost/benefit analysis similar to what follows, but aggressive confrontation is not advisable.

Tallying up the costs and benefits

If you have Hoarding OCD, you usually have trouble with many decisions, and the decision to seek treatment is an especially difficult one. Ambivalence concerning change is quite common. You may be able to resolve that ambivalence with a cost/benefit analysis.

A cost/benefit analysis is pretty much what it sounds like. First you review all the possible benefits that your hoarding entails — every way in which you believe that hoarding improves your life or feelings in some manner. Then you list every imaginable cost — all the ways in which you believe that hoarding may negatively impact your life and emotions. Finally, you reflect on these two lists and ask yourself which one feels most persuasive to you. The following steps explain how to proceed. See Appendix A for a blank form you can use to conduct your own cost/benefit analysis.

1. **On a piece of paper or in a notebook, designate space for the creation of two columns plus a block of space after the columns for writing a summary.**

   Label the first column "Benefits." Label the second column "Costs." Label the block of space "My Reflections."

2. **Under "Benefits," write down all the imaginable advantages of hoarding and the ways in which it feels useful to you.**

   Include how it makes things easier or better and/or how it may help you feel better, safer, or more secure.

3. **Under "Costs," write down all the ways that your hoarding may hold you back, cost you something, or cause you harm.**

   Don't forget to include how hoarding may cause negative emotions, such as shame or embarrassment.

4. **Under "My Reflections," summarize what you can deduce from your cost/benefit analysis.**

   Which argument seems more formidable — the costs or the benefits of your hoarding?

Matt's example in the following story demonstrates how someone with Hoarding OCD feels horribly ambivalent about whether or not he wants to seek treatment. A cost/benefit analysis helps him find the answer.

Matt hoards lots of things — tools, car parts, batteries, nails, screws, paper clips, rubber bands, scrap metal, wood of almost any type, old shingles, broken glass, string, wire, and scraps of plastic. He is a handyman and never wants to find himself without exactly the right item for any project he undertakes. His collections overflow his entire garage and recently have overtaken his living room and kitchen from floor to ceiling. He also feels attached to all of these "treasures." He picks up a copy of *OCD For Dummies* and decides to fill out a cost/benefit analysis for his hoarding, as shown in Table 16-1.

Table 16-1	Cost/Benefit Analysis of Matt's Hoarding
Benefits	**Costs**
I never find myself without the right tool or part.	I can't always find what I need in all of these piles.
I'm not embarrassed by not having what I need.	I am deeply embarrassed to have anyone see my home.
I never run out of things.	I can barely get through my house lately.
I save time by not having to run to the store for every little thing I need.	I spend huge amounts of time going through all my stuff in order to remember what I have and where it is.
Throwing things away makes me feel nervous.	I'm starting to fear that if someone sees my house, they might call me in to the health department.
Having all this stuff makes me feel more like a true handyman.	I can't have friends over because they'd think that I'm crazy.
	I could never date anyone seriously because of how my house looks.
	Some of the piles are so tall that I'm afraid they could fall and hurt my cat.

My Reflections
Wow. This is difficult. I don't want to start throwing things away. But I can see from this exercise that my hoarding is really starting to cost me a lot. It's getting out of hand. I'd feel horrible if my cat got hurt by a pile of junk falling on her. And if I ever do run out of something, it wouldn't be horrible to go and buy it. Also, I miss having people over. I want to feel like a normal person again.

As a result of weighing the costs against the benefits, Matt chooses to go ahead and seek treatment. Besides, he knows he can always stop the treatment if he just can't stand it. He believes that treatment looks worth undertaking. Now he's ready for the next step in dealing with his Hoarding OCD — challenging his beliefs about hoarding.

Questioning beliefs about hoarding

If you have Hoarding OCD, you probably carry around some interesting beliefs in your mind that give you reasons for continuing your hoarding. Following, we list a few of the most important of these beliefs. Then we give you a list of questions that you can use to challenge them. With practice, you're likely to find that these beliefs start losing their ability to control your hoarding behavior. Two additional beliefs frequently associated with hoarding (perfectionism and being excessively responsible) can be found in Chapter 8.

- ✔ **Hoarding gives me comfort.** This concern focuses on the discomfort hoarders usually feel when they throw possessions out. They feel they cannot stand to let go of their stuff.

- ✔ **I need to see things in order to remember them.** This belief comes about because many of those with Hoarding OCD don't trust their memories. They believe that they must keep things in sight or they will forget them.

- ✔ **My collections define who I am.** Those with this hoarding belief think that their possessions define who they are. They worry that tossing things out will cause them to lose part of their identity.

- ✔ **My possessions have real value.** This compulsive credo tells the person that all possessions have value even if that value is small. If you have fallen prey to this idea, you're probably capable of assigning value to almost anything. Thus, losing something feels like it could be calamitous.

We recommend that you review these beliefs and figure out which ones (if any) apply to you. If one or more do (and they likely will!), then subject your beliefs to further scrutiny by asking yourself the following questions:

- ✔ Can I think of any evidence or past experiences that might contradict this belief?

- ✔ Can I think of anything illogical about this belief and consider a more logical alternative? Would other people see this belief as illogical?

- ✔ Would I be willing to consider testing this belief out by throwing things away (see the later section "Developing New Strategies for Keeping and Tossing Things") and seeing whether my fears actually come true?

Teresa suffers from the common hoarding belief that her possessions have real value. The following example shows you how she uses the preceding questions to evaluate her belief.

Teresa has hoarded magazines, newspapers, books, flyers, and ads for years. She also accumulates cleaning supplies at an astounding rate. Her apartment is filled to the bursting point. She goes to a therapist after she discovers herself unable to use her dining room to eat or her kitchen to cook. Her therapist asks her to confront her belief about the value of her possessions. Here are her responses:

✔ **Can you think of any evidence or past experiences that might contradict this belief?**

Well, I have to admit that I haven't used very many of the things I have accumulated. I'd guess that about 98 percent of the items in my piles never actually get used, so their real value must be a little questionable.

✔ **Can you think of anything illogical about this belief and consider a more logical alternative? Would other people see this belief as illogical?**

I know that other people see my belief as illogical. I guess I do know in my head that no one would buy these papers, so they must be less valuable than I feel they are.

✔ **Would you be willing to consider testing this belief out by throwing things away and seeing whether your fears actually come true?**

It's gotten to the point where I think I have to try. I fear losing these things and the effects of tossing them out. But I guess I don't actually know that any disasters will occur by eliminating these things. So, yes, it's time to take a run at this thing and confront my beliefs head on.

Tackling thoughts that fuel accumulating

Many folks with Hoarding OCD acquire their piles by buying or searching for huge quantities of stuff. If you tend to pursue the procurement of possessions endlessly, the problem may be related to difficulty in distinguishing between needs and wants. We suggest that you ask yourself these questions prior to making almost any purchase:

✔ Do I actually have the time to deal with this purchase (in relation to books, magazines, camera equipment, and anything else that requires time, study, or involvement)?

✔ Do most people have this item and consider it essential?

✔ Will I feel substantially happier three months from now if I obtain this item?

✔ Will this item enhance the quality of my life significantly?

✔ Would not having this thing put my safety, health, or well-being in danger?

We suspect that answering these questions will help you see that many of the things you find yourself desiring or wanting are actually of limited importance to your life. And because almost everything consumes space, resources, and/or time, perhaps you're better off without many of these things. Distinguishing between wants and needs helps prepare you for the later section, "Developing New Strategies for Keeping and Tossing Things."

Learning to organize

This final hoarding rethinking strategy also helps you prepare for tackling your hoarding behavior. Because those with Hoarding OCD frequently struggle with organization, we recommend that you compile a list of categories for your possessions. Then go through each category and make a decision about where you want to keep items in that category. For example, keeping canned foods in your kitchen pantry makes sense.

We recommend that you make a list of 20 or 30 categories for your stuff. Table 16-2 provides some ideas for these categories, but you're free to come up with your own list as long as it makes sense.

Table 16-2	Sample Categories for Your Stuff	
Clothes and shoes	Bills	Nostalgia, souvenirs, and family pictures
Books and magazines	Legal papers	Fresh food
Canned food	Glassware	Silverware and utensils
Pots and pans	Cleaning supplies	Dishes
Sheets and towels	Games and toys	Toiletries
Office supplies	Garden tools	Nails, screws, washers, nuts, bolts, and such
Plastic bags and storage containers	CDs and DVDs	Lawn chemicals and pesticides

Don't forget to note where you plan to store all the items in each category. Keep this list handy so you know where things are without having to go through all your piles!

You may also find it useful to develop your organization skills further by reading *Organizing For Dummies* by Eileen Roth (Wiley).

Developing New Strategies for Keeping and Tossing Things

Behavioral techniques for Hoarding OCD start with setting specific goals and then slowly moving forward, one at a time. One reason that hoarders often resist treatment is because they worry that someone's going to come by with a dumpster during the first session. But the idea behind exposure and response prevention (ERP), the most commonly used treatment, is to start with tasks that are not unbearable and build up tolerance. In this section, we give you some ideas on how to do that.

Before you attempt ERP, refer to the complete, step-by-step directions we provide in Chapter 10.

Resisting accumulating

Figure 16-2 illustrates an exposure staircase that involves resisting accumulating. If a hoarder keeps getting more stuff, the problem becomes pretty daunting to solve in a hurry. Some people with Hoarding OCD accumulate by not throwing out junk mail, newspapers, or trash. Others accumulate largely through buying things compulsively. The staircase in Figure 16-2 deals with the latter. See Figure 16-3 in the section "Doing a real cleanup" for an illustration of an exposure staircase that deals with tossing things out. Your staircases will contain different items and ratings — ours are intended to give you an idea of how to proceed.

If you have trouble going into stores, flea markets, or surfing the Internet without buying something, ask yourself the following questions: "Do I really need this?" "Do I already have this?" "Will I use this?" "Would I get sick or die without this?" "Am I buying this just to make myself feel better?"

Figure 16-2:
Hoarding
OCD
exposure
staircase:
Resisting
accumu-
lating.

Spending 1 hour in a dollar store without buying anything (90 Ugh Factor Rating)
Watching the shopping channel for 1 hour without buying anything (85 Ugh Factor Rating)
Stopping at my favorite used clothing store and picking up only one piece of clothing (80 Ugh Factor Rating)
Canceling subscriptions to magazines (or journals) I don't read (75 Ugh Factor Rating)
Going to the dollar store and buying only 1 thing (65 Ugh Factor Rating)
Callling the number on the back of two catalogs and telling them to take me off the list (50 Ugh Factor Rating)
Stopping at my favorite used clothing store and only buying two pieces of clothing (40 Ugh Factor Rating)
Looking at eBay for 30 minutes without buying anything (40 Ugh Factor Rating)
Getting three bills to be sent by e-mail and paid electronically to reduce paper (30 Ugh Factor Rating)
Not printing paper copies of every e-mail (30 Ugh Factor Rating)

Imagining tossing stuff out

Some exposure hierarchies can be done in the imagination. Starting with an imaginary hierarchy can help warm you up for a real life exposure hierarchy, which you'll need to do next. For most people, a therapist or a trained coach needs to be present to assist in the exercise. The assisting person can ask questions, add details, and keep track of the time and the Ugh Factor Ratings. The following example gives you an idea of some possible steps for this type of exposure hierarchy.

✔ Imagine throwing out all my newspapers (90 Ugh Factor Rating)

✔ Imagine giving away my duplicate tools (85 Ugh Factor Rating)

✔ Think about how I would feel throwing away some of my children's drawings from elementary school (80 Ugh Factor Rating)

✔ Describe in detail what my bedroom closet looks like and what is in it (75 Ugh Factor Rating)

✔ Think about missing important articles if I cancel my subscriptions (65 Ugh Factor Rating)

✔ Imagine sending three bags of clothes to a charity (50 Ugh Factor Rating)

✔ Imagine filling a box with books and taking them to the library (40 Ugh Factor Rating)

✔ Think about going through papers and discarding the ones not on the "What to Save" list (40 Ugh Factor Rating)

✔ Imagine what it would be like to pay all the bills electronically and not have paper records (30 Ugh Factor Rating)

✔ Imagine throwing away Christmas cards from years ago (30 Ugh Factor Rating)

Doing a real cleanup

The biggest challenge is actually sorting, giving away, and discarding things. Just imagining the job often causes anxiety. The task of cleaning a house stuffed with stuff can be overwhelming. Therefore, breaking the tasks into small steps and tackling the easier areas first are very important.

Before you start your own cleanup, decide what you'll do with your items — list which items you'll throw away, give to charity, sell, recycle, give to a friend, and put in storage. You must make a decision. Not making a decision is making a decision to keep hoarding.

The exposure staircase in Figure 16-3 can provide you with some ideas on how to approach the process of cleaning up, but the staircase you create should be consistent with your own hoarding habits.

What papers to keep

Regardless of whether you have a problem with hoarding, there are lots of papers that have to be kept and filed in a lifetime. The IRS says that if you don't file a tax return or you file a fraudulent tax return, there's no limit to how long they can come after you. So keep those records of your fraudulent activity forever. Hmmm, hopefully that situation doesn't apply to you. But the IRS says that if you filed a return but forgot to report a quarter of your income or if you claimed a loss from a worthless security (but it wasn't clearly fraudulent), they have seven years to challenge you. So keeping your tax-related records for seven years is probably a good idea. For most people, the IRS says that tax records need to be kept for three years. That's how long the IRS has to come after you for typical audits or challenges. But if you like to play it safe and you aren't a crook, we suggest maintaining tax records for seven years.

Keep certificates and papers related to birth, marriage, divorce (and settlement agreements), adoptions, custody, citizenship, military service, wills, advance directives, current passports, social security, employment records, and death in safe places permanently. House- and car-related documents (such as ownership papers, deeds, and contracts) should be kept while you own the property and until the tax consequences have been addressed. For example, if you sell a home and claim a tax deduction, you need to keep the papers three years past the time you file your tax return (unless you do something fraudulent — then keep the papers forever, but again, we don't really recommend fraud).

Stocks, bonds, bank accounts, certificates of deposit, insurance policies, and securities should be kept during your ownership or for up to seven years for tax purposes. Cancelled checks that have no relation to taxes can be tossed after three years. Pay stubs can be thrown out at the end of each year after you've compared them to your W-2. Throw out credit card slips and sales receipts after 30 days unless there are applicable warranties or tax implications.

Other paper (or video) documentation that should be stored in a safe place includes a list of all the valuables in your home, such as jewelry, appliances, art, and so on. You should also develop a list of contacts (family, attorney, physician) that you can leave with a trusted friend should anything happen to you.

When you begin working on your exposure staircase, don't try to do too much in one day. Regularly working for short periods of time is better than working until exhaustion. Plan to work about an hour or two on sorting, throwing away, and storing items. Then take the rest of the day off to do something pleasant (not getting more things). Keep at this until you can reclaim your life.

Consider writing out some reminders on index cards to carry with you when you are sorting, discarding, or storing, for example, "I must donate, throw away, or store," "I have never used this," "People are more important than things," and "I will benefit from living a simpler life." Let these messages become mantras.

REMEMBER

OCD Hoarding is challenging to treat. Most people need the help of an experienced, well-trained mental-health professional to successfully overcome it.

Figure 16-3:
Hoarding
OCD
exposure
staircase:
Tossing
for real.

Sorting through my boxes of sentimental items and throwing out 90% of them (90 Ugh Factor Rating)

Throwing away my soccer trophies (85 Ugh Factor Rating)

Getting rid of all but a few office supplies that I will definitely use in the next six months (85 Ugh Factor Rating)

Discarding all my magazines that are older than two months (80 Ugh Factor Rating)

Getting rid of all but two sets of sheets for each bed (75 Ugh Factor Rating)

Giving all of the clothes in my closet that I haven't worn in two years to charity (75 Ugh Factor Rating)

Throwing away all my old college papers (65 Ugh Factor Rating)

Throwing away articles that I keep because I think I might want to read them later (60 Ugh Factor Rating)

Cleaning out the linen closet and keeping three sets of towels for each bathroom (50 Ugh Factor Rating)

Getting rid of old novels that I probably won't read again (40 Ugh Factor Rating)

Going through two boxes of papers and discarding the ones not on the "What to Save" list (40 Ugh Factor Rating)

Paying all the bills electronically and not having paper records (30 Ugh Factor Rating)

Throwing away Christmas cards from years ago (30 Ugh Factor Rating)

Chapter 17

Shrinking Superstitious OCD

. . . .

In This Chapter

▶ Believing in magic

▶ Examining some typical superstitions

▶ Overcoming superstitions

. . . .

God bless you! Gesundheit (which is German for "good health")! These phrases are examples of the custom of giving a blessing to others after they sneeze. Most people say something when in the company of a sneezer, even if they aren't sure why. Such responses to sneezing, like many superstitions, probably have some origins that make a little sense.

The expression "God bless you" may have begun during the bubonic plague in Europe. Sneezing could be the first sign of an illness that often led to death. The blessing was an attempt to stop the disease or provide some spiritual comfort if, in fact, the sneezer was infected. Other beliefs about sneezing include that when someone sneezes, the soul tries to escape, the heart stops, or the devil tries to inhabit the body. What we really know is that sneezing causes zillions of germs to spew out of your nose at about 100 miles an hour!

In this chapter, we discuss Superstitious OCD. Lots of people have superstitions. We tell you the difference between "normal" beliefs, superstitions, and OCD superstitions. We discuss the most common superstitions associated with Superstitious OCD, and we give you techniques for challenging Superstitious OCD thinking and behavior.

Seeing When Superstitions Constitute OCD

A popular old song asks the question, "Do you believe in magic?" You probably base most of your beliefs on what you observe, what you can prove, and what you have been taught. So you observe that the sky is blue, you can prove that apples fall to the ground, and you have been taught that Abraham Lincoln was the president of the United States during the Civil War.

You've probably heard that some people consider the number 13 to be associated with bad luck. Do you believe that? If you do, then what do you base your belief on? If you think about it, you can't observe, prove, or base a belief that the number 13 is connected to bad luck on any real or factual evidence. When a belief is disconnected from any proof or facts, it is very likely a superstition.

Maybe the number 13 makes you a bit uncomfortable, but you really don't live most of your life thinking about the number 13. If that's the case, your superstition about the number doesn't interfere with your life. Thus, you have a superstition, but it's not Superstitious OCD.

If you have Superstitious OCD and view 13 as something to be avoided, you may refuse to go outside on the 13th day of each month. You may feel compelled to avoid looking at the number 13 or refuse to exit the elevator onto the 13th floor. You may find yourself avoiding groups of 13 people at meetings or restaurants. You strongly believe that the number 13 must be avoided or it will in some way hurt you or people you care about. You may struggle to get through this paragraph because of all the number 13s that appear in it. We thought about making this Chapter 13, but decided not to take the risk!

The difference between general superstition and Superstitious OCD is that OCD consumes your mind and steals significant time from enjoying your life. Think of a continuum of belief. At one end is not taking something too seriously (like bad luck associated with the number 13); at the other end is believing in something wholeheartedly despite a lack of evidence or experience — and then taking time-consuming actions to avoid the superstition.

Those with Superstitious OCD have unwanted *obsessions* — thoughts, images, or urges — about their superstition. They also have *compulsions* — mental rituals or patterns of actions — that they perform in order to neutralize or decrease the discomfort of the obsession.

Various types of OCD overlap with each other. Seeing elements of Superstitious OCD associated with other types of OCD is particularly common. However, we present Superstitious OCD separately because some people suffer primarily from this type of OCD and show few or no signs of other types of OCD.

Revealing Common OCD Superstitions and Rituals

Like most expressions of OCD, those involving superstitions are infinite and mostly unique. Obsessions and compulsions often start with common superstitions, such as thinking that 13 is unlucky, but become odder and increasingly complex. A few superstition themes are particularly common. Here are some examples, along with a few of the ways that people try to neutralize them through various compulsive rituals:

✔ **Cats:** Cats are a common worry among those with Superstitious OCD. Black cats, of course, stand out and are seen as inflicting bad luck or harm when they cross one's path. Some also believe that cats can suck the breath out of babies if left unattended for even a moment around an infant. Those with Superstitious OCD sometimes feel inclined to "undo" the effects of cat encounters by carrying lucky symbols, turning in circles seven times, or saying "tac" seven times in their minds in order to cancel out the cat because *tac* is cat spelled backwards.

✔ **Cemeteries and death:** Cemeteries, words related to death, and symbols of death often create consternation for many of those with Superstitious OCD. These folks typically avoid driving by funeral homes and cemeteries. They try to avoid passing by a hearse or even letting their eyes pass over the obituary section in a newspaper. When they do have the misfortune of confronting one or more of these death-related objects or symbols, they feel driven to neutralize the event. Some may need to chant the word "life" over and over again. Others may need to plant nine new flowers in their gardens — you can imagine how full those gardens become.

✔ **Colors:** For many, black means death and evil. Red represents blood and injury or ill health. If these colors are thought about or encountered, the person may feel a need to neutralize them by performing any number of rituals, such as tapping a foot, praying, imagining another color, or spelling the color backwards.

✔ **Numbers:** Those with Superstitious OCD commonly believe in lucky numbers and unlucky numbers. Numbers can have any kind of significance. For example, a man may read license plate numbers and have to stop his car whenever he encounters a plate with the number three in it. A woman may fear the number four and worry that thinking about the number or encountering it in her daily life will cause harm to herself or her family unless she finds a way to neutralize the number. When she sees or thinks about four, she must walk in counterclockwise circles eight times to neutralize the number's effects.

✔ **Symbols:** Some carry around grave concerns about the meaning of various symbols that, like certain words, can convey either positive or negative powers. Symbols frequently associated with positive energy and good luck include four-leafclovers, rabbits' feet, ankhs, horseshoes, rosary beads, shamrocks, and swallows. Symbols viewed as bad or evil include the inverted pentagram, the zodiac, a goat's head, an upside-down cross, and a hand held in a horned position. When people encounter negative or evil symbols, they often feel compelled to neutralize their effects either by bringing out a positive symbol or by engaging in one or more rituals, such as chanting "God please protect me and those I love" 14 times.

✔ **Words:** Some people believe that certain words transmit good energy and other words have bad, or even evil, power. Words often thought to be infused with inherent good energy include: "good," "God," "beneficent," "love," "sharing," "kindness," "soothe," and "relax." Sometimes bad words actually have no inherently negative meaning at all for most people. They become seen as bad because they are associated with an unpleasant event in the person's life. For example, a woman may associate the word "table" with hearing about a loved one's death because she was sitting at a table when she was told about the death. Thus, she may feel compelled to cross herself three times whenever she hears that word.

The preceding list is very incomplete. Superstitions come in a dizzying array of forms. Following are just a few miscellaneous superstitions to give you an idea:

✔ Breaking a mirror brings seven years of bad luck.

✔ Leaving your shoes upside down causes bad luck to visit.

✔ Dropping a pair of scissors causes your spouse to be unfaithful.

✔ Failing to compensate anyone who gives you a knife or anything sharp causes harm to come to you.

✔ Walking under a ladder brings bad luck.

✔ Failing to lift your feet up when driving over a railroad track causes bad luck.

Those with Superstitious OCD take these superstitions very seriously and feel compelled to do all kinds of strange things to undo them when the feared events occur. We give you only a few sample rituals. Trying to think up a ritual that no one actually uses is a little like trying to find a username that no one else has ever used.

Evil in Washington, D.C.?

The *Washington Post* reported on a superstition that some people believe about the capitol of the United States — Washington, D.C. Apparently, these folks believe that the city harbors profound satanic forces because one can draw a demonic pentagram by connecting the dots formed by these important landmarks: Dupont Circle, Logan Circle, Mount Vernon Square, the White House, and Washington Circle. Others add to this "evidence" by pointing to the fact that the Freemasons had an important hand in designing major structures throughout the city. They assume that the Freemasons collaborated with Satan. Like many Americans, we're not all that pleased by some of what goes on in Washington, but we sort of doubt it has a lot to do with landmark configurations and Freemasonry. We won't presume to speak for Satan!

When people use neutralizing rituals, they typically believe that they must be performed with perfect precision. If anything goes wrong in the execution of a ritual, it must be repeated over and over until it feels perfect. This repeating until perfect is similar to "Just So" OCD, which we discuss in Chapter 15.

Changing Thinking about OCD Superstitions

People with Superstitious OCD are pretty darned convinced that giving up their ways will result in harm to others or themselves. Because they believe that not adhering to their superstitious beliefs and behaviors will allow something bad to happen, they don't often volunteer for treatment. Why step on that crack when you never know if the one time you do . . . oops, there goes your mother's back. The point is that because people tend to avoid checking out, challenging, or testing the validity of their superstitions, they never find out whether or not they're true.

A problem with Superstitious OCD is that the feared consequence is usually vague, can't be disproven, or lies in the distant future. Maybe you worry that opening an umbrella inside, seeing an open umbrella, or hearing the word "umbrella" in your home will cause bad luck. As a result, you basically never go out of the house when it rains and avoid watching the weather on the news.

On Tuesday, you hear the word "umbrella" on the lead into the local news; you immediately engage in elaborate exorcisms, turning on all the lights in the house, arranging the hangers in your closet in a particular way, and chanting a prayer 32 times. But, after all that, you go outside and see that the car has a flat tire. Your OCD mind convinces you that the flat tire was caused by hearing the word "umbrella." Wow. That brain is pretty clever. Even if your tire isn't flat, you aren't off the hook. You go to work and at the lunch table, a colleague mentions that her cousin has been diagnosed with cancer. Your OCD mind tells you the cancer is caused by the utterance of "umbrella."

You can challenge superstitions in a couple of ways:

- ✔ One way is to make up competing superstitions and create playful scenes.
- ✔ Another is to learn to handle moderate feelings of discomfort.

We discuss these two change strategies in the next two sections.

All OCD change strategies have a slight risk of making you feel worse for a little while. That's especially true for exposure and response prevention (ERP), which we discuss in detail in Chapter 10. If you experience any excessive uptick in your distress or harbor any concerns or worries about conducting any of these exercises, please consult a mental-health professional for additional help.

Creating competing superstitions

One way to challenge your Superstitious OCD thinking is to make up competing stories and practice them. We assume that you have a few troubling superstitions in your head. When you are exposed to these superstitions, you feel uncomfortable. You have some neutralizing rituals like chants, tapping, and counter words.

The idea here is to create what essentially are "fake" superstitions. You choose the object of this fake superstition and you decide how it works. Because you are making up these competing superstitions, you know they really can't impact you or anyone else. However, by examining these fake superstitions and pretending how you would feel if they were real, hopefully you'll gain insight into how to overcome your active superstitions.

Make this fun. Be creative and silly.

Get out your notebook and try the following exercise:

1. **Pick a neutral word, event, color, or happening that is not connected to your superstitions in any way.**

2. **Write a few sentences (purely fiction) that turn these words, events, or happenings into superstitions.**

3. **Choose a few bad outcomes for encountering this word, event, or happening.**

4. **Write out the actions or mental rituals that are necessary in order to protect you from the new superstition.**

   Make sure these actions are not ones you use for your current, active superstitions.

5. **After you've completed Steps 1 through 4, reflect on how you feel.**

   Can you think differently about your active superstitions? Are your real superstitions any more logical than the fake one you made up? Yet, does the fake one feel a little less worrisome? If so, what does that tell you? Write down your reflections.

6. **Consider designing three, four, or more of these new, fictional superstitions.**

Being silly with neutral, fake superstitions can loosen up your thinking. You're probably not ready to give up your active superstitions, but maybe you're closer. The next example shows you how one woman used this exercise. It also illustrates how Superstitious OCD can become quite quirky.

> **Kate** is required by her OCD to drive at a certain speed that always involves her lucky number 6. The speed depends on what is on the radio when she starts her car. If there is music, she drives 6 miles faster than the posted speed limit. If there is news or talk, she drives 6 miles slower than the speed limit. If she does not follow this rule, she believes her children will be kidnapped. You can imagine how many times she is harassed while driving, which increases her discomfort, as well as her certainty that many bad drivers out there may be watching her in order to take her children.
>
> Kate consults a psychologist who suggests that she try designing new superstitions. This idea sounds a little strange to Kate at first, but she decides to give it a try. Here are two brand new superstitions she comes up with:
>
> **New superstition #1:** Yellow lines must be avoided. This is because white lines are suggestive of cocaine, an illegal and immoral drug, plus, yellow is the color of urine. Yellow lines, therefore, are a double whammy. They are both contaminated and evil. If you encounter a yellow line, you must cross yourself eight times while thinking, "blue square, blue square, blue square . . . ." Saying "blue square" neutralizes the yellow line by symbolically blocking its path and turning it green.

New superstition #2: If you go through the left door to a store, you will lose all your money. The reason? "Left" sounds like "leave." You may leave your wallet or purse in the store. So you must enter through the right door. If that door is locked, you need to go to another entrance. If that isn't possible, you must not go to that store. Even when you go through the right door, you may have bad luck because some of your energy may have gone in the left door. Thus, you need to touch eight things using your right hand to prevent bad things from happening.

Kate concludes by thinking about what this exercise has taught her. She tells her psychologist, "I can see how these new superstitions are almost identical to the nature of my real superstitions. I was surprised how easy it was to come up with them. Yet, these new ones don't really bother me all that much because I know I made them up. I guess the point is that my OCD mind came up with my original superstitions too. Maybe I can start challenging these things."

Kate's story shows you how easily the mind can spin into superstitious thinking. You can make up these things out of thin air. If you try your hand at this, you're likely to see how creative your OCD mind really is. Creative, but wrong.

Managing discomfort differently

At the beginning of this chapter, we talk about the way most people automatically respond when they hear a sneeze. Most people do some sort of blessing that doesn't really have much to do with religious belief, superstition, or consideration of the other person. Saying "bless you" when someone nearby sneezes is a habit.

Nothing is inherently wrong with habits. Habits can be useful. You may brush your teeth every day without really thinking about what you're doing. That's a good habit. If you're like most people, not engaging in a habit is somewhat uncomfortable. For instance, if you're unable to brush your teeth before you go to bed, you probably don't feel right. And if you have the habit of saying "bless you" after a sneeze, then stopping yourself from saying "bless you" after someone sneezes is difficult, if not uncomfortable — try it and see.

Smoking cigarettes is often a habit and one that is very hard to break. People struggle for years and suffer significant discomfort when attempting to quit smoking, partly because smoking is a habit and partly because nicotine is highly addictive, which compounds the problem.

Superstitious OCD can be thought of as a habit, too. This superstitious habit is not so helpful. If you don't comply with what your OCD mind tells you to do, you're likely to feel some discomfort — sometimes a lot of discomfort at first.

To manage the discomfort you encounter while working to overcome your Superstitious OCD, constantly remind yourself of the following points:

- All discomfort lessens as you continue to cease your old habitual rituals.
- Tolerating discomfort is like building muscles — you have to feel the burn and increase weights slowly over time — no pain, no gain.
- No one has ever died as a result of confronting their superstitions.

Yes, bad habits and superstitions are hard to break. But persistence and willingness to tolerate discomfort will eventually break them down. Consider reading Chapter 9 on mindfulness for ideas about how to tolerate discomfort.

Deflating the Power of OCD Superstitions with ERP

Exposure and response prevention (ERP) is the cornerstone for the treatment of most types of OCD. And that's the case for Superstitious OCD as well. ERP involves facing your OCD triggers head on, but don't worry; you won't crash. Odds of success are high when using ERP. However, most people will experience greater success if they work in collaboration with a mental-health professional trained in this approach.

We discuss ERP in considerable detail in Chapter 10. Please review that chapter prior to attempting ERP for your Superstitious OCD.

Facing off with scary superstitions

Here we present a typical exposure hierarchy/staircase that exemplifies the use of ERP in dealing with suspicions. (The difference between an exposure hierarchy and a staircase is simply that an exposure hierarchy is a list of steps to be taken, while a staircase is an illustration of this list.) The exact nature of your staircase will depend very much upon the nature of your individual Superstitious OCD. However, this example hierarchy gives you an idea of how to proceed.

✔ Sitting in a cemetery for an hour and touching the headstones (Ugh Factor Rating 95)

✔ Walking in a cemetery for an hour without touching any headstones (Ugh Factor Rating 90)

✔ Walking around the perimeter of a cemetery for an hour (Ugh Factor Rating 85)

✔ Reading a collection of obituaries in the newspaper over and over for an hour (Ugh Factor Rating 75)

✔ Writing the word "die" on paper over and over for an hour (Ugh Factor Rating 65)

✔ Looking at pictures of funeral homes and cemeteries on the Internet for an hour (Ugh Factor Rating 60)

✔ Walking around the parking lots of several funeral homes for at least an hour altogether (Ugh Factor Rating 55)

✔ Driving around various cemeteries for an hour (Ugh Factor Rating 50)

✔ Looking at the yellow page ads for funeral homes for an hour (Ugh Factor Rating 45)

✔ Imagining scenes of people dying for 45 minutes with my therapist (Ugh Factor Rating 40)

✔ Discussing all the details of my superstitions with my therapist for 50 minutes (Ugh Factor Rating 30)

Defeating the power of superstitious charms

Not all superstitions are scary. For example, wishing someone good luck is not necessarily a bad thing and it conveys a positive sentiment. Charms don't make luck, but many people carry them just in case.

Most people with Superstitious OCD believe in the power of good-luck symbols. However, they often turn to good-luck charms in compulsive ways — as a means of reducing distress associated with their obsessional, superstitious fears. Since overcoming OCD typically involves letting go of compulsions, we have a strategy for dealing with these superstitious symbols — even though they may appear positive at first glance. This exercise could appear silly to those who don't have Superstitious OCD, but those who suffer from it will find it difficult.

Figure 17-1 illustrates some good-luck charms, which are quite likely to apply if you have almost any type of Superstitious OCD.

We want you to do something very different than what your OCD mind wants you to do with these illustrations. We suggest that you spend some serious time on the following exercise:

1. **Carefully look at, review, and read each and every symbol, picture, or word.**

2. **Say the words out loud.**

3. **When you feel ready, cross off the words. You may even consider cutting up a photocopy of the page.**

   (Please don't deface the book if it doesn't belong to you — for example, if you've borrowed it from a library.)

4. **As you cross the words out (or cut up the page), notice your feelings.**

5. **Stay with this exercise until your feelings of distress are reduced.**

   You can either make multiple copies of the page and slowly destroy each one, or you can continue to cross the words out, over and over. You can even repeat phrases such as "I don't want good luck!" again and again. Try to stay with the exercise until your feelings come down by 50 percent or more.

6. **Consider making an alternative, bad-luck page with the help of a therapist.**

   You can make this page by surfing the Internet for all kinds of bad-luck symbols and words that give you trouble with your Superstitious OCD.

7. **After you've made your alternative page, expose yourself to each word and symbol the way you did with the good-luck symbols.**

   However, in this case, you don't destroy the page, but rather, you expose yourself to it. Read the words and observe the evil symbols. You may even consider rubbing the page over your arms and hands.

Figure 17-1:
A variety of
good luck
charms.

Chapter 18

Uncovering OCD Accomplices

Counting, touching, doodling, and compulsive slowness often accompany the other specific types of OCD we cover in earlier chapters. For example, some people with hit-and-run issues who fear running someone over with their car may count compulsively while driving in order to shut out their obsessive images. Others with Doubting and Checking OCD may feel a need to repeatedly touch door handles in specific ways in order to check whether the door is locked. Or, someone with Contamination OCD may take slow, hour-long showers in order to feel clean enough.

In all such cases, the counting, doodling, touching, and slowness are not really distinctly separate types of OCD, although they occasionally present as the primary symptom. These symptoms are quite common and often difficult to treat. Furthermore, counting, doodling, touching, and compulsive slowness tend to capture so much of people's attention and resources that they find themselves unable to carry out important tasks in their lives. So we pay special attention to them in this chapter.

We describe people who suffer from these particular OCD symptoms. Each of these four types of behaviors can be treated using a two-step approach that involves changing how the behaviors are done and then not doing them!

Concerning Counting

The staircase to our private practice offices has 19 stairs. How did we know this fascinating fact? Well, umm, as we were writing this chapter, we lapsed into a discussion about how common counting compulsions are among those with and without full-blown OCD. In our discussion, we discovered that we both count steps from time to time. And we recognized that we do so more often at times when we're feeling a little worried about something, such as running late for an appointment or having work pile up on us.

Many people count stairs, steps, and ceiling tiles. Frequently, counting does not result in a diagnosis of OCD because it doesn't take lots of time or cause major interference with a person's life. It may serve to reduce or distract people from worrisome, anxious thoughts, or it may just alleviate the boredom of sitting in a doctor's waiting room.

At other times, counting grows to the point that it greatly disrupts a person's life. Those who have this problem count all kinds of things, such as:

- Books on a bookshelf
- Cars passing
- Change and money
- Letters in words, names, sentences, or paragraphs
- Highway markings and signs
- Lines in the sidewalk
- Streetlights

Some people count consecutively; others like to count in sets of specific numbers, such as groups of four or seven. For example, a man may count four sets of seven steps. Or a woman may look out the window and feel compelled to count cars in sets of five until she has logged six sets.

Counting effectively blocks out other thoughts. That's not a problem as long as it's brief or occasional. When counting gets out of control, however, the person cannot focus on work or other important life tasks. Counting becomes a disturbing compulsion in those cases.

Preparation for combating compulsive counting involves self-monitoring. Jot down notes about what it is you actually find yourself counting and when you usually do it. You may need to spend a few days collecting data to catalog your counting.

After you've collected information about what and when you count, you're prepared to tackle your counting head-on. We have a couple of strategies for you to try in the following two sections:

- Misdirecting counting behavior through miscounting
- Stopping counting by resisting counting

By the way, how many "c's" appeared in the past two paragraphs? Well, maybe you shouldn't answer that question.

Miscounting on purpose

One of the best ways to mess up your counting problem is to practice the art of miscounting. Miscounting involves intentionally screwing up. Thus, you could skip counting a few steps, count one step as three, or count totally out of order. The OCD mind doesn't like messing up in this manner. If you attempt this technique, be sure to

- ✔ Miscount for ever increasingly large blocks of time.
- ✔ Expect some discomfort and rate that discomfort (see Ugh Factor Rating in Chapter 10) each time you miscount.
- ✔ Pat yourself on the back for each successful attempt to miscount.

Once you've experienced some success and a decrease in discomfort from miscounting, you're ready for the next step — resisting counting (see the next section).

If you do not experience success, consider seeking professional help.

Resisting the act of counting

Resisting counting is rather similar to exposure and response prevention (ERP — see Chapter 10 for details). However, unlike most other compulsions, counting crops up almost anywhere, anytime. This makes it harder to design a set of increasingly difficult steps for an ERP hierarchy or staircase.

Instead, we recommend that you set aside blocks of time when you do not count. You can start with brief periods, perhaps as short as five minutes if you're currently counting almost all the time. Then aim for successively larger blocks of time in which you resist all counting. Try to do this exercise as often as you can — at least several times a day. If you do find yourself starting to count, stop. Don't get upset with yourself; just gently remind your OCD mind that you are in charge and will not count for now. Remind yourself that the counting isn't "you," but merely a product of your OCD mind.

In Chapter 8 and elsewhere, we warn about not attempting to suppress obsessive thoughts because they will merely increase if you do. *Resisting* compulsive counting is not the same thing as thought *suppression*. That's because obsessions are unwanted, intrusive thoughts that really can't be effectively suppressed. However, counting is a mental compulsion that is designed to decrease anxiety and distress. This kind of compulsion can be effectively resisted.

Taking Charge of Touching

If you've ever watched the popular television series *Monk,* you may have seen detective Monk touch various objects such as parking meters or posts while walking down the street. Many people without OCD ritualistically touch a series of items from time to time. Again, touching only becomes OCD when it takes lots of time or interferes with your life.

Troubling touching can consist of constant tapping of fingers in certain sequences, touching every third railing and needing to go back if one is missed, tapping wood ritualistically, rubbing smooth or rough surfaces over and over, or complicated combinations of foot tapping and hand movements.

Distinguishing between motor tics (see Chapters 3 and 19) and touching symptoms of OCD can be tricky. Motor tics involve quick, uncontrollable movements of various types, but are usually not accompanied by obsessive thoughts. You may want to consult a professional trained in OCD diagnosis and treatment for help with making this distinction.

The first step in taking charge of your touching is self-monitoring. Spend a day or two noticing all the ways in which you ritualistically touch, tap, or rub various items or surfaces. Take notes and record when, where, and how you touch. Then you can apply a two-step method for addressing OCD touching:

✔ Mixing up your touching patterns

✔ Stopping touching

Messing with your touching

Similar to miscounting noted earlier in this chapter, messing with your touching entails changing your touching patterns. Thus, you can:

✔ Change the rhythm of your tapping.

✔ Change the typical surfaces you rub.

✔ Instead of tapping your right foot, try tapping your left foot.

✔ Intentionally miss tapping a few items in a sequence (like lampposts).

✔ Tap harder than usual.

✔ Tap more slowly than you want to.

Notice how you feel when you change your touching patterns. Expect some discomfort at first, and be aware that the discomfort is highly likely to decrease as you continue.

Discontinuing touching

After you've mastered messing with your touching, as we describe in the preceding section, you're ready for the next step, discontinuing touching. When you feel like touching something, don't do it! Of course, it isn't quite that simple. You will probably find it useful to start by not engaging in your compulsive touching for an hour or so. Write down your success. Then up your goal to an hour and a half, then two hours, then three. You get the idea. Ultimately, your compulsion to touch will decrease after you've made it through an entire day or two. However, you will need to remain vigilant, because touching OCD loves to creep back in through the back door when you're not looking.

Doing Away with Doodling

Everyone doodles now and then. Harmless, right? Well, yes, in some cases. But with OCD, things tend to run out of control. And it happens with doodling just like it does with other OCD symptoms. Compulsive doodlers sometimes have favorite themes for their doodling, such as circles, weapons, or mazes.

Those with a doodling problem often become so wrapped up in their doodling that the rest of the world is shut out. This symptom often shows up in students. They sit at their desks doodling and may not even hear the lecture they're attending. Even if they do, they certainly can't take notes. The same problem shows up at the office. Some office workers doodle their days away and run into trouble with their supervisors for a lack of productivity.

The techniques for doing away with doodling look much like the strategies we outline for counting and touching earlier in this chapter. Start by jotting down how often, where, and when you doodle. Get a feel for just how much trouble it causes you. Then try the following two techniques:

- ✔ Doodle differently.
- ✔ Don't doodle.

Doodling in different ways

Change your doodling patterns in every way you can think of. Most people who doodle compulsively have preferred pens, pencils, paper, designs, and patterns for their doodling. Regularly change all these things in some way or another. The goal is to make doodling as unsatisfying to your OCD mind as possible.

Denying the urge to doodle

Stopping doodling is best executed after you've been doodling differently for a time. The strategy of just saying no to doodling demands increasing amounts of time in which you consciously resist the urge to doodle. You slowly build up your tolerance while taking notes, working on your tasks, and so on. It helps if you monitor your successes as well as the amount of discomfort you feel when you don't doodle for each block of time (see Chapter 10 for details on the Ugh Factor Rating).

Speeding Up Slowness

OCD inevitably slows people down, if for no other reason than because it consumes so much of their time. However, sometimes slowness becomes the primary problem. Showering can take over an hour — or until all the hot water is used up. Getting ready for work can require two or three hours, making you chronically late for work. Eating a meal can drag on and on, and not just because you're savoring the food. Some people with compulsive slowness speak . . . very . . . very . . . ever so very . . . slowly. You can imagine how slowness not only interferes with completing life's tasks, but also can be exquisitely annoying to others.

Those with this OCD symptom are not particularly slow thinkers per se. Typically, their slowness represents an attempt to reduce their doubts and uncertainty and/or obtain perfection. These people want to make sure they complete tasks in a correct or "just so" manner.

A few neurological disorders include symptoms of motor slowness as a prominent feature. These include Parkinson's disease and Binswanger's disease, which is a form of vascular dementia. If you or someone you love demonstrates problems with compulsive slowness, check it out with your family doctor, who may choose to refer you to a neurologist.

Compulsive slowness is a little tricky to treat with standard ERP. However, you can address the issues of doubting, uncertainty, and perfectionism (which frequently drive this problem) by working carefully through Chapter 8. Just don't take too long to work through your issue!

Two types of exposure strategies can be successfully applied to problems with slowness — mixing things up and speeding things up.

Mixing things up

Each person's slowness problem is unique. There are more variations on this theme than books in the library. However, most people who live in slow motion are looking for certainty and perfection. Therefore, it's often helpful to experiment with an exposure staircase that pushes you to engage in the activities that you're slow at with increasing amounts of uncertainty and imperfection.

Before you begin, read Chapter 10 for important instructions on how to use exposure staircases / hierarchies within ERP. Austin's story illustrates how he uses an exposure hierarchy to speed up his life.

> **Austin** is a freshman in college. He is gifted, but graduated from high school with only mediocre grades because of his compulsive slowness. He's often late to class because he is so slow getting ready to leave — he combs each hair into place, straightens his clothes, and polishes his shoes to perfection. He takes notes slowly and retraces each word to make sure that it's clear. However, this note-taking strategy prevents him from getting much of the important material on paper. He passed high school because he was bright enough to get away with this inefficiency. But now he finds that his notes don't give him the information he needs to pass his tests. His slowness also bogs him down because he reads and rereads all his textbook assignments out of fear of not understanding everything. He's behind in all his classes. He seeks counseling at the student mental-health center. His therapist persuades him to try an exposure hierarchy. Here's what they come up with:

- ✔ Not combing my hair at all and going out in public (Ugh Factor Rating 90)

- ✔ Taking really sloppy notes with misspelled words (Ugh Factor Rating 85)

- ✔ Reading a section in my textbook only once (Ugh Factor Rating 80)

- ✔ Intentionally mussing up my clothes (Ugh Factor Rating 75)

- ✔ Taking notes quickly without tracing over letters (Ugh Factor Rating 70)

- ✔ Polishing one shoe and not the other (Ugh Factor Rating 70)

- ✔ Turning in a paper that I briefly edit only once (Ugh Factor Rating 65)

- ✔ Reading a section in my textbook only twice (Ugh Factor Rating 65)

- ✔ Not folding my underwear (Ugh Factor Rating 50)

- ✔ Wearing one blue sock and one brown sock (Ugh Factor Rating 45)

- ✔ Not ironing my bluejeans (Ugh Factor Rating 35)

Austin completes his hierarchy, which helps him speed up because it gives him practice with making mistakes and engaging in imperfection — both of which fuel his slowness. Austin's treatment also involves talking about his experiences with the exposure exercises.

Speeding things up

Survey a few close friends or family members and ask them how long they spend doing basic tasks such as eating, showering, shaving, brushing teeth, getting dressed, grooming, or whatever it is that you're slow at. Then write down the average of their reports and make it your goal to meet or beat those lengths of time. Each time you succeed, be sure to reward yourself.

The key here is to try and not go um, er . . . too fast! What we mean is, try and speed up about 10 to 20 percent with each attempt until you've reached your goal. You don't have to accomplish the goals all at once, but neither do you need to take forever getting there.

Here are a few of our suggestions for goals on some basic life tasks. These are not set in granite and not based on scientific research — just common sense.

- **Baths:** Under 20 minutes unless you're wanting an occasional relaxing treat
- **Eating most meals:** 30 minutes
- **Putting on make-up:** Under 15 minutes
- **Selecting clothes and getting dressed:** Under 15 minutes
- **Showering:** Under 10 minutes
- **Brushing your teeth:** 2 minutes (a typical electric toothbrush times out then)

Other tasks that involve slowness, like writing or reading, are more difficult to assign exact goals to. Review your own particular slowness issues and try to design some common-sense solutions. If you have trouble doing so, consider seeing a therapist for some help.

Chapter 19

Dealing with OCD-Related Impulsive Problems

*T*ics, Tourette's syndrome, trichotillomania, skin-picking, and nail-biting all fall under the category of *impulsive problems* — tics and habits that are driven by sudden impulses. Tics are repetitive, rapid vocalizations or movements that are difficult to suppress. Such noises include grunts, groans, barks, and swear words, whereas movements may involve rapid head jerks, eye blinks, facial grimaces, and so on. Impulsive habits are repetitive and difficult to suppress, including pulling out one's hair (trichotillomania), picking at one's skin, and biting one's nails. (See Chapter 3 for more detailed descriptions of each of these disorders.)

Many experts believe that these problems have some connection to OCD, but they are not officially considered to be part of OCD at this time. They do, however, frequently co-occur with OCD. Like OCD, people report that they have great difficulty stopping these behaviors. Unlike OCD, these behaviors are largely thought to occur as a way of self-soothing or obtaining a pleasurable feeling rather than reducing fear, anxiety, and distress. However, some people with these habits report engaging in them as a way of reducing distress, so the distinction may not hold for everyone.

In this chapter, we review the primary strategies for undoing these problematic behaviors and habits. Most importantly, we tell you about a treatment that was developed in the 1970s by Drs. Nathan Azrin and Gregory Nunn called Habit Reversal Training (HRT). Today HRT remains one of the most widely employed treatment approaches to these issues. We conclude with a discussion of important thinking habits to acquire in order to succeed and maintain your gains.

We review other cousins of OCD in Chapter 3 that we do not discuss in this chapter because treating them entails greater complexity. These problem areas include body dysmorphic disorder, eating disorders, pathological gambling, kleptomania, hypochondriasis, pyromania, and various paraphilias. If one of these problems seems to apply to you, we recommend that you seek professional help.

Changing Behavior to Reduce Impulsive Problems

Addressing OCD-related impulsive problems can be difficult. That's because these impulsive habits tend to occur with little or no conscious thought or awareness. They are well-ingrained habits, and most people have them for years before they attempt to change them.

Habit Reversal Training (HRT) has been the most heavily researched strategy for these problems and usually works quite well. HRT, like exposure and response prevention (ERP) therapy (see Chapter 10), involves extended periods of time in which the person refrains from the problematic behavior. However, unlike ERP, it attempts to instill a new behavior that competes with the habit.

HRT consists of four major components:

- **Increasing your awareness of when your problematic behaviors and habits are occurring.**

   Many people report that they are almost completely unaware of when they have tics, pull their hair, or pick at their skin.

- **Learning how to relax as a way of handling stressors that sometimes set off problematic behaviors and habits.**

- **Learning new, alternative behaviors.**

   This strategy is particularly important.

- **Seeing how to keep yourself motivated with self-rewards.**

Some professionals used to believe that if you eliminated problematic behaviors such as tics and hair pulling, you would simply find another bad habit to replace it. However, studies have consistently failed to verify this concern. Thus, if you succeed in ridding yourself of a problem behavior, you are good to go.

Increasing awareness of your impulsive problems

Increasing awareness of your tics and habits helps prepare you for the rest of HRT. We recommend at least a week of careful monitoring. Although it's something of a pain, make note of the following during that time:

- ✔ The time of day you feel an urge.

- ✔ Where you are when an urge strikes.

- ✔ How you feel when you have an urge (happy, sad, anxious, angry, and so on).

- ✔ What you are doing when you feel an urge (watching television, reading, and so forth).

- ✔ How you feel after you engage in your tic or habit, or how you feel if you don't engage in the problematic behavior.

- ✔ Describe your behavior in detail. If it's a tic, note which part of the body is moving or what sound is made. If it's hair-pulling, note where you're pulling the hair from and whether you use one hand or two.

 Some people worry that increasing awareness of their tics, urges, and habits will make them all increase. If you have that concern, relax. Studies show that increasing awareness does nothing to increase symptoms and sometimes reduces them somewhat, at least for a while. However, you need to carry out the rest of HRT in order to reduce symptoms permanently.

Relaxing away impulsive problems

The second step in HRT is what's known as progressive muscle relaxation training. Dr. Edmund Jacobsen developed this strategy more than 50 years ago. Literally hundreds of studies have shown that this technique can improve anxiety and health in numerous ways, although among the four components of HRT, relaxation may be the least important. Here is a set of instructions for progressive muscle relaxation that appeared in our earlier book, *Overcoming Anxiety For Dummies* (also from Wiley):

1. **Take a deep breath, hold, imagine, and let the tension go.**

   Pulling the air in from your abdomen, breathe deeply. Hold your breath for three or four seconds and slowly let the air out. Imagine your whole body is a balloon losing air as you exhale and let tension go out with the air. Take three more such breaths and feel your entire body getting more limp with each one.

2. Squeeze your hands tight and then relax.

Squeeze your fingers into a fist. Feel the tension and hold it for six to ten seconds. Then, all at once, release your hands and let them go limp. Allow the tension in your hands to flow out. Let the relaxation deepen for 10 to 15 seconds.

3. Tighten your arms and relax.

Bring your lower arms up almost to your shoulders and tighten the muscles. Make sure you tense the muscles on the inside and outside of both the upper and lower arms. If you're not sure you're doing that, use one hand to do a tension check on the other arm. Hold the tension a little while and then drop your arms as though you cut a string holding them up. Let the tension flow out and the relaxation flow in.

4. Raise up your shoulders, tighten, and then relax.

Raise your shoulders up as though you were a turtle trying to get into its shell. Hold the tension and then let your shoulders drop. Feel the relaxation deepen for 10 to 15 seconds.

5. Tighten and relax the muscles in your upper back.

Pull your shoulders back and bring your shoulder blades closer together. Hold that tension a little while . . . and let it go.

6. Scrunch up your entire face and then relax.

Squeeze your forehead down, bring your jaws together, tighten your eyes and eyebrows, and contract your tongue and lips. Let the tension grow and hold it . . . then relax and let go.

7. Tighten and relax your neck in the back of your head.

Without causing any pain, gently pull your head back toward your back and feel the muscles tighten in the back of your neck. Notice that tension and hold it, let go, and relax. Feel relaxation deepening and repeat it if you want.

8. Contract the front neck muscles and then loosen.

Gently move your chin toward your chest. Tighten your neck muscles and let the tension increase and maintain it; then relax. Feel the tension melting away like candle wax.

9. Tighten the muscles in your stomach and chest and maintain the tension. Then let it go.

10. Arch your back, hang on to the contraction, and then relax.

Be gentle with your lower back and skip it entirely if you've ever had trouble with this part of your body. Tighten these muscles by arching your lower back, pressing it back against the chair, or tensing the muscles any way you want. Gently increase and maintain the tension, but not too much. Now, relax and allow the waves to roll in.

11. Contract and relax your buttocks muscles.

Tighten your buttocks so as to gently lift yourself up in your chair. Hold the tension. Then let tension melt and relaxation grow.

12. Squeeze and relax your thigh muscles.

Tighten and hold these muscles. Then relax and feel the tension draining out; let the calm deepen and spread.

13. Contract and relax your calves.

Tighten the muscles in your calves by pulling your toes toward your face. Take care; if you ever get muscle cramps, don't overdo. Hold the tension . . . let go. Let tension drain into the floor.

14. Gently curl your toes, maintain the tension, and then relax.

15. Take a little time to tour your entire body.

Notice whether you feel different than when you began. If you find any areas of tension, allow the relaxed areas around the tense areas to come in and replace them. If that doesn't work, repeat the tense-and-relax procedure for the tense area.

16. Spend a few minutes enjoying the relaxed feelings.

Let relaxation spread and penetrate every muscle fiber in your body. Notice any feelings you have. You may feel warmth, or you may feel a floating sensation. Perhaps you'll feel a sense of sinking down. Whatever it is, allow it to happen. When you want, you can open your eyes and go on with your day, perhaps feeling like you just returned from a brief vacation.

CDs and recordings of progressive muscle relaxation techniques are available on the Internet and in bookstores. Some people like to record their own version — if you want to go that way, feel free to use or change our wording and make your own, personalized recording.

Practice relaxation every day for at least a couple of weeks. As you get more skilled, you may discover that you can relax more quickly by condensing several muscle groups into one. For example, you could tighten your hands, arms, and shoulders together and relax them at the same time. Then you could tighten your upper back, face, and neck muscles simultaneously and relax them. After a while, you may find that you can completely relax within a few minutes.

You can find a number of additional relaxation techniques in *Overcoming Anxiety For Dummies*. No definitive studies suggest that one approach is far superior to others. What's important is finding a strategy that really works for you. Feel free to experiment.

If your impulsive problem involves any kind of intentional cutting on your body until bleeding occurs, you should seek professional help for the problem. HRT may ultimately play some role, but consulting a trained mental-health professional will likely be very helpful. We also recommend professional consultations if you do not make good progress on your own for any of the problems we describe in this chapter.

Sidetracking impulsive problems with something different

Possibly the most crucial aspect of HRT is designing a new response to compete with the old habit or behavior. Ideally, this new response uses virtually the same muscles as the tic or habit. It also needs to be something you can do in public without appearing obvious. It's best to take each tic or habit one at a time — after you've succeeded with one, you can move on to another one.

You may wonder what these competing responses look like. Table 19-1 shows you an array of possibilities. You may want to use one or more of these, but your own particular tic or habit may not be included. In that case, you can probably design your own by using these as a guide.

Table 19-1	Examples of Impulsive Problems and Suggested Competing Responses
Compulsive Problem	*Competing Responses*
Hair-pulling (habit — trichotillomania)	Make a fist; squeeze a soft ball; squeeze the arms of your chair
Facial grimace (tic)	Tighten your lips together; clench your teeth
Eye-blinking (tic)	Open your eyes as wide as possible
Nail-biting (habit)	Make a fist; squeeze a soft ball; squeeze the arms of your chair
Noises — grunts, groans, barks, and so on (tics)	Keeping your mouth closed, inhale slowly and deeply through the nose, then exhale slowly
Shoulder shrugs (tic)	Push shoulders back against chair; make a fist and push it into the palm of the other hand
Head jerks (tic)	Tilt head down toward the chest

(continued)

Table 19-1 (continued)	
Compulsive Problem	**Competing Responses**
Hand and arm jerks (tic)	Make a fist and push it into the palm of the other hand with some force
Skin-picking (habit)	Make a fist; squeeze a soft ball; squeeze the arms of your chair

Once you've designed and planned your competing responses, you're ready to start using them. Whenever you feel an urge or strong desire to engage in a tic or habit, immediately begin your competing response. Maintain that response for several minutes — later you can shorten the time to a minute or less. Try not to stop until the urge has lessened.

Reinforcing positive gains in overcoming impulsive problems

Now for the good part. Reinforcing or rewarding your good efforts is important. Of course you can always treat yourself in various ways such as indulging in a favorite food, going out to a movie, reading a great book, or buying yourself something special.

However, the best way of keeping your motivation high is to enlist the help of some trusted friends or family. Tell them what you're doing and ask them to encourage you and remind you to keep at it. See Chapter 22 for ideas about how to use coaches and support people — you certainly don't need them nagging you!

Changing Thinking to Reduce Impulsive Problems

Tackling tics and habits doesn't make any "Top Ten" lists of the "Easiest and Most Fun Things You Can Do." Rather, ridding yourself of these scoundrels takes hard work and determination. We find that it helps if you tinker with your thinking as a way of obtaining and maintaining momentum. In the following sections, we recommend a little work on four particular areas of thinking. These areas are:

✔ Choosing to change

✔ Confronting hopelessness

✔ Setting unfairness aside

✔ Being self-supporting

Finding reasons to change

Many people we see report that their tics or habits have hung around their necks since they were bordering on pubescence. And they come to us for help when they are middle-aged adults, meaning they have waited several decades or longer to finally deal with the issue. Such long delays in seeking treatment usually occur due to deep shame over the problem. Other people wait because they attempt to minimize the issue and pretend that it's no big deal.

In either case, you're likely to benefit from developing a list of reasons for dealing with your problematic habit or tic. Think of every imaginable motivation you have for finally loosening the chokehold your habits and tics have on your life. Here are a few such incentives that people have mentioned to us:

✔ I hate it when someone notices my problem and asks me about it.

✔ I live in constant fear of embarrassment and rejection.

✔ I no longer want to feel the constant pressure to hide and cover up my problem.

✔ I want to feel in charge of my life rather than feeling like my tics (or habits) have the upper hand.

✔ These habits distract me from tasks that I need to accomplish.

You get the idea. You likely have many reasons for making these changes. Remind yourself what those reasons are as you proceed. If your motivation happens to wane at any point, consider reading or rereading Chapter 6 for ideas on how to overcome obstacles and resistance to change.

Pushing hopelessness aside

Many people report slipping into thoughts of hopelessness when they try to break stubborn habits. If you find yourself having thoughts such as, "I'll never overcome this," "I thought I was getting somewhere, but this slip obviously means I haven't learned a thing," or "I can't even imagine getting over this problem," you need to jump on such self-defeating thoughts. You can start by answering the following questions:

- ✔ Have I ever tackled my tics or habits with professional assistance before?

- ✔ Have I ever experienced an extended time when I successfully dealt with my habits? If so, is it possible I can build upon that experience?

- ✔ Have I ever succeeded at anything that seemed impossible at the time?

- ✔ Have I ever tried HRT or ERP for these problems?

> **Scott** has a vocal tic in which he constantly clears his throat, and he bites his nails. He has had both of these problems since he was an adolescent and feels terribly embarrassed about them. He used the preceding questions to overcome his thoughts of hopelessness because he'd made a number of attempts to overcome these problems, but had failed each time. Here are Scott's answers to these questions:

✔ Have I ever tackled my tics or habits with professional assistance before?

My doctor put me on medication for smoking, but it didn't help. I have never seen a therapist for this stuff, but maybe that could help.

✔ Have I ever experienced an extended time when I successfully dealt with my habits? If so, is it possible I can build upon that experience?

I did manage to quit smoking after about 20 tries. And I did stop my nail-biting for three months once. So maybe if I keep at it . . . .

✔ Have I ever succeeded at anything that seemed impossible at the time?

Yes, I recall getting through graduate school. I never thought I'd make it.

✔ Have I ever tried HRT or ERP for these problems?

I'd never heard of HRT or ERP before I read Obsessive-Compulsive Disorder For Dummies. *Maybe it can help.*

Answering these questions helped Scott realize that changing habits is not a hopeless undertaking. He now feels more hopeful about making difficult, but desired, changes.

Undoing unfairness worries

Sometimes people defeat themselves by dwelling on how terribly unfair and unjust it is that they have one or more of these problems and have to work so hard to change them. They typically feel angry about the fact that the world has dealt them such a lousy hand.

If any of this thinking sounds like something you hear rattling around in your head, try to reconsider. Every person we've ever known struggles with difficult issues. Traumas, death, financial setbacks, and emotional struggles present formidable foes for everyone at one time or another throughout a lifetime. Focusing on the unfairness and injustice of it all merely takes your eye off the ball. Remind yourself, "Of course it isn't 'fair' that I have this problem, but I need to dwell on doing something about it, not on how unfair it is."

Designing supportive self-statements

Sometimes preparing a few straightforward self-statements helps you stay focused. Self-statements are simply thoughts that you say to yourself as reminders and motivators. Here are a few that you may find useful. Feel free to use our examples, change the wording a little, or design your own:

- ✔ I know I am entering a situation that sets my habit off; get ready!
- ✔ Urges are tough, but each and every time I resist them, I build up more strength.
- ✔ I want to take charge of my life again!
- ✔ Control takes time; patience is the key.
- ✔ When I "fail," I can still learn from the process if I simply don't beat up on myself.

Consider jotting down one or more of these statements on a 3"-x-5" card. Carry the card around with you as a reminder. You can do this!

Applying ERP to Impulsive Problems

Although far less studied than HRT for tics, ERP has shown promising results for this problem. Essentially, people with tics are asked to undergo multiple two-hour sessions in which they are exposed to situations that represent a high risk of causing tics to occur. The usual staircases are not used here because the high-risk situations typically are often not easily distinguished in terms of difficulty.

During these exposure sessions, the individuals try to suppress the tics and are also asked to concentrate on the body areas involved with their tics. Therapists usually act as coaches at first, and then clients are asked to practice religiously at home.

Treating Impulsive Problems with Medication

If you are considering taking medication for an impulse control disorder, make sure you go to a physician who has training and experience in managing these problems. The doctor may have to try several different drugs or drug combinations before finding the best treatment for you.

Tourette's syndrome and tics are difficult to treat with medication. Antipsychotic drugs are often helpful in controlling tics. However, the long-term use of these drugs can result in *tardive dyskinesia,* a serious disorder characterized by involuntary movements. These movements are repetitive and may include facial grimacing, sticking out the tongue, lip smacking, or purposeless movements of the arms, legs, or fingers. You can imagine that a person who already has tics is not going to want to suffer from these side effects.

Other newer drugs called atypical antipsychotics are also used. Side effects appear to be less severe, but concerns about the long-term use of these medications still exist. Clonidine, a drug designed to lower high blood pressure, sometimes works to control tics. The side effects can include fatigue, dry mouth, and dizziness.

Hair-pulling, skin-picking, and nail-biting have not been as well researched as tic disorders. Often, people with these habits have other problems going on as well, such as social anxiety, depression, or OCD. Selective serotonin reuptake inhibitors have been used with some success to treat the latter conditions, but not so much for hair-pulling, skin-picking, and nail-biting.

The best advice: Try working on your impulse control problem by using a behavioral treatment such as HRT. Work hard and get help from a therapist. If that doesn't work, then consider consulting with a psychiatrist, neurologist, or other physician who specializes in these problems.

Part V
Assisting Others with OCD

The 5th Wave   By Rich Tennant

"The funny thing is he's spent 9 hours organizing his computer desktop."

In this part . . .

OCD usually begins in childhood. This part enables you to see OCD symptoms emerging in a child. We highlight how symptoms may affect schoolwork, friendships, and family relationships. We explain what family members can do to help while avoiding common pitfalls. This part also provides information about helping friends and family who suffer from OCD.

Chapter 20

Determining Whether Your Child Has OCD

*M*illions of adults throughout the world suffer from OCD, and for most of them, the signs and symptoms began in childhood or adolescence. Unfortunately, OCD is under-diagnosed in children, just as it is in adults. Because kids with OCD often go untreated, they frequently experience bullying and social rejection by peers. Other kids often label their behavior "weird" or "crazy." The time consumed by obsessions and compulsions and their highly distracting nature often cause kids with OCD to do poorly in school.

In this chapter, we give you information about what OCD looks like in children and point out some common childhood disorders that can be confused with OCD. If you think your child may have OCD, we tell you where to go in order to know for sure. Although we can't tell you how to diagnose your child, we can give you information that should help you know whether your concerns should be checked out further.

Understanding Childhood OCD

Kids don't go to their parents saying, "I've been having lots of trouble with terrible obsessions and compulsions." In fact, they typically try to hide their symptoms out of shame and embarrassment. Sometimes they even think they might be crazy.

Obsessions are recurrent, unwanted thoughts, images, or urges. *Compulsions* are the actions (either mental or behavioral) that are practiced to decrease distress or neutralize obsessive thoughts.

Children may not be able to talk about obsessions because they don't have the vocabulary or insight necessary to do so. They describe obsessions only as powerful feelings of fear or of things just not being right. Compulsions are more likely than obsessions to be observed by parents.

Recognizing possible symptoms

If kids aren't likely to discuss their obsessive worries or compulsive actions, how can you, as a parent, know whether your child has OCD? Well, you can look for various signs. Don't become too obsessed with this list. All kids have a few of these sorts of problems from time to time. Nevertheless, the following signs and symptoms may be worth checking out:

- Asking parents or family members to repeat a phrase over and over
- Counting out loud repeatedly
- Demanding symmetry in objects, dinnerware, and furniture
- Being excessively concerned about their appearance and clothing
- Showing an excessive interest in feces or urine, including collecting them
- Spending an excessive amount of time getting ready for bed at night
- Worrying excessively about religion or going to hell
- Keeping completely unorganized collections of largely worthless stuff
- Displaying extreme irritability or anger when their usual routines are disrupted
- Fearing unlucky numbers and showing considerable interest in lucky numbers
- Needing frequent reassurance regarding their own health
- Worrying frequently about the fire alarms or home safety
- Making lots of erasures on schoolwork
- Being overly concerned with getting dirty
- Questioning parents about sanitation or cleanliness
- Checking door locks or windows repeatedly
- Asking questions repeatedly about parents' health and well-being
- Going through doorways over and over
- Touching items repeatedly in a ritualistic way

- Tracing over words repeatedly on schoolwork

- Repeating the same phrase over and over

- Needing an increasing amount of time to get ready in the morning

- Having trouble completing tests on time at school

- Spending unusually long periods of time washing hands or showering

- Adhering very strictly to routines

- Worrying about contamination from radiation or other toxins

This list is not exhaustive, nor does a single item allow for a diagnosis of OCD to be made. The difference between OCD and normality can be subtle. Plus, a fair amount of subjectivity is involved in discerning what is excessive or unusual as opposed to what's reasonable and normal. The key is to *determine whether these issues are starting to interfere with your child's or your family's life*. If you feel worried about the signs your child is demonstrating, you need to consult with a mental-health professional.

Ruling out normal growth and health issues

Rituals that are transient (meaning they fade over time) are a normal part of childhood around the ages of three to seven. For example, most kids enjoy specific bedtime routines. They also like to line up toys in specific patterns and even "order" their parents to sit in certain seats. Children typically outgrow these behaviors, and the behaviors don't significantly interfere with the family or the children's lives.

Childhood OCD most often starts before adolescence. In boys, it usually starts showing up by around the second or third grade. Girls typically show signs of OCD a little later. If symptoms start before the age of five, something else may be going on (see the sidebar "These PANDAS are not cute"), and you should check with your pediatrician.

Sorting through other childhood disorders

Diagnosing OCD can be complicated because the symptoms of OCD can look like symptoms of other childhood disorders, and children with OCD are likely to have other problems. That's why it is especially important to have your child assessed by a mental-health professional experienced in the diagnosis and treatment of OCD. OCD can either accompany or sometimes be confused with the following:

These PANDAS are not cute

Antibodies are designed to attack germs and aid in recovery. Sometimes these antibodies get out of control and attack normal, healthy parts of the body. The result of this phenomenon is called autoimmune disease. Strep throat, a common childhood illness, can produce antibodies that attack normal, healthy structures. This attack results in PANDAS or pediatric autoimmune neuropsychiatric disorders associated with streptococcal infection. Although there are no specific lab tests for PANDAS, a positive strep throat culture is one of the diagnostic criteria.

The symptoms mimic OCD. They come on quickly after the infection, are usually severe, and often include tremors, twitches, clumsiness, sensitivity, and extreme fear and anxiety. PANDAS can be successfully treated with medication and Cognitive-Behavioral Therapy (CBT). However, in several successful clinical trials, children have received treatment that removes the strep antibodies — resulting in a dramatic reduction of symptoms.

✔ **Anxiety disorders:** Although OCD is considered to be one of the anxiety disorders, other problems like separation anxiety (extreme fear of leaving a parent), social anxiety (extreme shyness and fear of rejection), or generalized anxiety (excessive worrying about many things) frequently accompany OCD.

✔ **Attention Deficit Hyperactivity Disorder (ADHD):** When children are consumed by obsessive thoughts and compulsive rituals, they fail to pay attention. Children are commonly given a diagnosis of ADHD when OCD is the real culprit. ADHD can also accompany OCD. Common symptoms of ADHD include distractibility, impulsivity (talking and behaving without thinking), and inattentiveness.

✔ **Behavior disorders (including Oppositional Defiant Disorder and conduct disorders):** Kids with one of these problems demonstrate defiance, disobedience, and disruptiveness. They break rules and are easily angered. Children with OCD sometimes seem defiant, but that's usually because parents, siblings, and teachers fail to understand their unusual behaviors and beliefs. For example, children can become very angry and stubborn when their parents push them to do homework, get ready for school or bedtime, and interrupt their compulsive routines.

✔ **Depression:** Kids with OCD may withdraw from others because they are embarrassed by their symptoms and that withdrawal may be mistaken as depression. On the other hand, kids with OCD may become clinically depressed as a result of or in addition to their OCD. Typical signs of depression include sadness, loss of interest, withdrawal, low energy, appetite changes, and problems with sleep.

✔ **Learning disabilities:** Kids with OCD can look like they have problems learning because they're not completing schoolwork or paying attention. Therefore, they may have poor grades. Learning disabilities are neurologically based problems and are diagnosed by a school or clinical psychologist.

✔ **Pervasive developmental disorders (including Asperger's Disorder and autism):** This set of problems involves severe impairment of social interactions and restricted interests. Thus, children with one of these problems may show unusual, keen interest in specific topics, such as airplanes or dinosaurs, but not in pleasing or getting to know other people. Kids with these pervasive developmental disorders also often have trouble with changes and transitions in routines and activities. The rigid interests and routines can sometimes look like obsessions and compulsions.

✔ **Tic disorders (including Tourette's syndrome):** Tics are sudden, recurrent motor movements or vocalizations (such as grunts, groans, snorts, words, barks, obscenities) that occur spontaneously and involuntarily. They can be suppressed for a little while, but are largely out of the person's control. OCD very often accompanies tics and Tourette's, but most of those with OCD do not have tics or Tourette's. Sometimes compulsive routines in OCD that involve tapping, making certain noises, or saying phrases can seem like tics.

✔ **Other disorders:** OCD symptoms can mimic or be confused with other disorders of childhood.

- OCD can disrupt eating. Children with OCD may not eat particular foods fearing contamination or even believing that the foods are somehow unlucky or that eating those foods could cause someone else harm. They may also need to line up their foods in strange patterns or orders. These problems with eating need to be carefully differentiated from eating disorders such as bulimia and anorexia. Bulimia and anorexia are serious and require professional treatment. You may want to get a copy of *Eating Disorders For Dummies* by Susan Schulherr (Wiley).

- Children with OCD can have problems with elimination, including a fear of using public toilets. This can result in toileting accidents and be confused with encopresis or enuresis (failure to control bowel movements and urine).

- Selective mutism is a disorder of childhood in which the child does not speak, except to close family members. Though unusual, children with OCD may behave in similar ways because of an obsessional fear of talking to strangers.

- Some children who have been separated from their parents, abused, or neglected develop attachment disorders in which they have trouble becoming securely attached to their caregivers. Kids with OCD may look like they have these problems because they're afraid that showing affection may cause harm or contaminate them or their parents in some way.

You can see that the diagnoses of childhood disorders can be quite complicated. If you're concerned about your child, make sure you choose a mental-health professional who has experience in assessment and diagnosis.

Some professionals are experts in assessment and diagnosis of emotional, neurological, learning, and behavior disorders. These professionals clarify the diagnosis, make specific recommendations, and then refer their clients to others for treatment.

Observing the Effects of OCD

The way OCD plays out in different contexts, settings, and relationships can vary, adding more difficulty to a diagnosis. As a parent, being aware of what's going on with your child in settings both in and out of your home is important. The next three sections show you how OCD affects home life, school performance, and relationships with peers. At least half of all kids with OCD find that one or more of these areas become highly impaired.

Having problems at home

OCD disturbs not only the kids who have it, but all of their family members as well. Morning routines can evolve into disasters. OCD makes kids take too long to wash, dress, eat, or gather materials for the day. When parents start to push or nag, children with OCD get extremely angry and sometimes throw tantrums. Bedtime can also be horrible, with rigid routines and rituals stealing time from homework. These delays also cause children to lose sleep and then feel tired the next morning. Tension, worry, and stress cause many kids with OCD to feel sick to their stomachs and have headaches or muscle aches.

OCD sucks in family members like an industrial-strength vacuum cleaner. Parents and/or siblings may become involved in supporting OCD rituals. For example, the kids may ask their parents to wash ostensibly contaminated clothes repeatedly. They may demand that meals be served in odd orders or containers. Brothers or sisters may be recruited to check doors and windows. And all family members may be required to provide frequent reassurance. We tell you what to do about all of these demands in Chapter 21.

On occasion, teachers report that they see none of the problems at school that the parents of OCD kids report seeing at home. When parents hear that their kids are doing just fine at school, they mistakenly assume that their kids are just being defiant. This assumption makes the parents irritated, which only worsens the situation. It's important to realize that OCD can show up only at home and still be OCD.

Experiencing problems at school

Although less common, OCD can appear at school and be minimally obvious at home. When OCD overtakes the mind, school can become a nightmare.

Children with OCD are usually bright and try to be well-behaved. Yet they may get into trouble for not paying attention, not completing work, and being off task. Teachers may not understand what is going on and believe that the OCD child is being disrespectful, uncooperative, and oppositional.

Children with OCD have recurring, distressing thoughts that keep them from paying attention to class work. These kids frequently have fears of making mistakes and are extreme perfectionists. They are tortured by the possibility of errors and therefore erase and redo the same problem over and over. This over-concern often keeps them from completing assignments.

Those children with fears about contamination may worry obsessively about getting sick from touching objects or other children. They may demand frequent bathroom breaks to wash. They may also refuse to participate in required classroom activities (such as cleaning up or collecting papers) due to fear of contact with dirt or germs.

Furthermore, children with OCD often have additional disorders, such as depression, attention deficit disorder, or tic disorders, that also interfere with learning. We discuss these other disorders in the section "Sorting through other childhood disorders."

Having difficulties with friends

Children with OCD are often isolated from others. They may have unusual rituals or behaviors, causing other children to tease or ridicule them. Full of fear, they are often victims of bullying.

Obsessions and compulsions take considerable time. Children with OCD don't have time to make and keep friends. Repetitive thoughts and rituals keep OCD children prisoners of their minds and outcasts among peers.

Finding the Right Help for Your Child

If you have a child who may have OCD or another disorder that is causing problems at home or at school, you must become informed and educated about the services in your area. We talk about the various professionals in Chapter 7, and in Appendix A, we list specific organizations and resources for you.

The good news is that research indicates that the first line of treatment for childhood OCD is CBT. Medications can be considered when risks and benefits are carefully weighed and follow-through is sufficient. We illustrate how these treatments can be applied to children in Chapter 21.

The bad news is that some mental-health professionals lack training and experience in the delivery of these research-backed, effective treatments. Finding a good therapist for your child depends on you doing some work. Talk to others, get referrals from your healthcare provider, check out the lists of resources in Appendix A, and then call providers and ask questions. If a provider does not answer phone calls, that's not a great sign. Here are some questions you may want to ask:

- ✔ Are you willing to cooperate with my child's physician, teacher, or school counselor?

- ✔ Are you willing to provide extra sessions, longer sessions, or sessions out of the office?

- ✔ Do you do exposure and response prevention (ERP) with children?

- ✔ Do you have training and experience in CBT for OCD?

- ✔ Do you work with children or adolescents?

- ✔ Will you develop work to complete outside of the therapy?

If you are satisfied with the answers to the questions above, then make arrangements to meet with the mental-health professional. Make sure that you feel comfortable and respected.

Your child may resist going to therapy at first, and may even throw a tantrum. After all, confronting fears and worries can be pretty scary. You have to balance your need to protect your child with what is best for your child. If your child needed a shot of antibiotics to treat a bad infection, you wouldn't hesitate to go to a doctor for the shot — even if it meant dragging your kicking, screaming child all the way to the doctor's office. OCD is a treatable disorder. Without treatment, it's likely to get worse and make your family's life more miserable. Be firm, and get your child help.

Chapter 21

Helping Your Child Overcome OCD

Maybe you've thought that your child has OCD, and a professional diagnosis has confirmed your fears. If so, we bet you're worried about your child. After all, obsessive-compulsive disorder sounds ominous, if not overwhelming. But take heart — all is not lost. Lots of famous, highly successful people have struggled with this problem.

If your child has been diagnosed with OCD, search the Internet together for a list of famous people with OCD as a way for both of you to understand that OCD is not only common, but doesn't need to stand in the way of a successful life. For starters, check out www.disabled-world.com/artman/publish/famous-ocd.shtml.

In this chapter, we first explain how important it is to separate the way you view your child from the way you view your child's disorder. Then we tell you how to negotiate your relationship with your child, and we explain your role in therapy. We also give important tips on the delicate dance between providing needed help versus attempting to rescue a child with OCD, however well-intended those misguided attempts may be.

Separating Who Your Child Is from the OCD

In order to prepare you for the hard work ahead to help your child emerge from OCD, it's important first to understand the difference between OCD and your child — they are not one and the same.

If your child has the measles, you can see the outbreak on his body. Any irritability and bad behavior are easily understood to be a reaction to how uncomfortable he feels. You can get specific medical help and medicines to treat the measles and ease your child's discomfort. When the disease is gone, so is the outbreak, and your child's behavior returns to normal. Through the entire ordeal, you are able to clearly distinguish between what the disease is doing to your child and who your child is as a person.

OCD is expressed not only through the behavior of your child, which you can see, but also through his thoughts, which you can't. Unlike a disease such as the measles or the mumps, OCD is more personal and intimate, meaning that it impacts and is expressed through the personality of the child. Yet, OCD should not *define* the personality of your child.

Take the measles again, for example. In some ways, OCD is like the measles. Although OCD is not usually caused directly by a virus, a mixture of biological factors does contribute to its development (see Chapter 4). Just as with the measles, *your child clearly did not ask for or desire to have OCD.*

Yet, when OCD afflicts your child, it can seem as though your child is choosing to intentionally act in childish, oppositional, and defiant ways such as:

- ✔ Displaying new, hard-to-explain fears

- ✔ Refusing to get out of the shower

- ✔ Having difficulty getting ready on time

- ✔ Taking forever to do homework

- ✔ Insisting on elaborate mealtime rituals

On the surface, these behaviors seem easy enough to change, and for many kids without OCD, they are. If your child has OCD, however, demanding immediate cessation of these symptoms is like insisting your child cure himself of the measles — now! Change is possible, but much more challenging. The good news is that a child with OCD who works hard has a good chance of substantial, if not virtually complete, recovery.

Think of it this way: Say your child was in an accident that broke his legs. You were told that recovery was possible, but that he might not be able to walk or do much of anything for weeks. Surgery was required to reset the bones and treat other injuries. Then he needed months of physical therapy to fully regain the use of his legs. He worked hard with the physical therapist and today finally walks with only a barely discernible limp. You certainly wouldn't blame him for the accident or for his residual limp. And you'd be darn proud of him for how brave he was during the long, sometimes painful recovery process.

Your child's OCD is no more under his control than being injured in an accident would be. The expressions of OCD that you see are not who your child truly is, just as injuries are not. With time and treatment, your child can emerge from the OCD, like the proverbial butterfly from the cocoon, to be the healthy person he really is deep down inside. That's the child you need to keep your eye on as you both work through his treatment.

If your child receives a diagnosis of OCD from a mental-health professional, it's important to understand that the OCD is not easily controlled by your child. It's not your fault or your child's fault. Blame and anger only make things worse.

Helping Your Child and Working with the Therapist

If you read this book carefully, you will have a good understanding of OCD and the treatment options that are available for it. You may think you have everything you need to treat your child on your own, but we don't recommend this. Certainly, you play an important role in your child's recovery, but we suggest you enlist the help of an experienced, professional therapist as well. Together, you and your child's therapist can be more effective than either of you working alone. In this section, we explain the advantages of enlisting a therapist's help and discuss your role in the recovery process. We explain the pitfalls to avoid when helping your child — falling into them is easy if you don't know what to look out for. Then we suggest some ways to boost your child's chances of a very successful outcome.

Note: We base our advice on the assumption that your child is receiving Cognitive-Behavioral Therapy (CBT) that includes exposure and response prevention (ERP). Refer to Chapters 8 and 10 for more information on these forms of therapy.

Parenting differently and not being the therapist

Although some self-help books seem to suggest that parents serving as their children's therapists can work, we strongly advise against this. We've seen very few parents who can deal with the emotional complexities and subtleties of attempting to serve as their own child's therapist. Simply put, parents love their children far too much to be able to have the necessary objectivity for planning and delivering treatment.

As a parent or caregiver of a child with OCD, you know your child more deeply, and under all sorts of circumstances, far better than a therapist who may only see your child a few dozen times. You want help, and when it comes to your child, you ultimately know what's best. But you may not know how to get there.

That's because you probably aren't an expert in treating OCD. Furthermore, the treatment of OCD does not always seem to make sense. So it's no wonder many parents feel uncomfortable when a therapist guides their children through exercises like sifting through garbage, walking on cracks, changing up bedtime routines, or wearing different colored socks. Sometimes, children find these tasks frightening and turn to their parents to help. How can anyone expect a parent to turn away from a child who is crying and in obvious distress?

Thus, you very well may feel tempted to argue with your child's therapist by suggesting that your child isn't ready or "just can't take it." Or you may undermine the therapist by comforting and reassuring your child every step of the way. These are natural parental instincts at work. And you must work hard to avoid these pitfalls. A few guidelines follow:

- **Avoid overprotection.** You have to keep your protective instincts in check. After thoroughly checking out your therapist (see Chapter 7 for how to do this), trust that the therapist knows how to treat OCD and trust that your child will be strong enough to gradually stand up and talk back to OCD. As your child progresses, the fear and anxiety will decrease.

- **Avoid impatience.** Positive results from treating OCD do not occur instantaneously. With children, the therapist may need a little more time to build up trust. And a few sessions of supportive therapy may be required to establish rapport before the real work begins.

- **Avoid rescue.** Parents feel sorry for their children with OCD; that's perfectly understandable. And, in fact, kids with OCD may need a little more help and structure at home and at school. However, it is not a good idea to rescue your child from activities such as cleaning up messy art projects, completing assignments on time, or doing chores around the house. Work with a therapist to develop reasonable expectations and then stick with them. Mastering the art of "not rescuing" is likely to take some practice.

Do your homework and make sure you pick a good therapist who is experienced in CBT, and then let the therapist take charge of the treatment.

If, even after checking your child's therapist out carefully, you develop alarming concerns about the therapy, get a second professional opinion before interfering with the therapy. If you feel it's necessary, you can put the therapy on temporary hold while getting that additional opinion.

Managing your emotions

Parenting any child is a difficult job. Parenting a child with OCD can be extremely hard. You don't always know what your child is thinking, and OCD behaviors can be frustrating, irritating, and annoying. At times you no doubt feel sorry for your child and cave in to demands — unfortunately, that only makes OCD worse.

Managing your own emotions will certainly help your child battle OCD. We suggest taking some deep breaths and calming down when you get upset. Here are a couple of the common feelings that parents of children with OCD experience and some ideas about what to do with them:

- ✔ **Anger:** Parents can get frustrated or angry because a child with OCD interferes with family life. There may be battles about getting ready to go somewhere, eating, or sleeping. Kids with OCD may demand certain foods, ask their parents to engage in rituals or special cleaning tasks, and have meltdowns for no reason. It is easy to see how even the most patient parent can get irritable. Another source of frustration for parents comes when their kids seem able to control aspects of their OCD for a while and then suddenly can't. Anger makes the whole situation worse. Try to understand, and get help from your child's therapist on how to handle these times. Reminding yourself that the OCD — rather than your child — is at work here may help.

- ✔ **Embarrassment:** Kids with OCD can look strange to other people. Imagine a child who starts to scream because a stranger accidentally bumps into him. Or a case where an unexpected sneeze triggers a frantic rush to a public restroom and elaborate cleansing rituals to decontaminate. Kids with OCD may have peculiar, inexplicable rituals that must be performed in order to go through doorways. Some children with OCD refuse to sit in car seats, can't climb certain stairs, refuse to dress for gym class, or spend hours mumbling to themselves. The public acting out of obsessions or compulsions can be quite difficult for a parent to handle or understand. Acceptance comes with education about the disorder. Again, reminding yourself that these behaviors are about OCD — and are not a reflection on you as a parent — can help.

Working with the therapist

How a therapist structures therapy with your child depends on many factors, such as your child's age, maturity, conversational skills, shyness, and independence. Some therapists have both parents and child together in the office throughout each session. Other therapists break the session up, having the child come in first and following with a summary for the parents. Teenagers are usually seen alone, with parents attending sessions only occasionally.

The bottom line is that therapy is built on a *collaborative, confidential* relationship between the client (child) and the therapist. The child must be comfortable confiding anything to the therapist. In general, parents need to know what is going on and what progress is being made, but it's counterproductive in most cases for them to be privy to all the details. Don't worry that your child may be talking about family embarrassments (such as the last fight you had with your spouse). Good therapists are not judgmental and keep information confidential. Furthermore, most therapists don't believe everything they hear.

When your child leaves the therapist's office, ask an open-ended question like, "How do you feel today?" rather than "What did you talk about?" Don't press your child for details about the therapy.

Collaborating on goals

Parents need to collaborate with their child and their child's therapist in setting appropriate goals. OCD is a formidable foe and is best tackled in small, sequential steps. Everyone needs to know what those steps will be and when they are going to occur. In most cases, some kind of exposure staircase (see Chapter 10) will be developed and times set aside for climbing each stair.

Parents can help the therapist by recording their kid's progress. They should also make note of any setbacks and/or distressing, unanticipated resistance shown by their child during this work. Furthermore, parents can usually be good historians and inform therapists about their child's early symptoms and how those have waxed and waned over the years.

Providing appropriate incentives

Everyone, including adults, feels more motivated to keep working on tasks when they can perceive some sort of payoff or incentive for all their hard work. For adults and even some mature teenagers, that payoff may be something intangible, such as taking pride in a job well done. Younger children often need more concrete, clearer rewards, such as special outings, a later bedtime, praise, money, stickers, or other treats. Most therapists who work with children have an array of interesting ideas for incentives that may work with your child.

Much as rewards may be useful in keeping your child on track, watch out for these pitfalls when designing your child's incentive plan:

- Don't overemphasize rewards and become excessively enthusiastic about each and every small gain. Kids sometimes learn to resist the pressure they feel when parents get too excited or push too hard — even with incentives.

- Rewards must not be the centerpiece of your child's OCD treatment plan. They are only a way to nudge along and encourage good, solid effort.

- Part of your reward plan needs to include ignoring lack of progress, off-task behavior, and even OCD backslides. Let the therapist deal with these issues. You will become too emotionally entangled if you get involved with telling your child to stop OCD behaviors.

✔ The younger your child, the more quickly you need to provide small rewards for specific efforts. Older children can be expected to work longer to obtain larger, less frequent rewards. Again, your child's therapist can provide a lot of guidance here.

Properly-designed reward plans are not bribes. Bribery is involved when parents dangle rewards and incentives in front of their kids with constant reminders and cajoling to obtain them. You don't want to remind your child about the reward plan very often at all.

Giving appropriate reassurance

A very common practice among children and adults with OCD is asking other people for reassurance. These questions are often repeated dozens of times every day. Examples of the type of questions asked include:

✔ Are the doors locked?

✔ Are you and daddy mad?

✔ Are you okay?

✔ Do I look sick?

✔ Do you still love me?

✔ Do you think a storm is coming?

✔ Do you think I hurt somebody?

✔ Is that dish really clean?

We recommend that you collaborate with your child's therapist in developing an automatic response to each of these questions. Also, tell your child ahead of time what the answer will be. Possible examples of such responses that avoid the reassurance trap include:

✔ I understand that you're worried, but I can't answer that.

✔ That's your OCD talking, what can you say back to it?

✔ You have to find the answer for that yourself.

✔ You know I can't answer that.

✔ You know the answer to that.

Perhaps these answers sound like they lack empathy and compassion to you. However, providing reassurance to an OCD child who asks for it only fuels OCD. Letting your child know that you understand his or her feelings is fine, but giving reassurance only ends up reinforcing your child's OCD.

Telling your child in advance what your responses will be helps reduce frustration on everyone's part and allows you as a parent to feel less guilt about not providing the reassurance that's been requested. Remind yourself of the old adage that sometimes you have to be just a little "cruel to be kind."

Acting as a coach and a cheerleader

We discourage parents from being therapists to their children with OCD. But in reality, parents are obviously involved and must take on some role. After all, parents spend many hours a day with their children. We like parents to act as coaches. Not as mean coaches who scream, discourage, and push, nor as coaches who overly praise and cajole. Rather, we suggest that parents be kind coaches who motivate through noticing progress and keeping a positive focus, while setting reasonable limits on OCD. Table 21-1 provides some ideas on what coaches should and shouldn't say.

Table 21-1	Bad Coach/Good Coach	
Child's Behavior	*Bad Coaching Response*	*Good Coaching Response*
Cuts showers down to three per day from six.	Fine, but when are you going to shower like everybody else in the world — once a day!?	Nice work, I see you've cut your showers down. What's your plan now?
Refuses to engage in an ERP exercise one day.	You'll never get better that way. Have you forgotten about the movie you can earn?	Maybe tomorrow will go better.
Says, "I'm not going to therapy anymore. I hate therapy."	If you go, I'll take you out for ice cream. And besides, I've already paid for it. You have to do this!	I know it's hard, but it's just what we all decided to do. There isn't really a choice here.
Child with contamination fears is able to clean up dog poop in the backyard and not wash for an hour.	Wow! That's so great! I can't believe you managed to do that! You are terrific. It looks like you've just about licked your OCD! Let's go and buy you that new video game you've wanted for so long. I'm so proud of you!	Wow, that looked hard. You must feel proud of yourself. I think you'll be ready for the next step soon. Would you like to pick out your reward from the list?
Child yells at parent for interrupting a bedtime ritual.	Who would ever marry you if you do these weird things all the time? Be normal! I can't stand it when you act crazy like this. Stop it!	I know you're frustrated, but we can't give in to your OCD mind. I want you to try and be more respectful.

As you can see in Table 21-1, bad coaches and good coaches behave differently. Bad coaches criticize, whereas good coaches refrain from criticism. Bad coaches go over the top with praise, cajoling, and reminders about incentives. Other times, they let their anger go out of control.

Good coaches praise with restraint and don't focus too much on rewards. Good coaches are leaders and role models for emotional control. They also set reasonable limits on their kids and their kids' OCD. Finally, they express positive expectations, but without undue pressure. Your child's therapist can help you figure out how to do all of that because it isn't always easy!

Explaining OCD to Family, Friends, and Schoolmates

Children with OCD work desperately hard to keep people from knowing about their problem. Only rarely do they fully succeed. And when others do see their OCD behaviors, they often fail to understand what's going on. All too often the net result is that the child with OCD experiences a lack of understanding, teasing, and social rejection. Feeling ostracized can lead to depression, anxiety, and failures in school.

So the questions become whom to tell, what to tell, and how to tell others about OCD. Unfortunately, there are no hard and fast rules. However, consider the following points:

- **Brothers and sisters:** There's no way that brothers and sisters living in the same household won't at some time and in some way know that their sibling has OCD, or at least some pretty odd behaviors. Sometimes brothers and sisters feel angry because they fear what others will think of them for having a sibling with OCD. They may also feel angry or jealous about the attention paid to the OCD or the fact that their sibling seems to get away with behaviors that they can't. And other times, they worry about catching the OCD. Acknowledging all of these feelings is important, yet limits must be set on how anger and jealousy get expressed.

  Explaining what OCD is all about is equally important. First, tell siblings of the child with OCD that OCD is no one's fault. Explain that the brain of the child with OCD misfires for various reasons. Further note that OCD is treatable, nothing to feel ashamed about, and that you can't "catch" OCD from someone else. Finally, try to spend a little special time with the siblings who don't suffer from OCD.

✔ **Relatives and close family friends:** Many people do not understand OCD very well. If your friends and family really want to be helpful, suggest that they educate themselves about OCD — reading this book is one way they could do that. However, if they don't want to spend that much time, you can at least explain a few things. Tell them the same things that siblings need to know: OCD involves a misfiring of the brain, it's usually very treatable, and it's not contagious. If relatives or close friends are directly involved with child care, you probably want to explain how treatment works in more detail so they don't inadvertently get in the way of what you're trying to do. If they show interest in helping, you may suggest that they read Chapter 22.

✔ **Schoolmates:** First, check with your child, your child's teacher, and the school counselor to see whether schoolmates are causing any problems, such as teasing or bullying due to your child's OCD. Some children have OCD and don't show much of it overtly at school. In that case, leave it alone. However, if problems do crop up, they can be handled a couple of ways:

- The school counselor may either give a talk about OCD to your child's class or recruit an expert to do so.

- If an individual child is causing problems with bullying and teasing, the counselor can probably deal with that.

Your child's therapist can collaborate with the counselor as well. What's important is to protect your child from becoming victimized.

OCD can easily affect your child's relationship with siblings, friends, and relatives. Help your child realize that any teasing or rejection is really about a misunderstanding of OCD, not about your child. Work with your child to fight back against the OCD.

In a few cases, OCD interferes significantly with learning and achievement in school. Usually, accommodations can be made for a while in the regular classroom. These accommodations may include providing a little extra time to complete tests or written work, seating the child near the front of the class to help with focus, and allowing extra breaks to check in with the counselor. If those accommodations are not sufficient and the child lags behind, a multi-disciplinary evaluation can be requested. Your child's therapist will no doubt want to be consulted on all of these accommodations and will help the school team provide needed help without inadvertently reinforcing the OCD.

Chapter 22

Helping Family and Friends Overcome OCD with Coaching

In This Chapter

▶ Knowing about OCD in order to help

▶ Understanding your role as coach

▶ Carrying out a game plan against OCD

*T*ackling OCD takes a team, and every team needs a coach — often more than one. If you're interested in helping a friend or family member overcome OCD, understand that it is not an opponent for the faint of heart or a single individual, no matter how brave. That's why we don't advocate a pure self-help approach in this book. It's not that people can't help themselves, but maintaining the focus, drive, and objectivity required to tackle OCD is easier and more effectively done with the help of others. For most OCD sufferers, that help includes one or more mental-health professionals as well as possibly friends or family. For a few, that help may come only from friends or family members who can serve as "coaches."

In this chapter, we tell you what you need to know if you're interested in helping a friend, loved one, child, or relative who suffers from OCD. We explain the task that lies ahead for you, including figuring out whether you're the right person to do the job and knowing what to look out for. We help you assess your coaching capabilities as well as offer techniques for effective coaching.

Discerning What It Takes to Be a Coach

One of the trendier terms in mental health, business, personal development, and physical fitness circles nowadays is "coach." When you think of the word "coach," you think of someone who listens, watches, provides feedback, models behavior, and instructs. That's a good analogy for the role that a friend or family member may play in helping someone with OCD. But there are two important points we want to clarify before we get into the nitty-gritty of coaching:

- ✔ **You don't have to be a professional to be a coach.** You don't need any sort of professional degree or license. Family and friends who agree to serve as coaches may be of great value in helping someone implement a game plan for fighting OCD.

- ✔ **Your role is to help implement — not develop — a treatment plan.** Unless those acting as coaches are trained and licensed mental-health professionals, they should not be responsible for *developing* an actual treatment plan for OCD. What we're discussing in this chapter is helping your friend or family member carry out a treatment plan that has been developed in cooperation with a therapist.

To be an effective coach, you need to understand the game that's being played. In this case, that means you need to become educated about OCD. Of course, we recommend reading this book — it really does provide a whole lot of information about OCD. It's also a good idea to find out about the specific type of OCD the person you're helping has. (See Chapter 2 as well as relevant chapters on specific types of OCD.)

Whatever type of OCD the person you care about has, your coaching will likely focus on helping that person to implement exposure and response prevention (ERP). We explain ERP fully in Chapter 10, and that chapter should be read carefully. There, you not only see what ERP is, but we also provide lots of examples, as well as advice on troubleshooting.

In brief, ERP involves guiding someone through a series of steps that all involve triggers for the OCD. The steps start out fairly easy and become sequentially more difficult. Although to a layperson some of the steps may look silly or easy, trust us — OCD can make them appear like Mt. Everest.

People with OCD must climb each step, one at a time. It's most helpful if they stay on that step until their distress levels (what we call Ugh Factor Ratings) come down a little. For example, imagine you're helping your friend Pete with Contamination OCD. Pete fears shaking hands and feels compelled to wash his hands for an hour if he happens to be forced into a handshaking encounter. The first step on the staircase may involve Pete agreeing to briefly shake hands with someone who has just washed up. Pete's next step may call for him to not wash his hands for one full hour. Your role as coach is to assist in that process — read on to discover how to do that right.

Understanding how OCD challenges you

Good coaches know which side they're on. If you're coaching a friend or relative with OCD, you take the side of that person and you work against the OCD. Sounds pretty obvious, doesn't it?

But sometimes OCD makes people act in ways that hook you into working against them. That happens when OCD hijacks someone's mind so much that the person fears and resists treatment of the OCD (see Chapter 6 for examples of such resistance).

Naturally, as a coach and helper, you want to see the person fight OCD with unbridled zeal and enthusiasm. Your intense desire to help may cause you to push, pressure, and prod your friend to increase effort and fight harder. If you see signs of hesitation or reluctance, you may want to confront, cajole, and conquer your friend's reluctance. That's a good idea, right?

Actually, it isn't. Psychologists now know that confronting and pressuring people to change typically causes them to dig in their heels and resist changing all the more. They may run from such "help" and avoid treatment entirely. Thus, if you push too hard, you actually end up serving your friend's OCD mind, not your friend.

Coaches don't coach people who don't want to be coached. They wait for people to seek their services. If resistance pops up, it's important to accept that position. Tell your friend or relative that you're ready to help when he or she wants it — not one minute before that.

The more you can accept people for who and where they are now, the more likely they are to accept the idea of making changes.

Assessing whether you're the right person to coach

Not everyone is born to coach. You may care about your friend or relative a great deal; yet, you may not be the right person to help implement OCD treatment. So how do you know if you'd be a good coach? Here are a few considerations:

- ✔ **Compassion:** You have to realize that OCD is a disorder that's not caused by weakness of character or malicious intentions. The person with OCD truly suffers and needs your empathic support (but not so much that you assuage and reassure).

✔ **Humor:** It really helps if you can laugh with the person you're coaching. Obviously, you don't want to laugh *at* the person you're coaching but rather at some of the humorous moments that pop up. Some exposure tasks can get a little silly, and it's okay to laugh so long as you're laughing together.

✔ **Temperament:** ERP requires great patience. Those with OCD can also test your mettle. If you're easily frustrated or have a short fuse, you probably ought to cheer from the sidelines rather than coach on the playing field.

✔ **Time:** Coaching takes some time. Depending on the case, ERP may consume a few hours each week for quite a few weeks or as much as a full day or two each week over a shorter time period. Sometimes ERP is scheduled to occur on a daily basis. Be clear about how much time is being asked of you and be certain you can commit without feeling resentful.

Think about how you and your life fit into the role of a coach. Don't volunteer if you aren't pretty sure you can follow through. It's okay to be a supportive bystander.

Knowing your limits

Until a few decades ago, OCD was thought to be a largely untreatable condition. Even today, sometimes OCD comes in a highly treatment-resistant mode. Although the odds are good that treatment will help, it can be difficult and require a lot of time and energy.

Don't take responsibility for the success or failure of the treatment plan. If you feel too personally involved, you may need to back off. You are facilitating, not taking over.

Know your own limits. If your frustration runs too high, it's time to walk away. You can still care and even cheerlead a little from the sidelines.

Applying Appropriate Coaching Techniques

If you choose to be a coach, you may become part of a team that includes your friend or relative, probably a mental-health professional, and perhaps other coaches. All of you will likely meet together and collaborate on the game plan. Feel free to toss out a few of your own ideas, but realize that responsibility for designing the game plan lies with the professional and the one who has OCD.

If you feel uncomfortable with any aspect of the ERP plan, express that discomfort. You don't want to agree to something that doesn't resonate with you. You may discover that the therapist uses some professional jargon that you don't follow. If that happens, don't hesitate to ask questions — it doesn't mean you're stupid. Sometimes professionals lapse into using shorthand that others shouldn't be expected to know.

Recognizing OCD's dirty tricks

As a coach (or supportive family member or friend), keep your eye on the ball. In this case, the opponent (OCD) is always trying to steal the ball. One way OCD tries to overtake the coach is by enticing the coach or other people to help perform checking or rituals or to provide reassurance. For example:

- A father repeatedly reassures and reasons with his daughter who has Superstitious OCD (see Chapter 17). He patiently explains that numbers have no power over events and that certain symbols and words cannot cause harm. He feels gratified when she feels temporarily relieved, not realizing how much fuel he has provided for her superstitions.

- A mother agrees to rewash the dishes and rerun the laundry for her son who has Contamination OCD (see Chapters 8, 9, & 10). The mom goes along because her son is so distraught if she doesn't.

- A teenager has his parents praying certain prayers with him before bed. If they don't do them "just so," he demands that they repeat the prayers. The parents comply so that their son goes to bed without screaming at them. Again, a simple act of kindness does nothing but make OCD stronger.

- A woman worries about her appearance. She repeatedly asks her husband whether she looks okay, whether her wrinkles are deeper, and whether he still finds her attractive. He wants her to feel better and consistently reassures her that he thinks she's beautiful. He doesn't realize that he's simply feeding his wife's OCD.

- Another person may have obsessions about closing up the house after leaving for work. That person calls a spouse or even a neighbor to check again. A half-hour later, the brief relief from the reassurance fades.

- Someone who repeatedly checks to see that appliances are off before going to bed may ask a concerned family member to check one more time. Rather than get into a squabble, that family member gives in. Unfortunately, giving in does not help the person with OCD. Rather, it empowers OCD. Although the person with the OCD feels temporarily assuaged and reassured, OCD doubts quickly return and grow stronger than ever.

Coaches must refrain from helping the person actually carry out checking or rituals. They also need to avoid reasoning with the person, no matter how rational doing so seems. OCD doesn't go away with reasoning; rather, it deepens. With permission from the person with OCD, coaches can also inform therapists about other friends or family members who are unwittingly feeding the OCD. The therapist can help design strategies to help everyone stop this vicious cycle.

Coaching with kindness

You've seen sports movies that portray really mean, arrogant coaches — sometimes they succeed and pull off miracles. But OCD coaching doesn't work with anything other than a kind, supportive approach. We discuss how to coach with kindness in the following sections.

Refraining from criticizing

ERP involves hard work. Some of the steps provoke a lot of distress and anxiety. The last thing people with OCD need to hear is that they aren't doing things right.

We're not suggesting that you can't provide a little corrective feedback, but any such messages must be worded carefully and gently. For example, instead of saying, "You didn't wait the full 30 minutes before washing," you could say, "You made it 20 minutes, that's good. The step calls for 30 minutes, and I'll bet you can get there next time."

Most people with OCD are quite intelligent, and they didn't ask to have OCD. The person you're coaching is probably working hard to get to a better place. Criticism undermines confidence.

Providing encouragement

It's not only okay, but also useful to express belief in your friend's or relative's ability to tackle OCD. A small dose of persuasion can do wonders too, but only if it is used very judiciously. You want to encourage and help the person to maintain a focus on each goal. But if you let your encouragement turn into pressure, it can be like trying to take a mountainous hairpin curve at high speed — you can easily fly off the edge of the road.

Leaving decision-making alone

People with OCD frequently ask for advice on what to do, when to do it, and how to do it — it's actually part of their OCD. If you're the coach, don't fall for this one. You want to keep firmly in your mind that part of good OCD treatment is to keep decision-making in the hands of the person with OCD.

For example, a woman with Shaming OCD may worry that she'll shout obscenities in public, or even worse, at church. Her exposure task is to go to a movie while actively focusing on and thinking about obscenities. She may ask you whether she should leave the movie if her anxiety becomes too great. Don't make that decision for her. It's okay to tell her that the general principle is to stay with an exposure step until distress comes down some, but how long she actually does so is always completely her decision to make.

Eliminating surprises by asking for permission

As a coach, keep in mind that treatment should be predictable and under the control of the person with OCD. Thus, if an exposure step calls for your friend to smear motor oil on her arm, you don't want to surprise her by unexpectedly sullying her arm with Penzoil. Rather, you should discuss the step and ideally allow her to do the dirty work. If she just can't bring herself to do it and *asks* you to, then you can. Her next step can then involve doing it herself.

Furthermore, you want to be sure you're both on the same page. Perhaps you're working with someone who has Hoarding OCD (see Chapter 16). If you go to that person's home, you'll probably encounter huge stacks of useless junk. Useless to you, perhaps, but likely seen as invaluable by the one you're coaching. The rule of thumb is: Don't touch a thing or toss out the most trivial, unusable item you've ever seen without explicit permission.

Those who have OCD don't give up their fundamental rights when they undergo treatment. Coaches can be effective only when they allow the people they are helping to control the steps being taken.

Avoiding arguing at all costs

Being a coach is tricky business. Sometimes the person you're coaching will suddenly balk and declare himself unable to take the next step. Perhaps you've actually seen him take steps that appear quite similar to the one he's resisting. Under such circumstances, you may be tempted to argue and convincingly demonstrate that his perspective is flawed. But whether he's right or wrong doesn't really matter.

A good coach doesn't take the bait. A good coach simply says, "You're ready when you're ready. You tell me when that is." Accept the position of the person you're helping and even express a little empathy.

You could easily think we're saying that you should never disagree with the person you're helping, but that's not quite true. We're saying that you should avoid *arguing* at almost any cost. You can express disagreement if you do so ever so gently — whether directly or with a question. Following are a few ways to express disagreement if you think doing so may be useful:

- ✔ "I hear you saying that you feel you're at an impasse. And clearly, you're only ready when you're ready. However, I wonder whether that's your OCD mind talking. What do you think?"

- ✔ "I know you feel rather hopeless right now. I'd feel frustrated too if I was in your shoes. Have you felt hopeless at other times and felt more hopeful later?"

- ✔ "You're right; the OCD does seem to be in charge right now. However, I do believe in you, and I suspect you're going to find a way to get where you want to be."

Sometimes you word your disagreement beautifully and your friend or relative still manages to argue back. When that happens, it's best to let go of the issue and allow the therapist to deal with it.

Coaches are not serving as therapists. It is not up to you as a coach to force the person you're coaching to stick with the treatment plan. You can express encouragement and belief in the person, but arguing is always counterproductive.

Sidestepping the word "should"

Dr. Albert Ellis was a psychologist who virtually made a career out of railing against the word "should." He aptly noted that there are few behaviors that people absolutely "should" or "should not" do. Obviously, many of us would argue that murder, stealing, and abuse belong on the "should not" do list. However, people have a strong proclivity to use the word "should" in an array of situations that really don't call for the harsh, judgmental tone the word conveys.

Most of the time, other words or phrases do the job of "should" without sounding so evaluative. If you plan to coach someone with OCD, we recommend that you start monitoring your use of the word "should." Try substituting other phrases, such as, "It would be better if . . . ," "I suspect you'd want to . . . ," or "It would be nice if . . ." The bottom line is that you don't want to tell those with OCD how they "should" feel, what they "should" be ready for, or what they "should" do. Check out the following list of some "should" statements, along with some improved ways of stating things:

"Should" statement: You should stay with this step for at least 30 minutes.

Improved statement: It has been 23 minutes. Just seven more to go. See if you can hang in there.

"Should" statement: You shouldn't feel that way.

Improved statement: I can tell you're feeling upset.

"Should" statement: You shouldn't wash your hands so much. They're starting to bleed!

Improved statement: I know it's hard, but it would help if you could stick with the plan of reducing that hand-washing.

"Should" statement: You shouldn't worry about numbers all the time; that's really silly.

Improved statement: I suspect you don't enjoy getting hooked by those number superstitions. It would be nice if you could work a little longer on this number repetition exercise.

 Don't beat yourself up for occasionally lapsing into using the word "should." We're sure you can find instances where we use it — it's ingrained in the human psyche. But do try to lessen your usage and, in general, avoid being judgmental.

Keeping difficult emotions in check

Watching someone you care about struggle with OCD can be frustrating. OCD is neither logical nor rational. When you see people being irrational, you may want to shake some sense into them. You may feel angry, upset, or distressed.

Try to appreciate the fact that the person you're coaching is likely to be consumed with fighting OCD and doesn't understand your turmoil. Furthermore, if you express your distress, things will only get worse. We suggest you read the earlier section in this chapter, "Knowing your limits," if you find yourself overwhelmed with negative emotions.

Developing alternatives to reassurance

In the section "Recognizing OCD's dirty tricks," we note that reassurance, assuaging, and giving into OCD demands only gives the OCD part of someone's mind more fuel. But how do you *not* reassure someone you care about who is in distress and begging for reassurance?

In fact, you'll probably find yourself unable to stop giving reassurance at first. Most kind people are programmed to provide reassurance to those who are in distress and ask for it. That's probably not a big problem for the average person. But OCD changes the game.

Work with the person you're coaching and the therapist on this issue. Everyone needs to know that you plan to respond differently from here on out. We recommend designing a list of automatic responses — ones that you can memorize and use reflexively. Table 22-1 provides a few examples of reassurance requests that may be asked of you and some reassurance-busting responses.

Table 22-1	Reassurance Requests and Reassurance Busters	
OCD Type	*Reassurance Request*	*Reassurance Buster*
Contamination	Do you think this table was wiped clean enough?	There's always a chance that germs remain anywhere, including on this table.
Checking and doubting	Do you think that bump we hit was a person?	Remember that your therapist said to say that it's always possible you did hit someone. Beyond that, I don't know.
Shaming	Will I go to hell?	I don't know.
Checking and doubting	Are you still attracted to me?	You know I can't answer that for you.
Shaming	Do you think I'm gay?	I can't answer that.
Superstitious	Do you think that hearse will bring us bad luck?	Probably.

Your list of reassurance busters needs to be planned in advance and agreed upon by the therapist and the person you're coaching. These are not pulled out as a surprise. And they're not intended to be sarcastic. Feel free to use judicious humor, but not disrespect.

Part VI
The Part of Tens

The 5th Wave

By Rich Tennant

"My mom asked me if I thought I had OCD. I'd tell her if she'd just ask me exactly eight times."

In this part . . .

The Part of Tens chapters are classic in all *For Dummies* books. Read about quick tips for combating OCD. See tips and ideas about what to do with your life after you've recovered from OCD. Finally, because Contamination OCD is so common, we thought you'd enjoy getting the real lowdown on dirt.

Chapter 23

Ten Quick OCD Tricks

A variety of chapters in this book give you detailed, comprehensive plans for dealing with your OCD. But sometimes you just want to make it through a minute, an hour, or a day. This chapter gives you some quick tips for dealing with your OCD. Use these tips to ease your journey.

Breathing Better

Breathing strategies can help you manage difficult feelings. Whether your feelings involve fear, anxiety, sadness, or urges, concentrating on your breath can decrease the intensity of your distress. First, take a deep breath through your nose. Notice the air going into your nostrils and flowing into your lungs. Fill the lower part of your lungs first by expanding your abdomen and your diaphragm. Hold that breath for a slow count of five. Then slowly release the air to a slow count of eight.

Many people find that making a slight hissing noise through their lips helps them slow down the exhalation. Continue breathing this way for five or six breaths. Notice how the breathing affects your feelings. Deep, slow breathing is a great alternative to other ways of trying to avoid feelings through compulsions.

Considering a Delay

Especially if you're early in the process of working on your OCD, stopping your compulsions may seem to border on the absurd or the impossible. That's okay — just delay. In other words, put off your compulsive behavior (such as hand-washing, chanting, arranging things, or cleaning) for 10 or 15 minutes. Later, try delaying for half an hour, then an hour. Give yourself credit for each and every delay. Soon you'll find yourself ready for full-blown exposure and response prevention (ERP — see Chapter 10).

Distracting Yourself

Although not an ideal strategy in the long run, distracting yourself during early ERP can help you get through the first steps. Try focusing on another competing activity, such as:

- Eating
- Going for a walk
- Knitting
- Reading
- Watching TV

After a while, we recommend that you drop your distraction strategies. But distraction can help get you started.

Accepting Discomfort

The OCD mind attempts to avoid discomfort of almost any kind all the time. The mind also labels discomfort as terrible and unacceptable. However, these attempts to avoid discomfort at all costs inevitably create even more discomfort in the long run.

Instead, open up a little room for discomfort in your life. When you feel distress, notice it and merely study it for a while, as though you were going to write a report about emotional upset. Remind yourself that some discomfort is inevitable in life. As you embrace negative feelings, you'll find that they paradoxically lessen their hold on you and your life.

Counting Every Exposure

Whether your ERP task is easy or difficult, takes 20 minutes or all day, appreciate the fact that every single success matters. Don't look at the big picture. Instead, focus on each attempt in and of itself. If you haven't done ERP for a few days, don't beat up on yourself; instead, design one small task and complete it.

Realizing It's Not You, It's Your OCD

OCD is not the same thing as who you are. OCD takes control of your brain and compels you to do things you don't like or want to do. OCD makes you feel that these actions are necessary, but you wouldn't choose to do them on your own. So it's important to remind yourself that you are not full of doubt, uncertainty, and avoidance of all risks — that's your OCD mind talking. As you step back and realize that it's just your OCD mind, you'll gain strength, confidence, and resolve.

Making Flashcards

When you're mired in the throes of an episode of OCD urges, thinking rationally and remembering what you're supposed to do is pretty hard. Therefore, we recommend that you write out a few ideas on some flashcards. Consider the following possibilities:

- Bad feelings eventually pass; just give them some time.
- Having bad thoughts doesn't make me a bad person.
- I've experienced this before and lived through it.
- The longer I delay a compulsion, the better off I'm going to be.
- Thoughts are just thoughts; just because I think something doesn't make it true.

Going to an Online Support Group

As you're working on your OCD, you'll experience your share of both successes and difficult times. When you feel discouraged, alone, or down, seeking some support is never a bad idea. One great place you can go almost anytime is online. We don't have any particular online support group to recommend to you — you need to explore and find one that feels like a good fit to you. Various networks online offer encouragement, education, and advice. Of course, they're not a substitute for professional help, but they can support your efforts. Always take care in terms of revealing personal information and data online that can reveal your identity.

Minding Meditation

Your OCD brain is primed to set off alarms excessively and in ways that feel outside of your control. Meditation teaches you to take control of your mind and focus it willfully. The skill of meditation can be acquired by almost anyone. Meditation is not an all or none phenomenon, but rather a skill that exists along a long continuum. We recommend that you consider an adult continuing education class and/or read *Meditation For Dummies,* 2nd Edition, by Stephan Bodian and Dean Ornish (Wiley) or other books on this topic.

Taking a Hot Bath

OCD got you down? Feeling stressed, frazzled, and out of control? Unless you have contamination OCD, we recommend you try a time-tested technique: Take a long soak in a hot bath, perhaps with oils, scents, or bubbles added. For those with contamination OCD, try throwing a handful of dirt into the tub and call it an exposure task!

Chapter 24

Ten Steps to Take After You Get Better

*O*bsessive-compulsive disorder (OCD) seriously damages the quality of the lives of those who suffer from it. Many people with OCD report that much of their day focuses on their obsessions and compulsions that involve cleaning, fears of contamination, checking on safety, and various superstitious worries and behaviors. Their OCD slams the door on more positive pursuits such as hobbies, recreation, charitable work, and social connections — most of what makes a life feel full and worthwhile.

However, the odds are high that you'll be able to substantially reduce the hold that OCD has over your life. Assuming you do, you'll have time and resources that you haven't had available to you in many years. You may find this new freedom confusing and not know what to do with it. This chapter gives you ten ideas for filling up the void.

Forgiving Yourself

Most people with OCD have a tendency to berate themselves for having the disorder in the first place. Making matters worse, they beat themselves up after they've improved from the OCD — often believing they have wasted years mired in their OCD and should be punished for doing so.

Being angry with yourself only keeps you from finding peace. Finding a way to forgive yourself is important. First, remember that you did not ask for your OCD. OCD is a complicated problem with many causes (see Chapters 4 and 5 for more information about the causes of OCD). For many decades no effective treatments even existed for OCD — proving just how formidable a foe OCD can really be.

You had to work hard to battle your OCD. If you have experienced significant success, you deserve praise, not punishment. Therefore, when you notice self-punishing thoughts going through your head, try answering back with one of these self-forgiving phrases:

- I am not the same as my OCD.
- I didn't ask for my OCD, but I did battle it well.
- I've made great progress; beating myself up will only make me backslide.
- If a friend of mine worked hard on his OCD, I'd praise him, not pummel him.
- It's time to focus on future successes, not past struggles.

Searching for Meaning

Many sufferers from OCD report that they feel as though their lives have no meaning outside of dealing with their OCD. But again, if you experience even partial success in battling your OCD, the possibility for discovering new meanings begins to emerge.

Think about what you want to be remembered for — it probably goes beyond your OCD. Do you want to be remembered for your clean house or your kind heart? You may find sources of meaning and ways you'd like to be remembered by considering the following possibilities:

- Advancing knowledge
- Being generous
- Being grateful
- Helping others who are less fortunate
- Improving the environment
- Taking care of rescue animals
- Teaching others

In addition, honor your personal faith. Believe in something larger than yourself or your OCD.

Strengthening Family Ties

OCD has a way of creating rifts in families. Friends and relatives of those with OCD often become frustrated and upset because they don't understand the disorder. And those who have OCD feel unfairly maligned and misunderstood.

If you've managed to overcome much of your OCD, it's time to mend those fences. Try having a monthly potluck with all family members invited. If you live some distance away, try to arrange family reunions every couple of years. If your family is willing to listen, you may want to explain OCD to them or suggest that they read this book. If your family is reasonably close, they may consider the value of family therapy — it can help. If you don't have a family, or your family is uninterested in reengaging, read the following section on finding friends.

Finding Friends

Your OCD may have dominated so much of your time and attention that you weren't able to develop good friendships. And finding friends, especially as an adult, can be difficult. People are busy with their jobs and immediate families.

Yet, the value of having a circle of friends is considerable. People with the support of friends tend to be much healthier, happier, and fulfilled. Friends give you a source of advice, enjoyable times, and encouragement.

Though the task may sound challenging, you can find friends if you work at it. Consider joining a neighborhood association and actively participating. Search for continuing education classes (see the section "Learning New Skills") and talk with your fellow classmates during breaks or after class. You can find social support groups at churches, synagogues, and mosques. Participate in politics. Be creative; you can do this.

Reaching Out to Others with OCD

If you've gone through exposure and response prevention therapy (ERP, see Chapter 10), you could make a great coach for someone else. Look for OCD support groups in your area. You can find them in your local newspaper or on the Internet (be sure to check out the OCD Foundation at www.ocfoundation.org).

Go to one of these support groups and tell them about your successes. You can also offer to coach. If someone takes you up on the offer, be sure to read Chapters 10 and 22 first.

Don't try to serve as a therapist for someone; that's the job of a mental-health professional.

Helping Others

You can help people who don't suffer from OCD, too! The benefit of helping someone else is reciprocal — you feel good and so does the person you're helping. The possibilities are endless, depending on what skills and interests you have, where you live, and what needs stand out in your community. Some suggestions for ways to help others include:

- ✔ Working with the American Cancer Society
- ✔ Joining Big Brothers or Big Sisters and mentoring a child
- ✔ Helping kids with their homework through Boys and Girls clubs
- ✔ Judging a school science fair
- ✔ Serving as a docent at a local museum
- ✔ Teaching English as a second language
- ✔ Teaching someone to read (whether a child or an adult) at your local community college
- ✔ Working with the local food bank

You can also go to www.volunteermatch.org. You enter where you live and your interests, and they match you up with available opportunities.

Benefiting from Exercise

OCD frequently takes up so much time that the thought of making time for exercise feels as likely as a cow jumping over the moon. But if you have reduced your OCD, you now have time available to you that you haven't seen in years. Now is the time to take advantage of it, and fill what used to be consumed by obsessions and compulsions with something much more positive — exercise!

The benefits of exercise abound. They include improved health, better sleep, increased energy, enhanced moods, and feeling more in control of your life.

If you haven't exercised regularly in quite some time, be sure to check with your doctor before you start an exercise regimen. Don't keep checking over and over, but do get your doctor's clearance.

Your options for exercise are numerous, but we recommend that you seek a mix of aerobic exercise (exercise that increases your heart rate) and anaerobic exercise (exercise focused on strength training). Many health clubs offer personal trainers who can design an individualized exercise plan. You can either carry out the plan on your own or, if you're lucky enough to be able to afford it, have your personal trainer work with you on a regular basis.

Learning New Skills

Another great way to put new, hard-won time to use is to learn a new skill. New skills keep your brain sharp and enhance your sense of mastery. You may even find that they help you in the workplace. Either way, learning is fun.

Consider taking classes at your local community college or university department of adult continuing education. The costs are usually reasonable. The choices are amazing — you can find classes on photography, writing, travel, dance, assertiveness, meditation, history, art, poetry, collecting (hmm, maybe not if you have Hoarding OCD), or bird-watching.

Pursuing Hobbies

What's a hobby? Hobbies are activities that you enjoy and that typically are not all that serious. A hobby can involve almost anything at all. You can look into arts and crafts, scrapbooking, painting, pottery, games (such as bridge, scrabble, or chess), gardening, aquariums, model railroads or airplanes, music, or genealogy. Collections can also be hobbies, but again, let us remind our Hoarding OCD readers to avoid this one.

The point of pursuing hobbies is that they can provide you with considerable enjoyment that you haven't experienced in quite a while. You may need to try a variety of hobbies in order to find one that fits you. Many hobbies are hard to appreciate until you take them out for a test ride.

Finding Healthy Pleasures

Pursuing pleasures is not only enjoyable, but good for you too. Numerous studies have shown that including a healthy dose of pleasures in your life decreases chronic pain, improves overall health, decreases risk of heart attacks, combats stress, and increases life expectancy. What pleases you is a rather idiosyncratic enterprise. Of course, hobbies (see preceding section) may please you, but other pleasurable activities may include eating a great meal; going to movies; reading great books; reading less-than-great, trashy books; taking long walks; and playing with your dogs.

Ben Franklin advised us about the need for moderation in all things. So if you love ice cream, great — just don't make it your main pleasurable pursuit. However, most people's scales tilt toward too little pleasure — especially people with OCD.

Chapter 25

Ten Dirty Little Secrets about Dirt

In This Chapter

▶ Digging up dirt

▶ Utilizing dirt

▶ Eating dirt

Dirt has a bad name. Those with OCD (especially the Contamination type) often view dirt as their arch enemy. They view each speck of dust with disdain and fear. But as the saying goes, you should "know your enemy." Read on to find out more about dirt.

Defining Dirt

The word "dirt" (or "dirty") generally has negative connotations. Dirt is filthy, squalid, obscene, corrupt, or malicious. Sometimes the term "dirt" refers to unseemly information about someone. Other times it is used to describe excrement, unsanitary conditions, dust, and general uncleanness. Soil is also a form of dirt, but obviously has more positive meanings. We need soil to grow crops. Soil consists of humus and disintegrated bits of rock. So, dirt isn't always a bad thing.

Living Dirt

Soil isn't simple, bland, or inert. Soil contains an entire ecosystem in a constant state of change. A square yard of soil can contain several hundred worms. Furthermore, bacteria, actinomycetes (disease-producing bacteria), fungi, micro-algae, nematodes (parasites), protozoa, and other organisms live, grow, and die in soil.

Digging Dirt

Preschoolers can spend hours digging in dirt and parents spend hours cleaning it up. At least a little dirt may actually help build up immune systems in children and protect them from getting allergies, asthma, and autoimmune diseases. Kids who have pets, a big family, or attend daycare in the first year of life are at lower risk of having allergies and asthma than kids brought up in pristine environments. Bet you didn't know that.

Dirt Just Isn't What It Used to Be

Don't take dirt for granted. Although scientists have developed super seeds that can increase food production across the world, people continue to starve. The main reason? Poor dirt. Over the years, nutrients have been taken from the soil and not put back. Without good soil, improvements in agriculture do little to increase the food supply to poor countries.

Chimps Who Eat Dirt

Although babies and toddlers often eat dirt, parents usually try to discourage the practice. However, in nature, chimpanzees have been observed eating dirt before and after eating certain plants. Researchers have found that the mixture of dirt and leaves boosts the chimps' immunity to malaria. Neither the dirt nor the leaves by themselves confer any anti-malaria properties.

Speaking of Washing Off Dirt

The American Society for Microbiology studied the hand-washing habits of 7,836 bathroom-goers in New York, Chicago, Atlanta, New Orleans, and San Francisco. Apparently, hand-washing is down since the previous study done in 1996. Less than half the men and slightly more than half the women observed washed their hands after using the public bathrooms. Overall, only 49 percent washed their hands compared to 60 percent in 1996. The researchers also asked people on the phone whether they washed their hands after using the bathroom. Of those who answered, 95 percent reported that indeed they do wash every time — an obvious exaggeration of the truth. However, we don't have reports of widespread contagions emanating from our decreased hand-washing.

Building with Dirt

People have used dirt as a building material for thousands of years. Clay, sand, and straw are mixed to form adobe bricks. Sometimes dung is even used instead of straw — apparently using dung repels insects. An adobe wall can make a surprisingly durable structure that's fireproof and insulating. Adobe structures have survived earthquakes and hundreds of years of exposure to the elements.

People Who Eat Dirt

Everyone consumes a little dirt — probably quite a few pounds of it over a lifetime. No matter how thoroughly you wash your veggies, a little dirt remains. However, some people actually eat dirt intentionally because, well, umm, they say they like it! Apparently, pregnant women are especially prone to this practice, which goes by the name of *geophagy*. Typically, they are most drawn to consuming clay. Why they crave clay is an open question. However, speculations include that dirt, and especially clay, contains various critical minerals such as iron, magnesium, and calcium — all of which may be needed in greater abundance during pregnancy. Furthermore, some clays contain kaolin, which used to be a major ingredient in Kaopectate. Apparently, many white clays are thus especially good at calming episodes of morning sickness.

So, are we recommending that you start chowing down on dirt or clay? Well, not really. See the next section for some of the potential downsides to geophagy.

Kids Who Eat Dirt

Mud pie. Really. Most kids eat dirt from time to time. In fact, it's considered quite normal for a toddler to ingest about 500 mg of dirt in one sitting. In case you haven't been around a toddler, they pretty much stuff everything they find into their mouths — dirt, paper, dog food, or dust. For the most part, this practice is harmless. But there are some exceptions. If you live on top of a landfill where nuclear waste, products with lead, gasoline, pesticides, old batteries, spent bullets, or other toxic waste products have been discarded, it's best not to let your young child eat dirt. Furthermore, if you have animals that use your garden or lawn for elimination, the dirt may contain some contaminates that could hurt your child. For the most part, letting little ones explore in a safe place, like clean sand, is a better idea.

Pica

A compulsion exists that causes kids to eat dirt that's *not* okay, as opposed to "normal" dirt eating (see the preceding section). This compulsion is called pica. *Pica* is the persistent eating of things that are *not* food. The word pica comes from the Latin word for magpie, a bird that picks up and eats anything. In order to be diagnosed with pica, a child must eat non-food items for longer than a month and in a greater-than-normal quantity. In fact, the child's eating habits must be really out of the ordinary. Many young children eat stuff that they pick up from the floor in the normal course of learning and crawling. To be diagnosed with dirt pica (also known as geophagy — see the section "People Who Eat Dirt"), a child must eat about 1 gram or more of dirt a day. Other substances that are ingested during bouts of pica include leaves, stones, paint, plaster, string, hair, insects, animal droppings, or cloth. Yum.

Part VII
Appendixes

The 5th Wave   By Rich Tennant

"I was cured of my OCD several sessions ago. I just need to keep coming until the bill adds up to an even number."

In this part . . .

In the appendixes we offer a listing of several additional resources, including books and Web sites, where you can gain more information on OCD. We also include the forms referenced in the book, which you can photocopy for your own use.

Appendix A

Resources for You

• •

*I*n this appendix, we provide a list of books, Web sites, and organizations that can give you important information about obsessive-compulsive disorder (OCD). We include resources for other emotional problems that often accompany OCD. Of course, this list cannot be a comprehensive compendium of every source of help, but it's a good start.

If you or someone you care about has OCD, information and education is critical to recovery. As comprehensive as this book is, we still recommend that you find out as much as you can about the disorder.

Books about OCD for the Public

- ✔ *The Boy Who Couldn't Stop Washing: The Experience and Treatment of Obsessive-Compulsive Disorder,* by Judith Rapoport (Plume)

- ✔ *Brain Lock: Free Yourself from Obsessive-Compulsive Behavior,* by Jeffrey Schwartz with Beverly Beyette (Harper Perennial)

- ✔ *Compulsive Hoarding and Acquiring: Workbook,* by Gail Steketee and Randy Frost (Oxford University Press)

- ✔ *Freedom from Obsessive-Compulsive Disorder: A Personalized Recovery Program for Living with Uncertainty,* by Jonathan Grayson (Berkley Trade)

- ✔ *Freeing Your Child from Obsessive-Compulsive Disorder,* by Tamar Chansky (Three Rivers Press)

- ✔ *Getting Control: Overcoming Your Obsessions and Compulsions,* by Lee Baer (Little Brown & Co.)

- ✔ *Obsessive-Compulsive Disorders: A Complete Guide to Getting Well and Staying Well,* by Fred Penzel (Oxford University Press)

- ✔ *The OCD Workbook: Your Guide to Breaking Free from Obsessive-Compulsive Disorder,* by Bruce Hyman and Cherry Pedrick (New Harbinger Publications)

- ✔ *Overcoming Compulsive Hoarding*, by Fugen Neziroglu, Jerome Bubrick, and Jose Yaryura-Tobias (New Harbinger Publications)

- ✔ *Overcoming Obsessive Thoughts*, by Christine Purdon and David Clark (New Harbinger Publications)

- ✔ *Stop Obsessing!: How to Overcome Your Obsessions and Compulsions*, by Edna Foa and Reid Wilson (Bantam)

- ✔ *Talking Back to OCD: The Program That Helps Kids and Teens Say "No Way" — and Parents Say "Way to Go,"* by John March with Christine Benton (The Guilford Press)

Books about OCD for Professionals

- ✔ *Beyond Reasonable Doubt: Reasoning Processes in Obsessive-Compulsive Disorder and Related Disorders*, by Kieron O'Connor, Frederick Aardema, and Marie-Claude Pélissier (Wiley)

- ✔ *Cognitive-Behavioral Therapy for OCD*, by David Clark (The Guilford Press)

- ✔ *Compulsive Hoarding and Acquiring: Therapist Guide*, by Gail Steketee and Randy Frost (Oxford University Press)

- ✔ *Concepts and Controversies in Obsessive-Compulsive Disorder*, edited by Jonathan Abramowitz and Arthur Houts (Springer)

- ✔ *Obsessive-Compulsive Disorder: The Latest Assessment and Treatment Strategies*, by Gail Steketee and Teresa Pigott, (Jones and Bartlett Publishers)

- ✔ *Psychological Treatment of Obsessive-Compulsive Disorder*, edited by Martin Antony, Christine Purdon, and Laura Summerfeldt (American Psychological Association)

Books about Anxiety and Depression

- ✔ *The Anxiety & Depression Workbook For Dummies*, by Charles Elliott and Laura Smith (Wiley)

- ✔ *The Anxiety and Phobia Workbook, 4th Edition*, by Edmund Bourne (New Harbinger Publications)

- ✔ *Depression For Dummies*, by Laura Smith and Charles Elliott (Wiley)

- ✔ *The Feeling Good Handbook: Using the New Mood Therapy in Everyday Life*, by David Burns (David Morrow and Company, Inc.)

- ✔ *Feeling Good: The New Mood Therapy Revised and Updated*, by David Burns (Harper)

✔ *Mind Over Mood: Change How You Feel by Changing the Way You Think,* by Dennis Greenberger and Christine Padesky (The Guilford Press)

✔ *Overcoming Anxiety For Dummies,* by Charles Elliott and Laura Smith (Wiley)

✔ *Seasonal Affective Disorder For Dummies,* by Laura Smith and Charles Elliott (Wiley)

✔ *The Worry Cure: Seven Steps to Stop Worry from Stopping You,* by Robert Leahy (Harmony)

Trusted Web Sites for OCD and Other Issues

As you know, the Internet has more information than anyone could ever hope to assimilate. And some of that information is either inaccurate or comes in the form of a poorly disguised sales pitch for some miracle cure that's too good to be true. The sites listed below, however, can be trusted.

✔ **Academy of Cognitive Therapy** (www.academyofct.org): Promotes the research and practice of Cognitive Therapy for the treatment of emotional disorders. The organization certifies the expertise of therapists who are skilled in this approach and lists the names of practitioners across the globe.

✔ **American Psychiatric Association** (www.psych.org/public info): Offers public access to information about OCD and other mental disorders.

✔ **American Psychological Association** (www.apa.org/pubinfo): Provides fact sheets and information about OCD and other emotional disorders. The association also offers continuing education for professionals.

✔ **Anxiety Disorders Association of America** (www.adaa.org): Provides a list of self-help groups. The association also offers various screening tools for self-assessment of anxiety. Most people with OCD report at least some difficulty with anxiety, so you may want to check this site out.

✔ **Association for Behavioral and Cognitive Therapies** (www.abct.org): Encourages the development of scientifically validated treatments for various emotional disorders, including OCD. The site has a section devoted to providing information about therapists all over the world.

✔ **National Alliance on Mental Illness** (www.nami.org): The largest organization in the United States dedicated to the improvement of people affected by mental illness. The alliance provides education and support to families and advocates on their behalf.

- ✔ **National Institute of Mental Health** (www.nimh.nih.gov): Offers educational materials on many mental-health issues, including OCD. It also offers summaries of research studies and notifications about clinical trials.

- ✔ **Obsessive Compulsive Foundation** (www.ocfoundation.org): An international, nonprofit organization dedicated to educating the public and professionals about OCD. The OC Foundation sponsors various conferences and workshops. It offers lists of support groups as well as informative articles.

- ✔ **WebMD** (www.webmd.com): Offers an encyclopedia of information about health and wellness, both physical and mental. This is a good source for looking up medications and getting a solid overview of a wide variety of ailments.

Appendix B

Forms to Use Against OCD

. . . .

*T*his appendix contains a few forms for your personal use. Feel free to make copies. Included are instructions on using these forms. We also note the chapter in which each form is first referenced in the book.

Cost/Benefit Analysis

In Chapter 6, we first suggest the value of what is called a cost/benefit analysis. You also see references to cost/benefit analysis in other chapters because it's a versatile, powerful strategy. When you think about changing or making a decision, reluctance and ambivalence often creep into your mind. A cost/benefit analysis can clarify the issue and motivate you to move forward.

You can use a cost/benefit analysis to change a belief, make a decision, rethink your perspective, decide about goals, and motivate your efforts. The process helps you to move past contemplating changes and actually start moving forward. Here's how to design a cost/benefit analysis for your issue or concern:

1. **At the top of the form, write a goal, problematic thought, or decision that you're pondering.**

2. **In the left-hand column, write about all the conceivable costs of making the changes you want to make.**

    Write out all the downsides and negatives for making this change that you can think of.

3. **In the right-hand column, write down all the potential benefits that your contemplated change could result in.**

    Dare to be creative.

4. **Under My Reflections, record conclusions, thoughts, and feelings that your cost/benefit analysis taught or clarified for you.**

    You can also write out any strategies for minimizing the costs in this section.

Cost/Benefit Analysis

Goal, problematic thought, belief, or decision:

Costs	*Benefits*

My Reflections:

Monitoring Self-Handicapping

When people start out to make changes, they often find themselves self-handicapping their efforts. See Chapter 6, where we discuss the various ways that people limit their efforts in order to have an excuse just in case they fail to make progress. These self-limitations obviously slow down improvement and change. Therefore, it's important to monitor your self-handicapping and design reasons for stopping this oppositional behavior.

1. **Write down the dates that you are monitoring your self-handicapping.**

2. **On the right side, indicate what behaviors or thoughts you had that indicated some type of self-handicapping.**

    Although you don't have to explicitly label your self-handicapping, you'll probably find it useful to review the list of ways people engage in self-handicapping found in Chapter 6.

3. **Respond to your self-handicapping by talking back to that part of your OCD mind. Formulate a reason not to engage in that type of self-handicapping.**

4. **After you have recorded your self-handicapping for at least a week, write down what you've learned from the exercise.**

My Monitoring of Self-Handicapping

Day	Self-Handicapping	Response
Monday		
Tuesday		
Wednesday		
Thursday		
Friday		
Saturday		
Sunday		

My Reflections:

Exposure Staircase

As first discussed in Chapter 10, you can take your OCD triggers and turn them into an OCD exposure staircase. Figure B-1 provides a blank staircase for you to fill in. Look for the item with the lowest Ugh Factor Rating and put it on the bottom stair. Continue to fill in the staircase with items from least difficult at the bottom of the staircase to most difficult at the top. Feel free to make extra copies as needed for your personal use.

Steps in your staircase should have reasonably even spacing between them in terms of their Ugh Factor Ratings. So if you have steps that are more than 10 or 15 Ugh Rating points apart, try to come up with another one to fit between them. Try breaking a difficult item into two or three parts. For example, if the idea of touching the doorknob of a health clinic feels terrifying, you can try starting with a glove on. Then work up to touching the knob with the back of your hand — anything that makes it easier, so long as you keep going after you master the easier item.

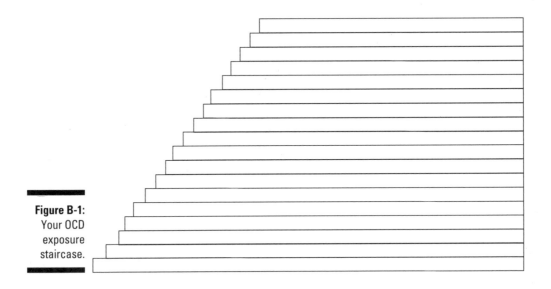

Figure B-1:
Your OCD
exposure
staircase.

Climbing and Checking Your ERP Progress Form

After you've completed filling in the steps, proceed with your staircase as follows:

1. Pick the lowest stair on your OCD staircase.

Some therapists recommend starting on a stair that has an Ugh Factor Rating of at least 50. You can do that, but we like the idea of starting slow, especially if you're doing this on your own.

2. **Write the label for the stair you're working on in the "Checking Your ERP Progress Form."**

A blank progress form follows for your use. See Chapter 10 for an example.

3. **Step on the stair.**

In other words, make contact with the OCD trigger.

4. **Record your Ugh Factor Rating when you first make contact with your stair.**

Refrain from resorting to a compulsion.

5. **Re-rate your Ugh Factor Rating every ten minutes.**

This rating may increase for a while, but stay in contact with your trigger anyway.

6. **Remain in contact with your trigger until your Ugh Factor Rating decreases.**

Generally, you'll find that takes anywhere from ten minutes up to an hour or so. Ideally, you want it to come down by 50 percent (or to an actual Ugh Factor Rating of 30 or below if your stair initially was 50 or above) before you move on to another step.

As you work through the preceding steps, keep the following tips in mind:

✔ Be on the lookout for subtle compulsions that you find yourself tempted to do in order to decrease your distress. For example, you may come up with a new compulsion such as wanting to count in your head or repeatedly say a poem or prayer.

✔ Don't try to suppress your obsessions. On the contrary, go ahead and let yourself worry about contamination or whatever. Notice the thoughts, but don't try to suppress them. In fact, it's a good idea to actively imagine the most feared and dire outcomes you can think of actually occurring — such as being stricken with a horrible disease and dying a slow, torturous death.

✔ Sometimes you may be able to climb two, three, or more steps in a single exposure session. Other times, one step will feel like plenty. You may even need to stay with one step for several sessions. Use drops in your Ugh Factor Ratings as your guide — slow and steady works just fine.

✔ Conduct at least two or three exposure sessions each week — the more the better.

Checking Your ERP Progress Form

Exposure Step	*Ugh Factor Ratings*

My Reflections:

Index

● **F** ●

BUSINESS, CAREERS & PERSONAL FINANCE

Accounting For Dummies, 4th Edition*
978-0-470-24600-9

Bookkeeping Workbook For Dummies†
978-0-470-16983-4

Commodities For Dummies
978-0-470-04928-0

Doing Business in China For Dummies
978-0-470-04929-7

E-Mail Marketing For Dummies
978-0-470-19087-6

Job Interviews For Dummies, 3rd Edition*†
978-0-470-17748-8

Personal Finance Workbook For Dummies*†
978-0-470-09933-9

Real Estate License Exams For Dummies
978-0-7645-7623-2

Six Sigma For Dummies
978-0-7645-6798-8

Small Business Kit For Dummies, 2nd Edition*†
978-0-7645-5984-6

Telephone Sales For Dummies
978-0-470-16836-3

BUSINESS PRODUCTIVITY & MICROSOFT OFFICE

Access 2007 For Dummies
978-0-470-03649-5

Excel 2007 For Dummies
978-0-470-03737-9

Office 2007 For Dummies
978-0-470-00923-9

Outlook 2007 For Dummies
978-0-470-03830-7

PowerPoint 2007 For Dummies
978-0-470-04059-1

Project 2007 For Dummies
978-0-470-03651-8

QuickBooks 2008 For Dummies
978-0-470-18470-7

Quicken 2008 For Dummies
978-0-470-17473-9

Salesforce.com For Dummies, 2nd Edition
978-0-470-04893-1

Word 2007 For Dummies
978-0-470-03658-7

EDUCATION, HISTORY, REFERENCE & TEST PREPARATION

African American History For Dummies
978-0-7645-5469-8

Algebra For Dummies
978-0-7645-5325-7

Algebra Workbook For Dummies
978-0-7645-8467-1

Art History For Dummies
978-0-470-09910-0

ASVAB For Dummies, 2nd Edition
978-0-470-10671-6

British Military History For Dummies
978-0-470-03213-8

Calculus For Dummies
978-0-7645-2498-1

Canadian History For Dummies, 2nd Edition
978-0-470-83656-9

Geometry Workbook For Dummies
978-0-471-79940-5

The SAT I For Dummies, 6th Edition
978-0-7645-7193-0

Series 7 Exam For Dummies
978-0-470-09932-2

World History For Dummies
978-0-7645-5242-7

FOOD, GARDEN, HOBBIES & HOME

Bridge For Dummies, 2nd Edition
978-0-471-92426-5

Coin Collecting For Dummies, 2nd Edition
978-0-470-22275-1

Cooking Basics For Dummies, 3rd Edition
978-0-7645-7206-7

Drawing For Dummies
978-0-7645-5476-6

Etiquette For Dummies, 2nd Edition
978-0-470-10672-3

Gardening Basics For Dummies*†
978-0-470-03749-2

Knitting Patterns For Dummies
978-0-470-04556-5

Living Gluten-Free For Dummies†
978-0-471-77383-2

Painting Do-It-Yourself For Dummies
978-0-470-17533-0

HEALTH, SELF HELP, PARENTING & PETS

Anger Management For Dummies
978-0-470-03715-7

Anxiety & Depression Workbook For Dummies
978-0-7645-9793-0

Dieting For Dummies, 2nd Edition
978-0-7645-4149-0

Dog Training For Dummies, 2nd Edition
978-0-7645-8418-3

Horseback Riding For Dummies
978-0-470-09719-9

Infertility For Dummies†
978-0-470-11518-3

Meditation For Dummies with CD-ROM, 2nd Edition
978-0-471-77774-8

Post-Traumatic Stress Disorder For Dummies
978-0-470-04922-8

Puppies For Dummies, 2nd Edition
978-0-470-03717-1

Thyroid For Dummies, 2nd Edition†
978-0-471-78755-6

Type 1 Diabetes For Dummies*†
978-0-470-17811-9

INTERNET & DIGITAL MEDIA

AdWords For Dummies
978-0-470-15252-2

Blogging For Dummies, 2nd Edition
978-0-470-23017-6

Digital Photography All-in-One Desk Reference For Dummies, 3rd Edition
978-0-470-03743-0

Digital Photography For Dummies, 5th Edition
978-0-7645-9802-9

Digital SLR Cameras & Photography For Dummies, 2nd Edition
978-0-470-14927-0

eBay Business All-in-One Desk Reference For Dummies
978-0-7645-8438-1

eBay For Dummies, 5th Edition*
978-0-470-04529-9

eBay Listings That Sell For Dummies
978-0-471-78912-3

Facebook For Dummies
978-0-470-26273-3

The Internet For Dummies, 11th Edition
978-0-470-12174-0

Investing Online For Dummies, 5th Edition
978-0-7645-8456-5

iPod & iTunes For Dummies, 5th Edition
978-0-470-17474-6

MySpace For Dummies
978-0-470-09529-4

Podcasting For Dummies
978-0-471-74898-4

Search Engine Optimization For Dummies, 2nd Edition
978-0-471-97998-2

Second Life For Dummies
978-0-470-18025-9

Starting an eBay Business For Dummies, 3rd Edition†
978-0-470-14924-9

GRAPHICS, DESIGN & WEB DEVELOPMENT

Adobe Creative Suite 3 Design Premium All-in-One Desk Reference For Dummies
978-0-470-11724-8

Adobe Web Suite CS3 All-in-One Desk Reference For Dummies
978-0-470-12099-6

AutoCAD 2008 For Dummies
978-0-470-11650-0

Building a Web Site For Dummies, 3rd Edition
978-0-470-14928-7

Creating Web Pages All-in-One Desk Reference For Dummies, 3rd Edition
978-0-470-09629-1

Creating Web Pages For Dummies, 8th Edition
978-0-470-08030-6

Dreamweaver CS3 For Dummies
978-0-470-11490-2

Flash CS3 For Dummies
978-0-470-12100-9

Google SketchUp For Dummies
978-0-470-13744-4

InDesign CS3 For Dummies
978-0-470-11865-8

Photoshop CS3 All-in-One Desk Reference For Dummies
978-0-470-11195-6

Photoshop CS3 For Dummies
978-0-470-11193-2

Photoshop Elements 5 For Dummies
978-0-470-09810-3

SolidWorks For Dummies
978-0-7645-9555-4

Visio 2007 For Dummies
978-0-470-08983-5

Web Design For Dummies, 2nd Edition
978-0-471-78117-2

Web Sites Do-It-Yourself For Dummies
978-0-470-16903-2

Web Stores Do-It-Yourself For Dummies
978-0-470-17443-2

LANGUAGES, RELIGION & SPIRITUALITY

Arabic For Dummies
978-0-471-77270-5

Chinese For Dummies, Audio Set
978-0-470-12766-7

French For Dummies
978-0-7645-5193-2

German For Dummies
978-0-7645-5195-6

Hebrew For Dummies
978-0-7645-5489-6

Ingles Para Dummies
978-0-7645-5427-8

Italian For Dummies, Audio Set
978-0-470-09586-7

Italian Verbs For Dummies
978-0-471-77389-4

Japanese For Dummies
978-0-7645-5429-2

Latin For Dummies
978-0-7645-5431-5

Portuguese For Dummies
978-0-471-78738-9

Russian For Dummies
978-0-471-78001-4

Spanish Phrases For Dummies
978-0-7645-7204-3

Spanish For Dummies
978-0-7645-5194-9

Spanish For Dummies, Audio Set
978-0-470-09585-0

The Bible For Dummies
978-0-7645-5296-0

Catholicism For Dummies
978-0-7645-5391-2

The Historical Jesus For Dummies
978-0-470-16785-4

Islam For Dummies
978-0-7645-5503-9

Spirituality For Dummies, 2nd Edition
978-0-470-19142-2

NETWORKING AND PROGRAMMING

ASP.NET 3.5 For Dummies
978-0-470-19592-5

C# 2008 For Dummies
978-0-470-19109-5

Hacking For Dummies, 2nd Edition
978-0-470-05235-8

Home Networking For Dummies, 4th Edition
978-0-470-11806-1

Java For Dummies, 4th Edition
978-0-470-08716-9

Microsoft® SQL Server™ 2008 All-in-One Desk Reference For Dummies
978-0-470-17954-3

Networking All-in-One Desk Reference For Dummies, 2nd Edition
978-0-7645-9939-2

Networking For Dummies, 8th Edition
978-0-470-05620-2

SharePoint 2007 For Dummies
978-0-470-09941-4

Wireless Home Networking For Dummies, 2nd Edition
978-0-471-74940-0

OPERATING SYSTEMS & COMPUTER BASICS

Mac For Dummies, 5th Edition
978-0-7645-8458-9

Laptops For Dummies, 2nd Edition
978-0-470-05432-1

Linux For Dummies, 8th Edition
978-0-470-11649-4

MacBook For Dummies
978-0-470-04859-7

**Mac OS X Leopard All-in-One
Desk Reference For Dummies**
978-0-470-05434-5

Mac OS X Leopard For Dummies
978-0-470-05433-8

Macs For Dummies, 9th Edition
978-0-470-04849-8

PCs For Dummies, 11th Edition
978-0-470-13728-4

Windows® Home Server For Dummies
978-0-470-18592-6

Windows Server 2008 For Dummies
978-0-470-18043-3

**Windows Vista All-in-One
Desk Reference For Dummies**
978-0-471-74941-7

Windows Vista For Dummies
978-0-471-75421-3

Windows Vista Security For Dummies
978-0-470-11805-4

SPORTS, FITNESS & MUSIC

Coaching Hockey For Dummies
978-0-470-83685-9

Coaching Soccer For Dummies
978-0-471-77381-8

Fitness For Dummies, 3rd Edition
978-0-7645-7851-9

Football For Dummies, 3rd Edition
978-0-470-12536-6

GarageBand For Dummies
978-0-7645-7323-1

Golf For Dummies, 3rd Edition
978-0-471-76871-5

Guitar For Dummies, 2nd Edition
978-0-7645-9904-0

**Home Recording For Musicians
For Dummies, 2nd Edition**
978-0-7645-8884-6

**iPod & iTunes For Dummies,
5th Edition**
978-0-470-17474-6

Music Theory For Dummies
978-0-7645-7838-0

Stretching For Dummies
978-0-470-06741-3

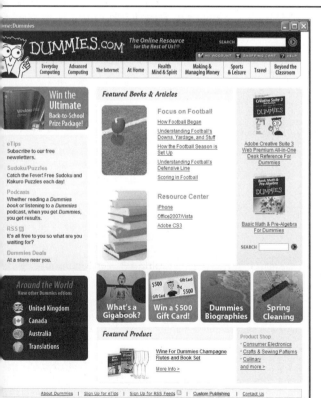

Get smart @ dummies.com®

- **Find a full list of Dummies titles**
- **Look into loads of FREE on-site articles**
- **Sign up for FREE eTips e-mailed to you weekly**
- **See what other products carry the Dummies name**
- **Shop directly from the Dummies bookstore**
- **Enter to win new prizes every month!**

Separate Canadian edition also available
Separate U.K. edition also available

Available wherever books are sold. For more information or to order direct: U.S. customers visit www.dummies.com or call 1-877-762-2974.
U.K. customers visit www.wileyeurope.com or call (0) 1243 843291. Canadian customers visit www.wiley.ca or call 1-800-567-4797.

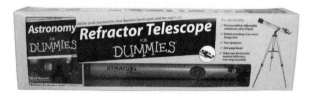